D1508055

Books by Stephen Birmingham

YOUNG MR. KEEFE

BARBARA GREER

THE TOWERS OF LOVE

THOSE HARPER WOMEN

FAST START, FAST FINISH

"OUR CROWD"

THE RIGHT PEOPLE

HEART TROUBLES

THE GRANDEES

THE LATE JOHN MARQUAND

THE RIGHT PLACES

THE
Right Places

THE
Right Places

by
Stephen Birmingham

ILLUSTRATED WITH PHOTOGRAPHS

Little, Brown and Company · Boston · Toronto

FIRST EDITION

T 03/73

Library of Congress Cataloging in Publication Data

Birmingham, Stephen.
   The right places.

   1. United States--Social life and customs--
1945-   2. Upper classes--United States.
I. Title.
E169.02.B542   301.44'1   72-10328
ISBN 0-316-09641-5

Published simultaneously in Canada
by Little, Brown & Company (Canada) Limited

PRINTED IN THE UNITED STATES OF AMERICA

For
Carol and Pavy

Contents

Illustrations

Part One

"WHO NEEDS PARIS?"

United Press International Photo

High jinks at Southampton — then and now

Photo by Elliott Erwitt, Magnu

1

The Money Nobody Knows

I THINK it started when Frank, the fresh-faced young man who delivers milk to our house on alternate days (I have never, alas, troubled to learn Frank's last name), announced that we would be having a substitute milkman for the next three weeks. He was taking his family on a skiing holiday to Val d'Isère. "Oh," I said. "That sounds very nice." I had never been to Val d'Isère.

Or possibly, from the other end of the scale, the incident that triggered my slow response was reading about a woman in Palm Beach named Mrs. William Wakeman who had shot her husband in the back because he had dared her to. He had, after all, just yanked her earrings out of her pierced ears. When she learned that he would be paralyzed from the waist down as a result, she cried, "Now what am I going to do for sex?" He later died.

Or perhaps it was when, also in Palm Beach, queen of winter resorts, I learned of a hostess who, for no particular reason, received her party guests reclining in an oversize baby carriage, sucking a pacifier.

Palm Beach seemed to be losing its grip on itself. Not long after that there had been, in the social columns of the Palm Beach *News,* a lengthy report of a "poodle wedding." The item noted: "The bride was attired in a dual-length ivory satin gown, short in front and long in back, trimmed with Alençon lace. Her long veil of French illusion fell to her turquoise-tinted toenails from the crown of seed pearls at-

tached to her topknot." Who was having a better time, I wondered —
those people in Palm Beach, or Frank in the Alps?

Nor was what was happening, or appeared to be happening, restricted to choice acreage of Florida real estate. In Southampton, New
York, a queen, reportedly, of northeastern resorts, a man said: "It's
fun here for a while, at the beginning of the season, when everyone is
opening up their houses, and you see all the people you haven't seen
for a while. People all work on their tans, and the parties are fun. But
after a few weeks it gets kind of boring. You see the same people
again and again, and by the end of the season this is a hateful place.
All the love affairs that were fresh and fun at the start of the season
have gone stale, husbands and wives are at each others' throats, there's
nothing new to talk about, and everybody literally despises everybody
else. By September, nobody can wait to get away."

What it is, of course, is that things are not as they once were. Society, or the idea of society — in the sense of a group of attractive and
well-heeled people enjoying each other in certain attractive and generally expensive places — is not dead, exactly. But it has spread to include a great many other people who would never before have been
considered a part of society and who, furthermore, would never have
wanted to be considered as such. It is not that no one has the where-
withal (what with taxes and all) to enjoy the good life. On the contrary, it has got so that almost anyone beyond the level of poverty
can enjoy it, or at least some of it. In the process, the old notion of
"exclusivity" has almost completely disappeared. The resorts and the
clubs and the suburbs and the compounds of the wealthy and wellborn
have lost their old meanings and, in the process, their power to impress.
The barriers — of money, character, class, or breeding — have van-
ished, if they ever really existed, and those who had tried so hard to
establish and confirm their existence are now left stranded and adrift,
left with nothing to do but finger revolvers and munch on pacifiers —
anything to provide distraction from the tedium at hand. The old idea
of society in America was based on keeping the others out, the wrong
people, as it were. But it is futile to erect a barricade when no one
wants to get in. It is pointless to be exclusive when there is no one
to exclude. Abandoned in places like Palm Beach and Southampton,
the men and women who once thought of themselves as America's

social leaders are now looking at each other somewhat dazedly and wondering where it all went, how it all happened so fast, what became of F. Scott Fitzgerald and the days when the very rich were different from you and me. And, in the meantime, the people who have money to enjoy are, for the most part, people nobody knows from places where nobody goes.

At the same time, the *right* places are really in the mind, aren't they? Aren't they *where you are?* They are in Kansas City, for example, or in Bakersfield, or on a deserted beach in Mexico. Nobody is going to tell Fresno that it is *wrong* and get away with it. The right place may still be the top of the money and social heap, but today almost anybody anywhere can find the top of that heap without too many directions. Today, when a once-fashionable specialty store such as Bergdorf Goodman has opened a shop for the hippie trade, when a once-disreputable Third Avenue saloon is now one of the most popular spots in town, and when yachting is a sport of corporations, isn't it silly to talk about "nobodies" from "nowhere"? So let's stop all that, now that everybody's in the act. And let's look at some of the lovely deltas and oases, mental and otherwise, where the good life is flourishing at full strength.

As a writer, I've looked at some of these places in the last year or so, and have jotted down some of my impressions and opinions of this new and still changing mood and style. You can even glimpse it in Colusa and in all the way stations of the lecture circuit. But wait.

In a blurred rush of feeling, the bemused priest in Fitzgerald's short story "Absolution" cries out: "When a whole lot of people get together in the best places things go glimmering all the time." One rather quickly guesses that this was also the author's belief, or fond hope — that when clean-limbed youths and slender girls of good name and decent expectations met under the stars, with an orchestra playing, at the country club dance, or strolled together on a green lawn beside a sparkling pool, life flickered, expanded, lifted to a kind of gauzy climax. These were the best people, the right people in the right places. These were people who not only knew but cared which St. Paul's was the right boys' school and which was not. These were people in John O'Hara's novels, always careful to wear shoes from Peel's and to carry Vuitton luggage. (Never Vuitton shoes and Peel's luggage.) To these people, things mattered. And things went glimmering — all the time.

There were, furthermore, a lot of people who subscribed to this pretty view, who felt it had solidity and substance. But it was like, to use an earthbound comparison, the great soybean scandal of a few years back. Huge fortunes were gambled — a whole Wall Street underwriting firm staked itself — on huge storage tanks that were allegedly filled with valuable oil. In the excitement (dreams of riches, visions of power) no one thought to apply the simplest sort of test — to pick up a stick and bang the side of one of the tankers to see whether it was really filled with oil or not.

Some time ago, testing the worth and value of what had been touted as society, someone banged the side of the barrel with a stick and heard it echo, hollowly: empty. News of this discovery has been passed around. Whatever may once have been there has drained away. It doesn't matter any more, and there's nothing to fear. The market for swimming pools, where Fitzgerald characters once lounged so charmingly, is now the homeowner in the ten-thousand-dollar-and-up income bracket, according to the president of the Lebow Advertising Company, and that's not so very rich. The rich *are* you and me.

And, what's more, they can go just about anywhere they want. The right places are the places where they have the best times. These are the places that "count" now. They're going to count even more. Watch.

Christmas spectacular at Kansas City's Country Club Plaza

2

Kansas City:
Seville on the Missouri

THERE are at least two kinds of anonymous (or at least unpub-
licized) wealth — the kind that is perfectly happy with its anonymity, and the kind that isn't, that would do anything to see itself
better advertised. There is a lot of the latter variety in Kansas City.

First, Kansas City tells you, you must go to the bluff. Beyond the
bluff, the land rises and falls in a series of hills and valleys which, by
their ordinariness, give the bluff emphasis. Great importance is attached to this bluff. If, it is argued, the Missouri River had not encountered the bluff at this particular point in its course, the river
would doubtless have continued southward, along a more or less
straight path into the Gulf of Mexico. But the river met the bluff
and was diverted by it and bent eastward. Its eastward thrust continues for some two hundred miles until the Missouri joins the Mis-
sissippi at St. Louis. This, if one continues to pursue this hypothesis,
may have had a profound effect upon the course of American history.
If the river had continued straight south and into the Gulf, if it had
not been turned in a new direction by the sturdy bluff that leaps out
of the plains, the North American continent might easily have remained a land divided into three parts by two great rivers, and under
three flags — the British, the French, and the Spanish. This rationale
might sound farfetched to some. But it does not to the citizens of
Kansas City, which rises, straight and tall and proud, from the summit
of this bluff. Parents take their children for Sunday picnics on the

bluff where there is a sweeping view of unparalleled splendor. The river does seem to hesitate, irked to find this mighty obstacle thwarting it; then, resigned, it turns and presses on another way. The view from the bluff offers a kind of reassurance that Kansas City stands and has always stood — and firmly — at a point pivotal to the course of men's affairs. As one man puts it, "We may not be fashionable, but goddamn it, we're *meaningful!*"

The ideal, if impractical, way to approach Kansas City is on foot. A visitor who misses the experience of encountering the city in this fashion runs the risk of missing the point. To those willing to come as pedestrians across the apparently limitless miles of dusty plains that border the city on all sides, the city presents itself gradually, climbing out of the level horizon as a cluster of slender towers that cling together and pierce the sky like exclamation points, a strangely developing mirage of power and promise in the middle of the desert. The size and the strength and, at the same time, the elegance of Kansas City's splendid skyline offer one of the city's first surprises. To the arriving motorist, this is simply a more rapidly emerging phenomenon, and quite enough to pull the motorist's eyes off the road. Newcomers have arrived here breathtaken. The view of Kansas City from across the plains has been compared, without tongue in cheek, to that of the spires of Chartres Cathedral as they lift from the flat farmlands of central France. And yet, how can Kansas City bear such a romantic comparison? After all, this is Kansas City, Missouri, symbol of the homely and the cornball, unfashionable in the extreme. Its founding fathers wanted to name it Possum Trot, and very nearly did. Kansas City is, isn't it, the original cow town, home of the square, the lummox, the nasal-voiced booster and Babbitt, the graft-rich politician, the stockyard and the slaughterhouse? *New York* magazine once ran an advertisement asserting that readers would enjoy the publication "even if you live in Kansas City." It was supposed to be a joke. Kansas City is a joke city, and all the Kansas City jokes are tired ones. No one, it is commonly assumed, would go to Kansas City unless he had to. And yet some surprisingly fresh breezes blow across the bluff.

"People are always so terribly surprised to find that Kansas City is a beautiful city, and that we have bright and attractive people here who have beautiful things," says Mrs. Kenneth Spencer, a Kansas City *grande dame,* the widow of one of its leading industrialists (the Spencer Chemical Company, among other interests) and one of the leading supporters of local philanthropies, art, and culture. Mrs. Spencer is herself the possessor of quite a few of the beautiful things in Kansas City, including a vast duplex apartment filled with a museum-quality collection of eighteenth-century French and English antique furniture, Oriental rugs, Chinese porcelains, and a cabochon-cut emerald very nearly as big as the Ritz. "People from other places act as though they feel sorry for me, as though I *had* to live in Kansas City," Mrs. Spencer says. "Obviously I don't *have* to live in Kansas City. I live here because I simply love it!" Kansas City, so much maligned, evokes this kind of passionate love from among its citizens who defend their city — and defend it, and remind all who will listen, again and again, that Kansas City simply is not what it is so often made out to be. "Don't you think my house is pretty?" asks Mrs. Spencer. "Don't you think my view is pretty?" Her view is of a green and leafy park. "Why should I live in Paris when I have all this?"

The reasons why Kansas City is so often maligned and misunderstood are subtle and complicated, but one of them is simple: the rival city of St. Louis to the east. "The typical image of a Kansas City man is a guy chewing on a corncob pipe," says one Kansas City man. "In St. Louis, they're pictured riding to the hounds. Damn it, we ride to the hounds here too." Another Kansas Citian asked at a Chamber of Commerce meeting not long ago, "How does St. Louis get away with calling itself 'The Gateway to the West'? St. Louis is *not* the Gateway to the West. Kansas City is the Gateway to the West. We were always the most important junction in the western movement, and St. Louis *never* was. We were where the covered wagons provisioned for their journeys, and then we became a great rail center. Now, with TWA based here, we're the great air center. St. Louis has just arbitrarily put up that Gateway Arch, just to have itself a tourist attraction. And it's just as arbitrarily decided to call itself 'The Gateway to the West.' Gentlemen, we have got to do something to fight back."

St. Louis and Kansas City see eye to eye on almost nothing. St. Louis, the older of the two cities ("but only *slightly* older," one is immediately reminded when this touchy point comes up, since there is a mere thirty-year difference between the dates of the two cities' char-

ters) has, partly from being on the easterly side of the state, managed
to convey a more East Coast impression of seemliness, cultivation, and
tone. There is also a touch of Old South charm radiated by "old St.
Louis," and St. Louis society is frequently included among the perfumed upper circles of such social capitals as Philadelphia, Charleston,
Savannah, and New Orleans. An edition of the *Social Register* is published for St. Louis. None is for Kansas City. There is even something distinctly different in the *sound* of the names of the two cities —
St. Louis, soft and sibilant; Kansas City, rawboned, rough-and-tumble.

At the same time, Kansas City's special character, and its special
character problems, have much to do with several dynamic and strong-
willed men who have successively left their personal stamps upon the
city over the years. One of these was William Rockhill Nelson, the
owner and publisher of the Kansas City *Star*. Mr. Nelson was something of a despot, with decidedly paternalistic notions, and, among
other innovations, installed his *Star* employees in neat, old-English-
style stone houses hard by his own mansion so that everyone on the
paper could live "as one big happy family." It worked, at least for a
while, and though the houses have passed out of the *Star*'s control,
they still stand and are highly regarded as residences. Nelson had
grandiose ideas for Kansas City, and it was under his aegis that a German engineer and city planner named George Kessler was imported
to create a master design for the city before it was too late. It was
Kessler who saw a way to make brilliant use of the many natural valleys that ribboned the city; they would contain parks and broad tree-
lined boulevards, and residential areas would be placed on the hills
above, overlooking greenery. Thanks to Kessler's planning genius, and
the staunch backing of William Rockhill Nelson, Kansas Citians now
enjoy more than fifty parks and over a hundred miles of inner-city
boulevards and parkways. André Maurois once wrote, "Who in Europe, or in America for that matter, knows Kansas City is one of the
loveliest cities on earth?" The man to thank for this is Mr. Nelson.
When he died, he left a substantial trust for the establishment of the
William Rockhill Nelson Gallery of Art, which has become the city's
major art museum with a smallish but important permanent collection.
Rather typically, Nelson left no funds for the maintenance of his gift,
on the theory that if Kansas City citizens wanted a worthwhile mu-

seum they had better work for it. Today, fund-raising parties and benefits for the ever-needy Nelson Gallery have provided Kansas City social climbers with their most rewarding avenue.

Kansas City was supposed to expand to the northeast. Instead, it has done just the opposite, and the costliest and most fashionable districts are now on the southwest side of the city — many of them, including the high-priced Mission Hills area, across the state line in Johnson County, Kansas. This situation, with many of the choicest taxpayers living in another state, has created a knotty problem for the Missouri-based city government, and was the doing of another high-powered and individualistic man, Mr. J. C. Nichols. Nichols came to Kansas City in the early nineteen-hundreds and bought the first few of what were to become thousands of Nichols-owned areas, most of them on the southwest side of town. It was he who developed the Mission Hills and Country Club districts where, today, all the richest people live in big sprawling houses, along twisting roads and lanes laid out by Nichols interests. In his developments, Nichols was fond of using fountains, statues, huge stone planters and ornamental sculpture. And the profusion of these Mediterranean touches in Kansas City is another of this Middle Western city's great surprises.

But Nichols's masterwork was the creation of Country Club Plaza, and it did indeed represent a totally new concept in American architecture and commerce. It was nothing other than the first suburban shopping center in the world and, begun in 1920, it was foresightedly designed for the automobile age. Extensive parking space was planned for rooftops and within and beneath buildings. Today, the Country Club Plaza sprawls across forty southwestern acres and contains branches of all the best shops and restaurants, as well as professional offices. Because Mr. Nichols admired the Moorish style of southern Spain, he designed his shopping center with bell towers, minarets, courtyards, more fountains, more statuary, a scale replica of Seville's Giralda Tower, and one fountain that is an exact copy of the Seville Light. In the years since, as a result of all this, Seville has been adopted as Kansas City's "sister city," a designation that technically doesn't mean much other than to give city-proud Kansas Citians still another reason to crow, "Who needs Paris? Who needs Europe?" At Christmastime, the Country Club Plaza is decorated with thousands upon thousands of sparkling lights, and incoming planes on clear nights traditionally dip from side to side above the Plaza to let their passengers view the spectacle.

Not everyone in Kansas City admires the Country Club Plaza's style of architecture, and many people point out, with some justification, that the Spanish style is not really appropriate to a river city in the American Middle West. Missouri is not, after all, California, and though the state did have a brief Spanish regime this left no lasting impression on the place or people. Particularly disparaging of the Plaza are those connected with the Kansas City Art Institute and School of Design, and those with the various museums. Craig Craven, a young member of the Nelson Gallery staff, describes the Country Club Plaza as "the capitol of *kitsch*." When an outdoor art show was presented there, Craven denounced it as "open-air *kitsch*." On the other hand, there is no question that the Country Club Plaza has become a successful real estate venture, and that it is continuing to become more so. Miller Nichols, J. C. Nichols's son who now heads the giant company, has announced that the Plaza will before long contain a three-hundred-and-fifty-room hotel. Without question, it will be built in a style that would look right at home in Andalusia.

During the nineteen-twenties and -thirties, one of the most enthusiastic supporters of Mr. Nichols's building projects, and of the lavish use of concrete in highways (to say nothing of in fountains, statues, and ornamental urns) was Kansas City's notorious political boss, Thomas J. ("Big Tom") Pendergast, and his Pendergast Cement Company. Until the Pendergast machine's inglorious end in 1938 — when more than two hundred and fifty people were indicted on charges of voting frauds, and the corruption of the Pendergast regime lay dismally exposed with the Big Boss himself sentenced to prison for tax evasion — developers like Nichols received Pendergast's full cooperation, which was of important help. But, of course, "Nobody" in Kansas City talks about that now.

Also of significant help to the builders and developers of Kansas City have been various members of the Kemper banking family. The Pendergasts were hardly among Kansas City's "right people," but the Kempers very definitely are, and they have been for some time. When you think banking in Kansas City, you think Kemper. The first

Kemper, William T., arrived here in 1893, with his wife, the former Charlotte Crosby, a lady of inherited means who was also a shrewd businesswoman. Charlotte Kemper made cautious loans of money from a tin strongbox which she kept under her bed. It was she and her husband who loaned J. C. Nichols the money to buy his first ten acres of land. The Kempers may have been a bit rough about the edges in the old days, but they have since acquired all the patina needed for entrance into the loftiest social circles, and they are said to consider themselves the grandest people in Kansas City.

To say that the Kempers have Kansas City banking pretty well sewn up would be putting it mildly. The Kempers own both the first and third largest banks in town: the City National Bank & Trust Company and the Commerce Trust Company. The second largest bank is thereby totally eclipsed by Kempers. Kempers also own or control some twenty-one smaller banks in Missouri, Kansas, Colorado, and Oklahoma. They also own a great many blocks of downtown Kansas City real estate and, through their other investments, the Kemper name decorates the lists of boards of directors of very nearly every important industry in town, plus such national firms as Owens-Corning Fiberglas and the Missouri Pacific Railroad. The Kempers of Kansas City are all very rich, but the family should not be regarded as a monolithic money structure. The Commerce Trust and the City National Bank are in fierce competition with each other, and the two brothers who for many years headed them — the late James M. Kemper of the former bank, and R. Crosby Kemper of the latter — were on such poor terms with each other that they rarely spoke. There have been other intrafamily ruckuses among the Kempers. When the young Crosby Kemper, Jrs., embarked on the building of a large and costly modern home, of a design so extreme in its use of glass and brick pylons that conservative Kansas Citians were horrified, many of the couple's relatives were critical and told them so. The storm grew to such proportions that the Kempers were angrily divorced before the house was finished. When the house was done, however, the pair patched things up and remarried each other.

"Boss" Pendergast was in favor of concrete streets and fountains, but of not much else that could be considered interesting or important, or even lasting. During the long two decades of his reign much of

Kansas City life — particularly its cultural life — slid into a slough of apathy and inactivity. World War II came soon after Pendergast's collapse, and so it has only been in the past twenty-odd years that Kansas City has been trying to pull itself back up to a level where it will have as much to offer culturally as other cities of half a million population or over. This has not been an easy task, because Kansas City businessmen, in whom strong traces of the free-for-all spirit of the Old Frontier still seem to linger, have always been frankly more interested in making money than in giving it away — particularly to something called "culture" which some men equate with downright sissy. The culture drive has received the endorsement of the faculty of the Art Institute and those connected with the museums — the so-called "artistic community" — but since some of these people have longish hair it is easy for a more conventional part of the community to dismiss them all as hippies or limp-wrists.

Several of the younger generation of Kansas City's older families have, however, been earnestly backing the cause of Art. As a result, the arts here have been becoming increasingly respectable and have even made their way into the society columns. Young Mrs. Irvine O. Hockaday, Jr., works as a volunteer at the Nelson Gallery, young Mrs. Patrick Graham toils on behalf of the opera, and young Mrs. Albert Lea is into anything that will benefit the Kansas City Philharmonic and so on. There are a number of wealthy young collectors who have set about with determination to prove that, as far as art is concerned, everything is very much up to date in Kansas City. One couple has a collection including works by Andy Warhol, Robert Rauschenberg, and Roy Lichtenstein. Mrs. Thomas McGreevy and her broker husband have focused their attention on op, or psychedelic art, and all the pieces in their otherwise traditional Kansas City house either glow, blink, flash, or emit unearthly sounds. Mrs. McGreevy, a former actress, has gone so far as to appear in an underground Kansas City film — and in the nude. Actually, she insists, it was a flesh-colored body stocking, but when her banker father-in-law saw the movie he was so shocked by what went on in it that he had the footage suppressed.

Another group of younger people has established the Performing Arts Foundation, dedicated to bringing better theater to Kansas City. The group includes the ubiquitous Mrs. McGreevy, Mrs. Crosby

Kemper, Jr., and David Stickelber, a witty bachelor who lives in an elegant apartment with upholstered walls and Oriental rugs everywhere, even in the kitchen because "it keeps the help happy." The Stickelber family fortune comes from the manufacturing of a bread-slicing machine — "It's the only kind there is, you can't slice bread without it," as the scion of the company says. Eyebrows went up in Kansas City when Maria Callas came to stay with David Stickelber "to forget" during the period when she was being replaced in the affections of Aristotle Onassis by Mrs. Jacqueline Kennedy. "Maria insisted on my creating the illusion that time was passing rapidly," Mr. Stickelber explains. "So each day I would go into her bedroom and say, 'This is December. Tomorrow it will be January. Thursday will be Valentine's Day' — and so on."

The bright young crowd in Kansas City speak often — and often bitterly — of their parents' generation which they feel, with some justification, is not doing what it might to support the arts in Kansas City. It is the older generation, of course, that still manages to hold most of the purse strings. The young group is particularly resentful of such people as the senior R. Crosby Kempers, who, it is felt, with their great wealth could have done much more for the city than they have and who, with the generally conservative banking policies they represent, have actually exerted a negative influence on the city's cultural life.

Still, for a number of years Mrs. Kemper senior headed the Jewel Ball, a debutante affair that benefits both the Nelson Art Gallery and the Kansas City Philharmonic. In fact, Mrs. Kemper *founded* the Jewel Ball — or so she says. The senior Mrs. Hockaday also says that *she* founded the Jewel Ball, and neither woman will give the other credit. What appears to have happened is that Mrs. Hockaday had the idea of having a ball, and Mrs. Kemper added the debutantes. In any case, it is still Kansas City's most important debutante affair — indeed, the only one that counts.

"The Kempers are worth millions and millions of dollars," says Molly McGreevy, "and so is Miller Nichols. Wouldn't you think people like that could spare just a *few hundred thousand* for the Performing Arts Foundation?" So far, the answer appears to be no.

Then there are rich Kansas Citians like Mr. Joyce C. Hall, the man who created Hallmark and guided it to where it is, one of the wealthiest corporations in the world. No one knows how rich Mr. Hall is because he is a reticent type and Hallmark is still a family-owned company, with its earnings a closely guarded family secret, but his holdings are said to be vast indeed. The Halls, who aren't particularly social, have contributed only minimal amounts to the city's cultural institutions, and the Kansas City Museum of History and Science was happy to receive, last year, a check for twenty-five hundred dollars from Mr. Hall. Meanwhile, the Nelson Gallery does somewhat better, and recently reported Mr. Hall's gift of fifty thousand dollars. Though the greeting card business might seem to align itself with art, the Halls at the moment are much more interested in a development called Crown Center (the Crown being from Hallmark's trademark), an eighty-five-acre urban renewal effort in downtown Kansas City encompassing nearly all the land between the old Union Station and the Hallmark headquarters, an area of real estate roughly two-thirds the size of Chicago's Loop. Crown Center has been designed to contain shops, apartments and office buildings, a new hotel, underground garages, and acres of parks and greenbelts. When completed, an estimated two hundred million dollars of Hallmark money will have been spent.

The older generation of Kansas City's rich continues, with a few exceptions, to do what it has always done. There are the hospitals to support. There is the Westport Garden Club to enjoy — probably the city's hardest-to-join club since no more than fifty women may belong at any one time. There is the River Club, a downtown eating club high on the bluff overlooking the river — also considered exclusive — which the men enjoy for lunch and couples enjoy for dinner. There is the Kansas City Country Club. There are, in other words, the traditional pleasures and pastimes of moneyed Middle Americans who have "settled in" to middle-sized cities. These families regard such eccentricities as the young McGreevys' blinking and beeping collection of art as harmless phases which the young will one day certainly outgrow.

And, in the meantime, Kansas City — as those in the young crowd are so painfully aware — lags a long way behind its rival city to the east when it comes to culture. Compared to what St. Louis can offer, Kansas City's History and Science Museum is, at best, a third-rate institution, though its energetic young director, Robert I. Johnson, is determined to do something about this situation. The Nelson Gallery has one of the three — the others are in Boston and Washington — finest collections of Oriental art in the country. But in other categories its collection is definitely a skimpy one. The most famous alumnus of the Kansas City Art Institute was the late Walt Disney. "Culturally, Kansas City has *got* to be given a shot in the arm," David Stickelber says. And the money to do it with is so maddeningly, frustratingly *there*. Mrs. Crosby Kemper, Jr., who ought to know, says, "This is a tough town in which to get people — the people who really have it — to put two nickels back to back."

Some Kansas Citians explain their situation by pointing out that Kansas City has never had a major rich-family benefactor — the way, for instance, Pittsburgh had Mellons, Wilmington had du Ponts, Detroit had Fords, and New York had Rockefellers. On the other hand, many people see it as a city with any number of potential big benefactors, each one too shy — if not too stingy — to make the first big step.

There is still another explanation. Years ago, St. Louis recognized the cultural wellsprings that could be tapped — and the purse strings that could be loosened — by turning to its large and well-heeled Jewish population. For many years, St. Louis has been inviting prominent Jews onto the boards of its museums and opera and philharmonic orchestra, and has made healthy use of the traditional Jewish interest in the arts and learning. Kansas City, perhaps for reasons of snobbery or ignorance going back to the rawboned frontier days, failed to tap this rich source. As a result, Kansas City's Jews withdrew into their own tight circle, with their own clubs and philanthropies and institutions. Recently, however, Kansas City became aware of what it was missing and losing, and a definite effort is now being made to draw Jews into the general community. The names of wealthy Jewish families — the Morton Soslands, the Paul Uhlmanns, the Aaron Levitts — now decorate the important boards and committees. Now Jewish girls are being taken into the Junior League and are presented at the Jewel Ball. A few of the old barriers remain, of course. There are no Jewish members of the Kansas City Country Club. Jews have their own, the Oakwood Country Club.

There is another breed of rich man in Kansas City who may be having a lot to do with shaping the city's future — the new-made millionaire. An example of this sort is Ewing M. Kauffman, whose Marion Laboratories, Inc., grew from where, some twenty years ago, Mr. Kauffman was mixing pills and cures and lixiviums in his own basement by the light of a sixty-watt bulb. Today it is a company worth about two hundred million dollars, and Mr. Kauffman himself says he is worth another hundred million. The Kauffman magic formula, according to the man who invented it, is profit-sharing. He operates a generous plan by which his employees are made to feel a part of the company they work for, and a part of its success. Kauffman boasts that at least twenty of his top men now have profit-sharing accounts in the millions. "My receptionist downstairs is worth half a million," he says. "I just retired a maintenance man who had a quarter of a million. Look at these people — happy, happy, happy!" And, as Mr. Kauffman gesticulates in their direction, his employees smile, and smile, and smile. Part two of the Kauffman formula is that you must work as hard for Kauffman as Kauffman works for Kauffman (often fifteen or sixteen hours a day), or out you go — with your profit-sharing account no more than a memory.

Ewing Marion Kauffman, who says, "I wanted to be Kauffman of Marion Laboratories, not Kauffman of Kauffman Laboratories, there's an important difference" (though business rivals hint darkly that he simply invented "Marion" as his middle name) is a man so totally lacking in modesty that his huge self-esteem more or less passes for charm. When he entertains, he urges his guests to make after-dinner speeches extolling Ewing Kauffman. After each tribute, he applauds approvingly. He lives in a huge brick fortress on a hill that prominently displays itself to the street below, and from his house he flies two big flags from two big flag poles, the American because he is proud to be an American, and the Canadian, because he is proud of his blondely beautiful and Canadian-born wife. His house is full of delights, including an Olympic-size swimming pool, a sauna and a steam bath, a pipe organ, a ballroom, and a fountain electronically geared to splash to the accompaniment of music and colored lights. "I'm just learning to use my wealth," he admits. "Now we give two hundred and fifty thousand dollars to charity every year." One of his most recent big outlays, however, was to purchase the Kansas City Royals, a baseball team, because "my wife wanted them."

There are, as they say in Kansas City, not many people around like Ewing Kauffman. At the same time, there are too few people in Kansas City like Mrs. Kenneth Spencer, whose husband died several years ago. In 1966, Mrs. Spencer wrote out a check for $2,125,000 to build a graduate research laboratory at the University of Kansas, her husband's alma mater. She continues to make sizable gifts to a long list of philanthropies. The Spencers had no children, and so one day Kansas City will doubtless benefit importantly from Mrs. Spencer's fortune.

Not long ago a group of young Kansas City businessmen sat at lunch at the Kansas City Club, the downtown eating club for men. The group included Jerry Jurden, vice president of ISC Industries, a securities outfit; George Kroh, a real estate developer, Bob Johnson of the History and Science Museum, Gordon Lenci, headmaster of the Barstow School, one of several private day schools in the city, and Irvine Hockaday, Jr., a young lawyer. No one at the table was over forty, and most were not more than thirty-five. And, as it almost inevitably does, the subject came up of what was wrong with Kansas City's "image."

"Kansas City had a lot of things going for it around the turn of the century," one man said. "The Armours were here with their meat business, Fred Harvey's headquarters were here, all the major truck lines came through here, and of course there was the river port. But look what's happened to Dallas, compared with what's happened to us! Compared with us, why should a city like Dallas even exist? Yet Dallas is known as the Big D, and everybody laughs at Kansas City."

"We've got to overcome apathy," George Kroh said. "We've still got a lot here. We've got cattle, oil, industry, a broad economic base — clean air, and no ghettoes. Of course there's not much glamour in being Mr. Clean. We've got the Mission Hunt, the Polo Club — and still we're thought of as a bunch of hicks in a nowhere cow town."

"One thing Kansas City is *not* — it's not provincial," Bob Johnson said. "I found that out when I moved here from Chicago. This is a very *aware* city. The people here know what's going on in the world."

"That," another man pointed out humorously, "is because of our location. We've got no ocean, no lakes, no mountains to go to — we've got to get *out* of Kansas City to find all that."

As for culture, the young men agreed that Kansas City has always been more oriented toward sports. "Still, you see a lot of people going to the theater now that you used to see at the ball games" — and there was general agreement that Big Tom Pendergast's influence on the city's cultural life had been disastrous. "And now," George Kroh said, "there's so damn much infighting going on among the various art groups. The Lyric Opera is fighting the Philharmonic, and the Performing Arts Foundation is fighting the Kempers, and all the different museum groups are fighting each other. We need some sort of unifying force." At the same time, it was pointed out, an exhibition of art owned by Kansas City collectors, held at the Nelson Gallery, had drawn some three hundred works from a hundred and ten different collections, with tastes ranging from Gainsborough to de Kooning and Warhol. And, someone else added, "I'd say that *at least ninety per cent* of those collectors were people under forty."

Irvine Hockaday, who is active in city politics, nodded emphatically and said, "Yes, this is a beautiful city, a great place to live. The only thing wrong with Kansas City is what Mayor Davis said. Did you hear what Mayor Davis said? He said, 'All this town needs is a few more funerals.'"

Senator Wherry, in a broadside against the Red Chinese, once said, "We will lift Shanghai up, up, up to Kansas City if it takes us a century!" So much for Senator Wherry, and so much for Shanghai. As for Kansas City, funerals are, alas, inevitable, and we shall see how high Kansas City climbs.

Courtesy of the Fresno County and City Chamber of Commerce

Luxury and livestock in California's Central Valley

3

California's Central Valley:
"Water, Wealth, Contentment, Health"

COLUSA, California, is not provincial either. Nor are Bakersfield, Fresno, Modesto, Stockton, Lodi, Sacramento, Chico, or Redding, to name a few other Central Valley places. And yet, like Kansas City, they are disparaged and made the butt of all the jokes. The lyric of a recent hit song runs, *"Oh, Lord, stuck in Lodi again!"* Not long ago, Herb Caen, the San Francisco columnist and chronicler, led off a column with "Lodi's leading playboy (and that's funny right there) . . ." And in a review of *Fat City*, a novel by Leonard Gardner, a news magazine wrote, "The place is Stockton, California, a city filled with a litter of lost people, most of whom pile on urine-smelling buses each morning and head for the onion, peach, or walnut fields for a killing day on skinny wages." In fiction, Colusa has fared no better.

Broadway producers say that if a reference to Canarsie gets a laugh in a New York show, the California road company can get an identical laugh by substituting "Modesto," or "Visalia," or "Yuba City." In fact, any Valley town will do.

The Central Valley of California contains some of the lushest agricultural land in the world, and the Valley's towns and cities are the homes of some of California's — and the country's — wealthiest families, who lead lives of quite splendid luxury. A "litter of lost people"? That would hardly apply to the Weber family of Stockton, founders of the city, who own vast ranches of peaches and tomatoes, or to Mrs. Tillie Lewis of the same city, another tomato tycoon, who made an enormous fortune when her canneries developed a way to take sugar out of canned fruits and juices, or to Mr. Peter Cook of Rio Vista, said to be "so rich that he doesn't lease out his gas wells — he drills them himself." Then there are people like the Alex Browns, so rich that they found it more practical to open their own bank than to bother with ordinary commercial accounts, and the McClatchys, owners of the Valley's largest newspaper and radio-TV chain for four generations.

In Modesto, there are the Gallos, largest wine producers in the world, and further south there are hugely wealthy families such as the Giffens of Fresno. Russell Giffen, from an office furnished with eighteenth-century antiques, directs a ranching operation with acreage in the hundreds of thousands (so many hundreds of thousands that he is not quite sure just how much land he owns), raising cotton, barley, wheat, safflower, alfalfa seed, melons, tomatoes, and a good deal else. Urine-smelling buses indeed! Central California garages practically overflow with air-conditioned Cadillacs and Rolls-Royces. The men who drive the big harvesters for Martin Wilmarth — who harvests, along with other produce, twelve hundred acres of rice in Colusa — sit in comfort in air-conditioned cabs. Another Valley farmer has a fleet of custom-made Cadillac pickup trucks, also air-conditioned, said to be the only vehicles of their sort in the world. At the same time, California's Central Valley, though it is the largest single region in the state, where over two hundred products are grown — products which become ten per cent of what America eats — the area has remained the one part of the state which hardly anyone outside it knows; which few outsiders see or visit, and which fewer understand.

Even Mrs. Ronald Reagan speaks without enthusiasm of her current address in Sacramento, the state capital and the Valley's largest city. "Thank heavens we can escape to Beverly Hills on the weekends!" Nancy Reagan says, adding that she *has* to go to Beverly Hills at least once a week to get her hair done. "No one in Sacramento can do hair," she sweepingly asserts. Like most people from Los Angeles and San Francisco, Nancy Reagan had never spent much time in the Valley and had never set foot in Sacramento until her husband was elected governor. When she did, she was horrified by what she found and has been complaining bitterly ever since, to anyone who will listen, about the house where she was expected to live.

The California governor's mansion, a turreted affair of Victorian gingerbread built in 1878 and painted a glittering wedding-cake white, was immediately unacceptable. "There are seven fireplaces, none of which can be lit," Mrs. Reagan has said. "The house is on a corner facing two gas stations and a motel, and it backs up on the American Legion Hall where I swear there are vile orgies every night. The house was condemned fifteen years ago. I said to Ronnie, I can't let my children live there!" Upon seeing it, Mrs. Reagan immediately refused to occupy the mansion, and the Governor indulged "Mommy" — as he calls her — and rented a house in the suburbs of the city. Since then, Nancy Reagan says that she has been "too busy" to get to know any of her Valley neighbors. She made one trip to the Sacramento branch of I. Magnin & Company, California's favorite fashion store, and found its contents inferior to those in the stores in Beverly Hills and San Francisco, where she still prefers to shop. "Here, everything is scaled down for these Valley farm women," she says.

These, needless to say, would be nothing short of fighting words to the women of the Central Valley who, among other things, are among Mrs. Reagan's husband's staunchest supporters. A great many Valley families are older-established than families in San Francisco and Los Angeles, and these consider themselves among the oldest of California's Old Guard. The first families of the Valley were here long before gold was discovered in the tailrace of Sutter's Mill, near Sacramento, and these families descend from men and women who crossed the Sierras on foot, before the days of the covered-wagon trains. And yet, as they are most acutely aware, young women from the Central Valley are not invited to join the debutante parties in San Francisco and Los Angeles, and Valley men languish far longer on the waiting lists of San Francisco's select clubs such as the Bohemian and the Pacific Union. "It's because of our cow-town image," they say with resignation, and they suffer from an inferiority complex even more severe than their counterparts in Kansas City.

Geographically, San Francisco and Los Angeles people have always treated the Valley as something to be endured, a place to be got through. You have to get through Bakersfield and Visalia in order to get from Los Angeles to Yosemite Park. From San Francisco, it was necessary to get through Sacramento in order to get to Lake Tahoe or

Squaw Valley — until the new freeway managed to speed the motorist over the rooftops of Sacramento without its really being visible. The old Route 99 that used to take you up and down the length of the Valley had, to be sure, a perverse way of leading the motorist through the most woebegone sections of each Valley town it encountered, and there was, as a result, no encouragement to turn off the main highway and explore. After a trip through or across the big Valley it was easy to leave it with the impression that it was little more than a flat — very flat — expanse of fields and orchards, punctuated by glum skid rows and trailer camps. Now, in a sense, the freeway system has made it worse. You can traverse the Valley without even knowing it's there.

And yet it is. Over the round, dry, coastal mountains that shelter San Francisco, through such a pass as the Altamont, and then down into the Valley, you know, when you encounter it, that you are in a somehow special place. There is a special smell, which changes with the seasons, from the smell of loamy earth to the perfume of blossoms and unfolding leaves to the drying of eucalyptus bark at the end of summer. Each harvest has its smell — sweet and winy grapes, dusty tomatoes. There is also a special hazy paleness to Valley sunlight and, in winter, special ghostly fogs and mists that rise from marshes and canals and river beds. There is also a special language here. Ask for directions, for example, and you might be told: "Head up about a mile past Harris's piece till you pass a prune orchard on your right and some apricots on your left. Then take your next right, which will put you up onto the levee, then go along the slough till you hit a grove of wild wormwood trees. . . ."

The Central Valley of California is actually a pair of valleys placed end to end, created by two rivers — the Sacramento, which flows south out of the Sierras, and the San Joaquin, which flows north. The two rivers merge in a fan-shaped delta east of San Francisco, and then empty to form San Francisco Bay. Like Kansas City's famous bluff, the much-advertised beauty of San Francisco Bay would not exist if it had not been created by the convergence of the Valley rivers which, of course, spill out at the end of their journey through the Golden Gate. The topography of the double valley, which is, on a relief map, as though a great scoop had been drawn down through the center of the state, is responsible for the Valley's special climate. Moist air from the Pacific is turned back by the coastal range of mountains and, on the eastern side, the towering Sierras collect westward-moving weather in the form of rain or snow. Thus the Valley remains hot and dry throughout most of the year, and it "never" rains from April to October. At least it's not supposed to rain during these months.

From the earliest days of California settlement, men struggled with the problems, and the promises, which this particular climate offered. During the long summers the rivers shrank to a trickle or dried up altogether, and the Valley became a desert. In spring, when the snows in the mountains melted, the rivers overflowed and the Valley became an inland swamp. You can tell which are the oldest of the Valley houses because they are built on high foundations, well above the ground, and are approached by long flights of steps, a reminder of the threat of high water that existed only a few years ago. Obviously, what the Central Valley needed was a way to store the spring floods and to distribute this water during the dry summer growing season, and from the first sandbagged levees along the Sacramento River and the digging of the first canals, ditches, and sloughs, this battle with water has been the Central Valley's major effort. In fact, the story of the Valley, and its economic success, has been written in water.

One of the first to recognize the Valley's potential in a large way was a man called Henry Miller (no kin to the novelist of the same name who also lives in California). Henry Miller remains, in some ways, a figure of mystery. His real name was Heinrich Alfred Kreiser. He was the son of a German (or perhaps Austrian) butcher. He came to the United States in 1847 at the age of nineteen, and when he heard of Sutter's gold he decided to head for California. When he went to pick up his steamer ticket to Panama he noticed that, for some reason, his ticket had been made out in the name of Henry Miller. This, at least, is what he claimed. Did he come upon the ticket dishonestly? In any case, the ticket was stamped "Non-Transferable," and so the young man, who spoke little English, decided that it was wisest to pretend to be Henry Miller rather than risk losing the ticket. He kept the name until he died.

In California, he worked for a while as a dishwasher and then as a sausage peddler, and it was as a sausage man that he first entered the

Central Valley and was struck with its possibilities. He was a quiet, reclusive young man, and as far as is known had no formal engineering training. Yet he began, in his spare time, to design levees and intricate irrigation systems. He also began to buy land which was considered worthless and which he could therefore buy dirt-cheap. Henry Miller — who, in his later years, developed grandiose ideas about his capacities and took to comparing himself with King Solomon — may have been a genius. He was certainly a clever salesman, and perhaps he was a scoundrel. In the days of feverish railroad-building and the speculation in land that was central to the allure of railroads, Miller was able to persuade various fledgling railroad companies to lay their tracks along certain routes. Then, when tracks were ready to be laid, Miller would discover a "better" route. The first route would then be abandoned, and its roadbed would become — by default — a ready-made levee for Miller's expanding irrigation system. Once, buying a parcel of land from a Spanish owner, Miller agreed to accept "as much land as a boat can circle in a day" in return for the price he offered. He then strapped a canoe to his wagon, set off at a fast clip across the countryside, and, by nightfall, had claimed a considerably larger portion than if his journey had been by water.

At the height of his career, Henry Miller and his partner, Charles Lux, another ex-butcher, owned over half a million acres of Valley land, on which a million head of cattle grazed. Miller and Lux were America's first cattle kings, and it was once claimed that whatever California real estate Henry Miller didn't own the Southern Pacific Railroad did. Miller liked to boast that he could ride from Mexico to the Oregon Border, on horseback, and never be required to sleep on land that was not his own. He was also responsible for the law of riparian rights, which provided that anyone owning land along a river can use the river's water. This gave Miller complete control of all the water in the San Joaquin Valley, a considerable resource. Today, Henry Miller's heirs and others who have inherited shares of the Miller-Lux holdings, are immensely rich. Henry Miller died in 1916, and the beneficiaries, direct and indirect, of his enterprises include such far-flung people as Mrs. William Wallace Mein, Jr., of San Francisco, who is Henry Miller's great-granddaughter, and Mr. Wilmarth S. Lewis of Farmington, Connecticut, the celebrated Walpole scholar, biographer, and collector of Walpoleiana.

Henry Miller pointed the way toward what could be done with water in terms of Central Valley agriculture. Since then, water has been at the heart of every Valley triumph, and every controversy. Feelings about water can be joyful; several years ago, when a new canal was opened carrying water from the Shasta Dam in the north into previously unirrigated southern areas, a bright indigo dye was thrown into the water at the source and, as the blued water made its way into each Valley settlement along the course of the new canal, the populace turned out and there were civic celebrations, speeches, parades, cheering, and all-night dancing in the streets.

Feelings about water can also run hard, stirring bitterness and resentment. In the southernmost part of the Central Valley, many people are angry about a plan to lift water out of the Delta and carry it, through a mountain tunnel, into Los Angeles, where it is badly needed because of that city's rapid growth. What right does Los Angeles have to "our" water? the northerners ask. A bit of graffiti in a Valley men's room reads, "Please flush after using. Los Angeles needs this water."

In the years since the pioneering Henry Miller, water has been chained behind a series of high dams and directed through hundreds of miles of canals and pumping stations, tunnels, reservoirs, and power systems. The Operations Control Center of this operation, in Sacramento, resembles the interior of a futuristic space ship, complete with wall-sized maps, flashing lights, computerized controls, all coordinating the release and flow of water throughout the Central Valley Project. The Control Center not only regulates the amounts of water that flow out, and where these gallonages go, but also the kinds of water — for drinking, for irrigation, or for industrial use — that are needed in any given part of the state of California at any given time. From here, the levels of rivers are controlled to keep barges afloat, to keep salt water from encroaching on peach orchards, to keep water temperatures at the proper levels to promote the spawning and the growth of fish. The Center is an operation of mind-boggling proportions, and it is getting bigger all the time. New dams are being built "that make Aswan look like just another PG&E project," according to one Valley engineer.

The Folsom Dam, west of Sacramento, already dwarfs the Aswan. The drawing boards teem with others.

With all these dams, and all the water they store, there has been a certain nervousness about what might happen in the case of a serious earthquake, and when, several years ago, there was an extended earthquake scare, a number of people hurried to higher ground, because if all the dams in California did break open at once, the entire Valley would certainly become a very damp place in which to live. In the meantime, the irrigation that the big dams provide has turned the Valley floor, in the spring, into a sea of billowing pink, white, blue, and orange blooms. And when they contemplate the wealth of agriculture that the Central Valley water system provides, Valley people are understandably resentful of city folk in San Francisco and Los Angeles who poke fun at Valley farmers. "Where would *they* be if it weren't for us?" one woman asks. That the Governor's wife feels she must go to Beverly Hills to get her hair done strikes Valley people as less an insult than a joke.

One way to grasp the special feeling of the California Central Valley is to begin in the south, in Bakersfield, a city which once belonged almost entirely to Henry Miller. Bakersfield is to the Valley what the bluff is to Kansas City, but the comparison cannot be stretched too far. Bakersfield is cotton, and Bakersfield is oil. Cotton has given Bakersfield a sense of permanence; cotton money, that is, is older money, rooted in the soil. Oil money gives Bakersfield a sense of transience, of come-and-go, because oil money is new money, based on a black substance that is always puddling up from beneath the substrata of the earth, and oil brings with it drillers and refiners and promoters and speculators, all of whom seem to have flown into Bakersfield from somewhere else. Today, virtually every oil company of any size has an office in Bakersfield, and it is hard to spend more than an hour in Bakersfield without a sense of the throbbing of pumps, refineries, and compressor plants that make gasoline out of natural gas, and of course a concurrent sense of oil-smelling money.

Money is a favorite topic of conversation in Bakersfield — who made how much, and when, and why, and who, because of failure to be in the right place at the right time, failed to make money. The Tevises and the Millers, for example, represent a long-standing money feud.

Like Henry Miller, the Tevis family were also big landowners in these parts (though on a somewhat lesser scale) and, in the 1930's, the Tevises found themselves land-poor. Miller, at that point, had succeeded in diversifying his interests. In order to recoup their fortunes, the Tevis family interests formed something called the Kern County Land Company, and shares were sold to the public — thereby departing from Tevis family control. Lo and behold, not long afterward, a bonanza in oil was discovered beneath Kern County Land Company acreage. Kern County Land Company shareholders found themselves rich overnight, and at least one man — Mr. C. Ray Robinson, the lawyer who had handled the Land Company's affairs — made himself a million dollars in legal fees alone, not counting what the jump in value of his stock netted him. Tevises moaned and gnashed their teeth but, alas, there was really nothing they could do; a fortune had slipped through their fingers. At one point, the Tevis mansion in Bakersfield had a private golf course, and the Tevises had actually entertained foreign royalty in their home. The big house had to be sold, and for a while it was used as the clubhouse for the Stockdale Country Club. Today, the site belongs to a San Franciscan named George Nickel, a Henry Miller heir — and a cousin of Mrs. William Wallace Mein — and none of the Miller-Lux heirs today feels the slightest guilt about gloating over the fact that Millers *still* outweigh the Tevises.

Moving north up the wide Valley, the next important town is Fresno. To many people, Fresno is more typically a Valley town than Bakersfield because it is solidly agricultural — vigorous, masculine, where cowboys wear their hats in the fanciest bars, yet a town with an elegant downtown shopping mall, reclaimed from a former slum, that has become a model for city planners everywhere, and a number of sleek new high-rise buildings. Fresno is at the geographic center of the state, and Fresno County is the richest agricultural county in the United States — as very few Fresnoisans will forget to remind you. The irrigated land around Fresno produces a great variety of crops, and it is here that the psychology of the California farmer is seen at its best. He is tough, pessimistic, politically conservative, fiercely independent. If there is one thing a Valley rancher resents it is "folks from outside trying to tell us what to do." The folks from outside are usually from the federal government, and at the heart of the continuous grumbling about the Central Valley irrigation project, and what kind of water will go where from which dam, is the fact that it is a U.S. Department of the Interior project — representing damned outsiders from Washington.

Stewart Udall — though long departed from his post as Secretary of the Interior — is still a dirty name in these parts, and a kind word for ex-Labor Secretary Willard Wirtz not long ago landed a man in a Valley rancher's heated pool — where he was discovered floating face down. Wirtz did away with the *bracero* program, which ranchers — now that it is no more — speak of in retrospect as though it once provided something like a second Eden. The *braceros* were Mexicans brought into California during peak-picking seasons to perform "stoop labor," the gathering of low-growing fruits and vegetables. "Why, the *braceros* were the greatest boost to the Mexican economy there ever was!" one rancher insisted not long ago. "The Mexicans who came up here loved the work, and they were wonderful workers. A good picker could make anywhere from sixty-five hundred dollars to ten thousand dollars a season! They came out here and said we should put heaters in the bunkhouses — *heaters!* A Mexican's not used to a heater! They said, 'Why aren't you feeding them meat? Why aren't you feeding them eggs?' My Lord, don't those damn fools in Washington know that a Mexican eats tortillas and beans?"

Valley ranchers admit that they may have used the wrong public relations tactic when Secretary Wirtz came out to California several years ago to look over the conditions in which the Mexican laborers worked and lived. The ranchers, hoping to woo Mr. Wirtz to their point of view, put on a big party for him, and that turned out to be a mistake. Wirtz was a teetotaler, or at least he rather frostily refused the many stiff drinks urged upon him, and Valley ranchers pride themselves on their capacity for alcohol. Wirtz also made a point of not eating a bite of the elaborate barbecue that was spread before him. He went back to Washington and canceled the *bracero* program.

Another Valley rancher said not long ago: "The national farm program has been conducted as a relief program for the South. Farm legislation on a national scale has been controlled by the South and the Midwest. California keeps getting the short end of the stick. The chairmen of both the House and the Senate agricultural committees are

Southerners. Meanwhile, we're caught here in a cost-price squeeze. Our taxes go higher, labor costs go up, but our customers have concentrated their buying power. There used to be, for example, hundreds of canneries for the cling-peach people to go to. Now there are nineteen or twenty. Those of us who sell direct to markets — well, there used to be thousands of little ones to shop from. Now there are just a few big super-chains. So it's harder for the farmer to fight for his price."

Adding to their woes, the farmers have lost control of the California Assembly and state Senate. The large landholders used to have great power in both, but under the one-man-one-vote system, their voice is much less effective. Now, though the Valley ranchers remain resolutely Republican, the Valley counties usually go Democratic.

And, needless to say, Valley ranchers had few kind words to say for Mr. Cesar Chavez and his striking table-grape pickers, whose headquarters were in Delano, some seventy-five miles south of Fresno. "We weren't *about* to have some labor organizer tell us what to do," one rancher says. "Why, California pays the number one farm wage in the country, and the grape pickers are paid the best! Why couldn't he pick on states that were behind?" Mrs. William Harkey, the wife of a wealthy peach rancher in the little town of Gridley, says, "Of course I bought grapes all through that whole darned thing. I didn't buy them to eat, of course, because they're terribly fattening, but I fed them to my pet raccoon." Of Senator Edward M. Kennedy's support of the table-grape boycott, the slightly sick Valley joke quickly became, "Confucius say, 'Man who boycott grapes should not play in Martha's Vineyard.' "

Valley ranchers are endlessly gloomy about their labor problems, and some insist that there can be no solutions. "The only people making money here are the developers," one rancher claims. "They're buying land at three thousand dollars an acre and selling it for housing at three thousand dollars a lot. Twenty-five years from now, this whole Valley will be nothing but houses, and all our fruits and vegetables will be coming from Africa." Still, despite the cities' sprawl, California's harvested acreage continues to increase. Another rancher says, "When they took away the *braceros,* they forced us to use the winos. Those decent hard-working Mexicans have been replaced by the dregs of society." It is true, during the harvest seasons, that trucks gathering up winos from the slums and backwaters of Valley towns for work in the fields make the image of "urine-smelling buses" an apt one. At the same time, the labor shortage has forced the farmers to increase the mechanization of their farms. More and more, computers are feeding cattle and machines are shaking peaches out of trees, replacing human hands. This has meant that, though the California farmer may not have been able to raise his prices by much, and though his machines are expensive, they have enabled him to increase his yields enormously. California farmland grows increasingly valuable. The average California farm, of 617 acres, is today worth $325,000. The national average is 389 acres — worth only $69,000. It seems likely that California farmers will continue to be able to afford their air-conditioned cars, their heated pools, their private planes, and their wives' seasonal forays into I. Magnin's, for some time to come.

One of the most difficult things, perhaps, for a Valley farmer to understand is why the average laborer is unwilling to work as hard as he, the farmer, does. During the harvest season, the farmer rolls up his sleeves and goes into the fields where he will work for fifteen or twenty hours a day, seven days a week. His wife, meanwhile, will put her Magnin's dresses aside and put on dungarees to work as a weighing master, while the rancher's sons and daughters are stooping and picking in the hot sun, side by side the winos. Why — the ranchers ask — aren't farm laborers happy to do the same?

The economic rule of the Valley is: the cheaper the water, the higher the value of the land. In the northern part of the Valley, where water is much more plentiful and thus cheaper, a farmer can operate quite profitably on a smaller acreage. The northern Valley is blessed with a larger river, the Sacramento, with more rainfall, and with the precious boon of a vast underground lake, called Lake Lassen, which makes irrigation possible through the use of wells. This means that the northern part of the Valley, from Sacramento north, is also the prettiest part. There are more and bigger trees, and there is a leafy shade in the northern towns that is not possible in the hotter, dryer south. Modesto — with its welcoming archway proclaiming, as one enters the town, "WATER, WEALTH, CONTENTMENT, HEALTH — MODESTO" — is a town of peach orchards and vineyards. Stockton and Sacramento concentrate on tomatoes. Further north, in Colusa and Chico, there is an emphasis on almonds and walnuts, whose larger and deeper root systems require a larger water supply.

When water first came to these towns, in some cases as recently as a generation ago, schoolchildren turned out in their Sunday best to plant seedlings of trees along the streets and highways, and today these have become tall stands of eucalyptus, sycamore, live oak, and pistachio trees (these turn a brilliant red in autumn). Sacramento is a particularly leafy city, with trees along both sides of most of the older streets, trees whose branches meet to form a solid canopy overhead, and a large central park, where the state capitol stands and where thousands of camellias burst into violent bloom in early spring.

Chico is another green place, and many of its streets are appropriately named after trees. At the heart of Chico is an extraordinary twenty-four-hundred-acre natural park where the original wilderness of the early Valley is carefully preserved. The park was donated by General John Bidwell, who founded the city. "He was mixed up with Sutter and all the rest," one local resident explains, "and his wife was big on Christianizing the Indians." Bidwell Park was the setting of the original *Robin Hood* film, with Errol Flynn, because its thickly clustered live oaks, festooned with grapevines, were considered the closest thing to Sherwood Forest. Hidden in Bidwell Park are two natural lakes and what Chico used to boast was "the World's Largest Oak." In 1963, the World's Largest Oak was split by a lightning bolt, and so now the Chamber of Commerce of Chico advertises that it has "Half of the World's Largest Oak." Chico's tree-lined Esplanade, with its handsome houses, provides one of the prettiest city entrances in America.

The northern Valley is full of surprises. "Down River" from Sacramento lies the rich and beautiful Delta region. Roads here wind narrowly along the tops of levees, across bridges, over sloughs and waterways that cross and split around islands in an endlessly complicated pattern. Boats have been known to lose themselves for days in these waters. Big, prosperous-looking farms, with handsome Victorian farmhouses, lie below the levees. (The roadways here are frequently at the level of a house's second-story windows, for many of these houses stand on land that has been reclaimed from the riverbed and is actually lower than the water table.) Each farm has its dock and pier where crops can be loaded into river barges. One gets the feeling that these farms have been operating in much the same fashion for at least a century, which turns out to be just the case. One suddenly crosses a bridge and a sign proclaims, "Locke — pop. 1002, elev. 13 ft." Locke is a Chinatown, a community of Chinese that was first established here when the railroads were being built and that has chosen to remain here. Above its Chinese lettering, one of Locke's shops proclaims itself to be a "Bakery and Lunch Parlor." Another sign exhorts, "DRINK! LIQUORS!" Down below the levee is an eating establishment of unprepossessing appearance but of great local celebrity called Al the Wop's. Al the Wop's is famous for its steak sandwiches and French fries.

North of Sacramento is the pretty river town of Colusa. Not long ago, Colusa celebrated the one hundredth anniversary of its incorporation, and visitors at this event were taken on tours of California's second oldest court house (1861), and the Will S. Green mansion (1868). Will S. Green founded Colusa and is venerated as this part of the Valley's "Father of Irrigation," since it was he who first surveyed the Grand Central Canal in 1860. Colusa also has a mini-mountain range all its own, the Sutter Buttes, which spring up surprisingly from the otherwise flat Valley floor to jagged peaks of over two thousand feet. With typical Valley pride and fondness for superlatives, the Sutter Buttes are promoted as "the World's Smallest Mountain Range."

It used to be that the Central Valley floor had a panoramic view of the snow-capped Sierras to the east and the lower coastal range of mountains to the west. Wherever you went in the Valley, the old-timers say, the mountains hung on two horizons. Today, they rarely show themselves, and this is the price the Valley has had to pay for irrigation. The air is no longer as dry as it was, and a misty haze nearly always obscures the mountains. Irrigation has also subtly changed Valley weather. It used, literally, never to rain in summer, but in recent years there have been sudden flash summer storms. These can be disastrous to certain crops. Peaches, for example, if hit by rain must be harvested within exactly seventy-two hours. Otherwise, brown spots appear, the peaches will not pass inspection, and an entire year's crop

— and income — will be lost. This happened to the peach ranchers of Modesto in 1969. Now, in addition to labor and Washington, the farmers bemoan the uncertainty of the weather — which, ironically, their own irrigation brought them.

Continuing north, one begins to encounter around the town of Corning, low, rolling hills. Then, through Red Bluff and Redding — lumber towns — one enters the high hills and pines, and the Valley is over. The Sacramento River, wide and sleepy as it spreads across the Delta, is a racing torrent here, a mountain stream. Climbing still higher, along a winding road with an Alpine feel to its bends, one comes to the Shasta Dam, from which the Sacramento River now issues through giant penstocks. At Shasta Dam, the visitor is barraged with statistics — how many thousands of kilowatts the dam generates (enough to light half the world), how many miles of recreational lakeshore the dam created, how many billions of gallons the man-made lake can store (enough to cover the entire state of California to the depth of one inch). On the horizon stands the white and symmetrical silhouette of Mount Shasta, whose seasonally melting snows help fill up the enormous lake.

Meanwhile, back in the state capital, young C. K. McClatchy is the fourth generation of his family to operate the "Bee" chain of Valley newspapers. There are *Bees* in Sacramento, Fresno, and Modesto, and Mr. McClatchy's wealthy maiden aunt, Miss Eleanor McClatchy, heads up McClatchy Enterprises, which includes radio and television stations. (A fifth generation of McClatchys is waiting eagerly in the wings.) C. K. McClatchy, typical of Valley men, has a special feeling about the place and what it means. "There is a sense, here," McClatchy says, "of the continuation of history — of the Gold Rush, of the opening up of the West, of the growth of California from the earliest pioneer days to where it is now the most populous state in the union. And you get a sense here of how history has moved — swept, been carried, into the present, and how the present has maintained the integrity of the past. The Valley has *kept up* with its history like no other place I know of. Just go and stand on the rim of Shasta Dam" — called "the Keystone of the Central Valley Project" — "and see the thing that is the source of so much that has happened to the Valley and beyond it, and you'll see what I mean, why I find this Valley, plain and flat and conservative as it is, one of the most thrilling places to be alive in that I know."

And so this is one of the right places, too. Who needs Paris here, either?

Photo by Prowell. Courtesy of t
Fort Lauderdale Chamber of Commerce and Pier (

The good life afloat — Pier 66, Fort Lauderdale

4

Fort Lauderdale:
"How Big Is Your Boat?"

MANY of the places where the money is new are affected to some degree by boosterism. But the point is, everybody knows this and nobody is ashamed of it. The new rich believe in living as they wish to live, not by any set of standards devised by a past generation. This is the way things are, and the devil take the hindmost.

For example, Mrs. Bernard Castro likes her champagne at room temperature. This is one of the social facts of life in Fort Lauderdale, Florida. Guests who prefer it chilled may add ice cubes. Most of the winter the Castros (who are very big in sofas) keep their yacht, the *Southern Trail,* tied up at the dock of Le Club International, which is the newest (some say the only) swinging place in Fort Lauderdale, and friends are always dropping in on Theresa Castro for a glass of warm champagne and a plate of pasta. Mrs. Castro keeps a freezer full of pasta on the yacht. Eddie Arcaro might come by, or Susan Hayward, or June Taylor (of the June Taylor Dancers), a mixed bag. Joe Namath's houseboat is usually berthed just a couple of slips away from the *Southern Trail* (Namath's houseboat has little slitty windows so you can't look in and see Joe, but Joe can look out and see you), and he and his friends — he has a lot of these — might pop over. At night the parties in and around the Club's dock get very loud, waking the herd of squirrel monkeys that nests in the trees, and causing the parrots to scream and complain. It is considered poor taste for a neighbor to complain.

The *Southern Trail* is one of the Castros' newest playthings, and is very much a part of the new Fort Lauderdale. Mrs. Castro loves to show it off to visitors, freezer and all. The staterooms, it goes without saying, are all furnished with Castro Convertibles. There is a big Castro Convertible in the grand saloon, upholstered in ranch mink. "If you've got it, flaunt it!" says Mrs. Castro with a big, happy smile. One end of this Convertible opens to reveal a bar, where the champagne is kept, and the other end converts into a stereophonic sound setup. The most ambitious Convertible in the saloon is a chair, a perfectly ordinary-looking overstuffed chair. At the press of a button, though, its back flings open and out comes an ironing board and, at the same time from under the seat an electric hair-dryer emerges. If she owns one of these chairs ("one of our newies," Mrs. Castro explains) the housewife can do her ironing and dry her hair at the same time. Mrs. Castro passes out handfuls of brochures to her guests describing other kinds of Castro Convertibles. "After all," she explains, "we make this boat tax-deducti-ble." As soon as it is warm again up North, where the Castros have a big house on the North Shore of Long Island, Mrs. Castro and her friends cruise up the Intracoastal Waterway aboard the *Southern Trail*, drinking champagne, eating pasta, and playing gin rummy all the way.

Everybody agrees that Fort Lauderdale isn't what it used to be. But then what Fort Lauderdale *is* is something of a problem. It certainly isn't another Palm Beach, and it certainly isn't Miami. Socially speak-ing, it is somewhere about halfway between the two, which is just about where it is geographically. That is, people who admire Miami regard Fort Lauderdale as hopelessly stuffy, Early Goldwater Conserva-tive, smugly snobby. Palm Beach, meanwhile, still clinging valiantly to the glitter of another era, refusing to admit that its chin is sagging, dismissed Fort Lauderdale long ago as garish, nouveau, tacky, and, as Palm Beach people have called it, "Kansas-City-by-the-sea." But for those who live there, and wouldn't live anywhere else, Fort Lauderdale has a style and a charm that are all its own.

For one thing, the place is booming. Its population has had a habit of doubling every five years, and Fort Lauderdale, barely fifty years old, is already a city of over 150,000 permanent residents. Physically and economically, its boosters say, it is the fastest-growing town in the United States, which may mean in the world. Land development is the name of the game if you are here to make a fortune (as most people frankly are and as it is in the California Valley), and the high-rise is what it's played with. Higher and higher rise the high-rises until they rake the heavens. They march along the oceanfront like so many gleaming white filing cabinets, and the sound of cement mixers is everywhere. The apartments and condominiums that these buildings contain sell so well that, in many cases, buildings have been completely sold before their foundations were even dug. It is said that this is the smart-money way to buy a condominium because, what with skyrocketing building costs, the same apartment you can buy from a builder's floor plan for fifty thousand dollars may wind up costing you seventy-five thousand dollars when the building is finished. Not long ago a man from Rye, New York, and his wife looked at a fulsomely decorated "model apartment" in a new Lauderdale high-rise, and offered to buy it just as it was — complete with everything it contained, right down to the ashtrays on the tables, pictures on the walls, books in the bookcases, and the plastic-flower centerpiece on the dining room table. When the builder demurred (he was, after all, using the model apartment as a selling tool, and to replace it would be costly and time-consuming), the Rye man offered twenty-five thousand dollars more, cash on the barrelhead, take it or leave it. The builder took it. The early-1970's business recession, spongy stock market, and tight money are said to have had "only a slight effect" on the Great Fort Lauderdale Boom.

With all this agitated growth, there have been, not surprisingly, growing pains. Developers, in the tradition of their breed, have tended to want to get their buildings up as rapidly as possible, the hell with what they look like. Some strange structural concoctions have resulted. Along one strip, the Gault Ocean Mile — which is beginning to resemble a mini-Miami Beach — the hotels and apartment houses have gone up Miami-fashion, cheek by jowl, with barely space to breathe between the buildings, and so crowded together that the tall buildings cast long afternoon shadows over what, perhaps, were intended to be sunny terraces and pools and beaches. Since Fort Lauderdale is on Florida's east coast, sun-worshippers must now get to the beach before midday; after that, the sun has set behind a mountain range of construction. From inland, what once were ocean views are now views of other buildings. Further south, in a section called Point of Americas, the developers have been somewhat more considerate in their use of the land and have left more space between their buildings. Still, when the last building in the Point of Americas complex was completed, it managed to block the southeasterly view of the Atlantic that many apartment owners bought in their original package.

One of the unusual things about Fort Lauderdale has always been its seven-mile stretch of public beach, skirted gracefully by Highway A-1A. Neither Miami nor Palm Beach has anything like this beach, which is permanently protected from the developer's hand. It is this beach that periodically attracts throngs of college kids — particularly during Easter vacation. (They still come in droves, though a strong contingent has defected to Delray Beach, farther north.) But recently a grim ecological note has been sounded. From the highest of the high-rises, it is appallingly visible: a wide and spreading tongue of livid water that flows out of the Inland Waterway and from New River, through Port Everglades (itself a sewage dump for cruise ships) and out into the Atlantic Ocean at the southernmost tip of the city. Each year, the swathe of red-black water seems to grow wider, stretch out its feathery fingers farther. Increased development has meant increased pollution, and it has been estimated that if nothing is done, Fort Lauderdale's famous beach will be unfit for swimming in less than five years' time.

Socially, Fort Lauderdale is changing, too. Fort Lauderdale has been called "the Venice of America," and for years it has been Florida's yachting capital. Within an area of thirty-five square miles of what was once a swamp, some two hundred and twenty miles of navigable canals and waterways have been carved, so that wherever you are in Fort Lauderdale you are never more than a few steps away from water (rather dirty water, to be sure), and you can tie up your boat in your backyard, as nearly everybody does. The yachting crowd that originally came to Fort Lauderdale was composed largely of Middle Westerners — retired executives of companies in Ohio, Michigan, Missouri, and Illinois, who may not have known much about yachting when they first arrived, but who had the cash and the time to learn. One-Upmanship in terms of yachts quickly became Fort Lauderdale's favorite parlor game, with "How big is your boat?" the commonest opening gambit.

It is said that a typical cocktail party conversation in Fort Lauderdale starts like this:

"Nice to meet you. How big is your boat?"

"Forty-seven feet. How big is yours?"

"Bigger."

These relatively old-time residents might be said to form the social backbone of such institutions as the Coral Ridge Yacht Club and, more particularly, the Fort Lauderdale Yacht Club, headquarters of what has been called "the Geritol Set." There is still a distinctly Middle Western flavor to life here. At the Parker Playhouse, the rule is "What goes over in Dayton will go over here," and such Broadway hits as *The Boys in the Band,* about a group of homosexuals, are deemed unfit for Fort Lauderdale audiences (though Lauderdale is not without its "gay" bars). Even the much tamer *You Know I Can't Hear You When the Water's Running* was ruled out as "too racy."

There has, however, long been evidence that Fort Lauderdale is wearying of its reputation as an enclave of Middle Western retirees who have taken to boating for lack of anything better to do, whose most flourishing enterprise was the local chapter of the John Birch Society, and who were, quite incongruously, joined once a year by thousands of long-haired and half-naked youngsters from Eastern campuses who lived it up on the beach with drink, drugs, and sex, much of it free. Fort Lauderdale wanted to be taken seriously as a *city,* and a place where at least some aspects of the good life could be discovered. The biggest boost in this direction which Fort Lauderdale has received has been the recent development of Le Club International with its infusion of new and frankly flashy money like — well, like the Bernard Castros'.

Le Club and its beamish young host, Paul Holm, have proved several things about Fort Lauderdale all at once. They proved that there was, after all, a sleekly handsome Younger Set in Fort Lauderdale — they had been there all along, with no place to go, very much like the thin person who is supposed to be inside every fat person, trying to get out.

Now they are at Le Club night after night, dancing to hard, loud, fast music, and they include some of the prettiest girls Fort Lauderdale has seen in decades. "I don't know where Paul finds them," confesses a friend. "I think they must come from a rental agency — a kind of Hertz Rent-a-Tart." When queried, Paul Holm merely smiles mysteriously. Le Club also contains a discreet number of guest rooms, accessible without the guest having to pass through the lobby, which many guests consider an advantage. Paul Holm has also proven that traditionally conservative Fort Lauderdale could make room for a club that has no religious or racial restrictions, and yet charges a fat one-thousand-dollar initiation fee for those who wish to join. The secret of Le Club's success, according to Holm, is simple. "People like to see celebrities," he says, and so he has kept the flow of celebrities coming in a steady and persistent stream, in what has been called the "Hey, there" system. ("Hey, there's Hugh O'Brian . . . Hey, there's Dinah Shore playing tennis with Elke Sommer . . . Hey, there comes Joe Namath out of his houseboat," and so on.) The formula certainly seems to be working.

Celebrities attract other celebrities as well as those who merely want to rub elbows with celebrities. Ann Miller, Groucho Marx, Danny Thomas, and dozens of others have been making their way to Fort Lauderdale, with so much partying going on that some people nickname it Fort Liquordale. Nancy Dickerson has taken an apartment there, and so, for a while at least, did Johnny Carson. Carson has a reputation for being a somewhat casual businessman. Not long ago his parents, Mr. and Mrs. "Kit" Carson, showed up at Ocean Manor, expecting to spend a few pleasant weeks in their son's apartment. An embarrassed management had to explain that the Carson lease had been allowed to expire several months before.

Fort Lauderdale has, in other words, become almost as glittery and glamorous as Palm Beach, without the latter's strained pomp and formality and endless emphasis on clothes-changing and gossip. And Fort Lauderdale has become as show-offy as Miami Beach, without the latter's strident vulgarity. There is, after all, a difference between wearing a mink stole on the beach and owning a mink-covered sofa bed — a subtle difference, perhaps, but still a difference. At the same time, Fort Lauderdale tries to keep one foot in its not-too-distant past, as can be seen from the crowds that turn up at the dog track, and in the intent faces of the purple-haired ladies who, night after night, fill up the Atlantic City–style auction rooms, feverishly bidding on second-hand diamond bracelets and "genuine antique" Chinese vases.

By day, Fort Lauderdale remains thoroughly dedicated to boats and boating, and Fort Lauderdale boating has developed its own breezy style. Where else but in Fort Lauderdale would you find a yacht with not one but two wood-burning fireplaces? Life for the yachtsman is comfortably upholstered wherever he turns, which has turned the Lauderdale marina business into an industry that takes in about a hundred million dollars a year. The Bahia Mar marina has dock space for three hundred private yachts and fifty sports-fishing boats. A yachting party can tie up here and, within minutes, be lolling on the wide Fort Lauderdale beach. Bahia Mar has its own shopping center with a self-service laundry, and a flossily got-out Patricia Murphy restaurant for indoor-outdoor dining. As insurance against a remote day when no yachts might show up, Bahia Mar also operates a 115-room motel.

If Bahia Mar seems too much like roughing it (with that self-service laundry, for example) there is always Pier 66, just up the canal. Pier 66 is the brainchild of Mr. Kenneth S. ("Boots") Adams, retired board chairman of the Phillips Petroleum Company, a yachtsman who needed a place to park his boat. The result is a kind of high-rise gas station that rises a full seventeen stories above the pumps, designed in a moonstruck style. This tower contains 156 deluxe guest suites, each with a balcony, and a rooftop revolving cocktail lounge. When your yacht steams into the Pier 66 marina, you are met by a uniformed dockman who registers you as you would be registered at a hotel. Immediately, a telephone is plugged in, and your boat has full hotel services, including room service and laundry, which if sent out by eight, will be delivered back to your stateroom by five P.M. (These details are outlined to you in honeyed tones by your super-dockman when you tie up.) Pier 66 facilities also include shops, a liquor store, ice cubes, two heated swimming pools, three more non-revolving cocktail lounges — and a great many other things. Sixty-six is the magic number for the Phillips Petroleum Company. (It seems that when testing their gasoline back in 1927, a car got up to 66 miles an hour.) The 66 theme is everywhere. The hotel-marina complex had its first full season in 1966. The diameter of the revolving cocktail lounge is 66 feet. It takes 66 minutes for the room to make a complete revolution. The glass-enclosed outside elevator that slithers up and down the building takes

66 seconds to complete a one-way trip. And so on. Even the telephone number of Pier 66 is composed of double sixes.

The watery orientation of Fort Lauderdale received additional impetus in the mid-1950's when it was pointed out that Port Everglades, which faces the city from the south, contains the deepest natural harbor of any Atlantic seaport south of Norfolk, Virginia. Proprietors of winter cruises, which had been departing from New York and losing business, knew that one reason for their woes was that passengers disliked having to spend two to three days at sea before reaching tropical weather. If, on the other hand, they flew to Fort Lauderdale to board their ships, they could be under sunny skies in a matter of hours. The Port Everglades cruise business has grown to such an extent since this idea was hatched that now some one hundred and fifty major Caribbean and South Atlantic cruises originate or terminate there. The arriving and departing cruise ships provide colorful sights from the terraces of the high-rises, and their passengers — since they are nearly always in a holiday mood — add zest and gaiety to Fort Lauderdale night life. One woman bubbles, "The cruise ships that come and go here give us an international air!" Well, perhaps not, but they do give Fort Lauderdale something it didn't have before.

Local boosters keep trying to pump more life into the tourist trade, which is, after all, the primary industry not only in Fort Lauderdale but in all of Florida. Because it was a boat, if for no other reason, the old *Queen Elizabeth* was for a while tied up at Port Everglades as a "tourist attraction." The *Queen* failed to attract, and went elsewhere to die. Another enterprise has also turned out to be something of a white elephant. This is an expensive-looking complex called the Swimming Hall of Fame, which features an Olympic-size pool and depictions of swimming "greats," plus exhibits and mementoes of the breaststroke, backstroke, and Australian crawl. Johnny Weissmuller, now a bit paunchier than when he was Tarzan, was made the Hall's director. "The general reception to the Swimming Hall of Fame has been sort of ho-hum," admits one resident.

It used to be, in Fort Lauderdale, with its generally WASP-y and Birch-y complexion, that Jews were "not encouraged" to buy houses in Fort Lauderdale proper. "You'd really be much happier, I think, in Hollywood," used to be the realtor's tactful approach to the situation, referring not to Hollywood, California, but the town in Florida, just a few miles below Fort Lauderdale. As a result, Hollywood Beach became a resort with a decidedly Jewish cast. Today, however — with social anti-Semitism not only unfashionable but unacceptable in most circles — all this has changed. Still, it is said that neither the Coral Ridge nor the Lauderdale Yacht Club really wants Jewish members, though there are a few in each club.

Real estate restrictions do, however, apply to blacks. This is a Southern city, and one hears the oft-repeated Florida refrain: "The Northerners who move down here start off with Northern ideas, but it's not long before they're even more Southern than the Southerners when it comes to how to treat the blacks."

The black ghetto of Fort Lauderdale is a dismal place — not far from the center of town and yet, as is the case in other Florida resort cities, conveniently out of the way and out of sight. You would have to be looking for it, or else be hopelessly lost, to find it. Whenever Lauderdale mayors have tried to do something to improve the lot of the blacks, these mayors have had poor luck getting reelected to office. Lauderdale has been proud, though, that it has had no riots. There was "trouble" a couple of summers ago, but it was cleared up, if in typically Southern fashion. The trouble began in a large vacant lot that black youths used for drag racing. There were complaints, and counter-complaints. A council was called to listen to the blacks' grievances; what they wanted, the blacks explained, was to have the city build a drag strip so that they would not have to use the vacant lot. A drag strip would have cost about forty thousand dollars. Instead, the city of Fort Lauderdale purchased a forty-three-thousand-dollar "monster" — a riot-control tank armed with guns, tear gas, grenades, and so on. The problem was declared solved.

As Fort Lauderdale has been growing from a cloistered resort to a fair-sized city with industries other than tourism, and a large permanent population, a number of people have been giving thought to what the city was losing, as well as to what it was gaining, in the process. Many observers felt that whereas Fort Lauderdale might be strong in terms of boats and boating, it was weak in terms of culture. They, like the young revolutionaries in Kansas City, have set about to change all this.

Today, as a result, Fort Lauderdale has a full-scale symphony orchestra. The Metropolitan Opera arrives regularly with a touring company, and performances are often sold out weeks in advance (but then, so are lectures by such as the "prophetess" Jeane Dixon). The War Memorial Auditorium, built for sports events, will soon be razed and rebuilt so that it can more comfortably accommodate the opera than it does at present. Nearby stands the Parker Playhouse, and there are plans to turn this entire area into a full-scale cultural center. All at once, everybody in Fort Lauderdale is *almost* as aware of the arts as of boats.

Two energetic ladies, Mrs. William Maurer and Mrs. Francis McCahill, each of whom has carved out a segment of Fort Lauderdale's cultural life for her own particular enthusiasm, exemplify what is currently going on.

Fort Lauderdale, for example, has never had a decent newspaper. A "pink section" of the Miami *Herald* devoted to Lauderdale is probably the place where most Lauderdale people turn for news of their city. Five years or so ago, Yolanda Maurer decided to publish a magazine devoted to Fort Lauderdale, called *Pictorial Life*. Admittedly, *Pictorial Life* concentrates primarily on social goings-on, sports, and the yachting world. "It's what sells magazines down here, after all," Mrs. Maurer admits, but the magazine has been successful. And, with success, it has been able to devote more of its pages to less frothy matters, to city government, problems of the local slums, pollution, education, economics. It is beginning to seem as though at last Fort Lauderdale has found a "voice." Mrs. Maurer's property has become a valuable one, and she has had offers to buy the magazine. She won't sell.

Mrs. Maurer charges through her daily schedule like an express train — selling ads and subscriptions, and chasing stories. Equally busy is Mrs. McCahill, whose crusade is for the Fort Lauderdale Museum of the Arts. At present, the art museum is housed in a small and unsatisfactory building, and has had the problems any new institution always has getting under way. Ten years ago, the idea of an art museum in Fort Lauderdale was considered insanity, but Mary McCahill has made the museum her personal project. A rich woman, she has for the last several years been personally paying the curator's salary, and if one day Fort Lauderdale does not have a first-class museum, Mary McCahill will know the reason why.

Like many strong-willed women, Mary McCahill has made enemies, but no one seriously questions her conviction nor the worthiness of her goal. She has been able to enlist the support of many of the newly-rich people who have come to Fort Lauderdale — Mrs. Theresa Castro, for one.

"This is a funny place," Mary McCahill said not long ago. "So many people come here from other places, and when you try to raise money there's an 'I-gave-at-the-office' kind of attitude. Because they gave to the museums and the symphonies back in Dayton and Cleveland, they don't see why they should now help Fort Lauderdale. They've come to Fort Lauderdale to be *through* with all that, and it's like pulling teeth to get them moving again, to convince them that they *can't* come to Fort Lauderdale to vote against school appropriations, just because they paid so many school taxes back in Detroit. It isn't fair to their new home. It's a *new attitude* we've got to try to build here — to get people to think of Fort Lauderdale not just as a place to *retire* to, but a place where people *live!*"

Both Mrs. McCahill and her husband — who is, technically, "retired" — put in a full day's work at the museum every day. The McCahills have a big house on Isla Bahia Drive, the "Millionaires' Row" of Fort Lauderdale, and their house, not surprisingly, backs up on one of Fort Lauderdale's myriad canals. But gesturing around her still-very-little museum downtown, Mary McCahill says, *"Here* is where we really live!"

Not long ago, the McCahills sold the big boat that used to park at the foot of their backyard garden. Indeed, a new wave may be coming.

"Jay" Rockefeller — the right place is West Virginia

5

West Virginia:
"In These Hills and Hollows"

W HY would the heir to one of the largest private fortunes in the
world choose — indeed eagerly elect — to make his home on
the fringes of Appalachia? It is all a part of the new style and meaning of wealth in America, where the value of all the old trappings of
money is rapidly disappearing, and where the wrong places are becoming the right places.

It all began, oddly enough, with a rumor that a nudist colony for
"Northern swingers" was about to be built in the heart of these bleak
and profitless hills. It seemed hardly possible, but that was the talk.
There had been a sudden and mysterious flurry of land-buying in the
wild, green, mountainous, and — if one can overlook the periodic
stains of poverty that streak the hillsides — extraordinarily beautiful
vastness of Pocahontas County, West Virginia, a region so remote and
silent that it was thought to be worthless for anything other than rabbit and quail shooting and, perhaps, the discreet manufacture of a bit
of moonshine whisky. Who was buying this land, and why? Almost
anyone who wants to purchase land almost anywhere in West Virginia creates some sort of stir, because he must either have discovered
a new vein of bituminous coal, or else gone crazy. West Virginia is
one of the four poorest states in the country — only South Carolina,
Alabama, and Arkansas have a lower per capita income or a higher rate
of unemployment — and the possibility of new money finding its way
into the state is usually considered so remote that even West Virginians

despair of its ever happening. Here, where life at its best has for such a long time been hard and grim and sour, even the old-timers who love their "hills and hollows" wonder why anyone else would want to come to West Virginia. But Pocahontas County land was being bought up in parcels of hundreds of thousands of acres.

The purchaser or purchasers remained, meanwhile, shadowy and anonymous, and the deals were being negotiated with extreme secrecy through a series of New York law and real estate firms. More rumors billowed from hill to hollow. It was Howard Hughes, about to turn this corner of the state into another Las Vegas. It was Aristotle Onassis, planning to create a huge redoubt on the scale of his private island in the Aegean. It was the federal government, with a design to erect a super-penitentiary where — West Virginia being what it is — only the hardest and most incorrigible prisoners would be interned. There were a number of local people who wanly hoped that the wilderness would be the site of some sort of factory, where some of the dirt-poor menfolk of the region could find jobs. But the most "reliable" rumor insisted on a nude playground.

Needless to say, when printed invitations arrived in some five hundred Pocahontas County mailboxes, asking all and sundry in the region "to meet your new neighbors," there was a heavy turnout on the appointed day. The guests assembled, and presently a tall, slender, amiable-looking, dark-haired young man stepped up onto the make-shift stage, leading a pretty, blonde, blue-eyed young woman by the hand, smiled, and said, "Hi, I'm Jay Rockefeller, and this is my wife, Sharon. We want to build a house in this beautiful country of yours, and make it our home." A great cheer went up. It was just another example of the easy and winning charm of this youthful politician who swamped the Republican opposition in 1968 to become West Virginia's Democratic secretary of state (under a Republican governor), who in 1972 won the Democratic nomination for governor, and who could — as an active and growing band of Jay Rockefeller–watchers insist — be a winning candidate for President of the United States in 1980.

"Jay" Rockefeller is, of course, John Davison Rockefeller IV, great-grandson of the dynastic founder of the Standard Oil Company, and Jay's wife, Sharon, is the daughter of Illinois Senator Charles H. Percy, who is not exactly poor, either. The young Rockefellers' big barbecue-picnic at their new three-thousand-acre-plus spread in rural West Virginia was an immediate and enormous success. Sharon, golden hair swinging, was all bounce and smiles and earnestness, moving about from guest to guest, nibbling at a chicken leg and licking her fingers, asking questions ("Is there a good market nearby for fresh vegetables?" "Is there a diaper service?"), listening to the answers, performing introductions, showing an astonishing facility for remembering names, and, very quickly, getting on a first-name basis with everybody. Jay meanwhile, strolled about giving big, hearty handshakes, delivering friendly back-slaps to his neighbors, kissing babies, squeezing the shoulders and elbows of little old ladies (as a politician, he is even more of a toucher, a grabber, a hugger than his Uncle Nelson), and grinning down at the younger women with his big dark eyes and telling them just how gosh-darned pretty they looked. (Since moving to West Virginia, Jay Rockefeller has demonstrated something close to a professional actor's command of the local speech and idiom; it is certainly a far cry from any accent he might have picked up at Exeter or Harvard, and it works wonders). By the end of the afternoon, everyone was agreeing that — rich folks or no — Jay and Sharon Rockefeller were "just plain folks, no different than you and me." If these were nudists, they were certainly nice ones. This, of course, was just the impression Jay Rockefeller had been trying to cultivate in West Virginia from the beginning.

Even Jay's father, John D. Rockefeller III, managed to do himself proud at the party — and to some people's surprise. The senior Rockefeller is the shyest, the most withdrawn and introspective of the five Rockefeller brothers (which include Nelson, David, Winthrop, and Laurance). At large gatherings, Mr. Rockefeller often seems to be ill at ease, and this has been interpreted as snobbishness, or at least aristocratic aloofness. But at his son's picnic he mingled right in with the West Virginia farm folk, many of whom had never set foot outside their corner of the state. At the Rockefeller family estate in New York's Westchester County, John D. Three, as they call him, is something of a gentleman farmer, and that afternoon, talking with one of Jay's new neighbors, Mr. Rockefeller was overheard saying, "Why, I had that exact same trouble with my pigs!" The neighbors all wanted to know where Mr. Rockefeller was staying "out here in these hills and hollows," and he explained that he was putting up at the Greenbrier Hotel. Many West Virginians may be poor, but they are fiercely proud of their Southern hospitality, and the Pocahontas County farmers said to Mr. Rockefeller, "Now don't you waste your money any more at that Greenbrier. My Lord, they'll charge you forty dollars a day for a *room!* Next time, you-all just come and stay with *us.*"

"And if you get to New York," replied John D. Rockefeller III earnestly, "you-all come and stay with *me.*" Hearing this, Jay Rockefeller took his father aside and said, "Dad, down here they take these things literally. If you keep talking like that, you're going to have a whole slew of West Virginia farmers for house guests in New York."

Though Jay and Sharon Rockefeller have lived in West Virginia since 1964, enthusiastically insisting all the while that they find the place the most fascinating, challenging, and lovely in all the world, and that they would not willingly live anyplace else, there is still something outwardly a bit incongruous — to some of their parents' generation, at least — in the fact that these two enormously handsome and rich young people would have chosen this hardscrabble state in which to settle and make their future. Did they do so solely for *political* reasons? Bobby Kennedy, a few years ago, to establish himself politically, moved to New York City. Do the Rockefellers *really* like it here, or is there some hidden ulterior motive? Not long ago, out campaigning for governor against the incumbent Republican, Arch Moore, Jay Rockefeller tapped on the front door of a tiny house in a little West Virginia town named Sod (pop. 63). An elderly person, whose head was wrapped in a blue kerchief, looked pleased when she recognized her caller, and then complained that her toes were most certainly giving her misery.

Sod, West Virginia, is perhaps an even more woebegone place than its name implies. A derelict washing machine stood on the porch of the woman's tarpaper house, and behind the house an exhausted-looking privy leaned against a tree. A skinny chicken pecked in the dirt outside. In his J. Press jacket, button-down shirt, gray flannel slacks, Church's shoes, and a "sincere" regimental-striped necktie (for reasons he admits are political, Jay Rockefeller adopts the 1950's-collegiate style of dress), the Democratic candidate for governor was telling this par-

ticular voter about his dream of turning Lincoln County (one of the
state's very poorest) into — well, into something maybe a little better.
Down the road, a sign painted on an abandoned barn commanded:
CHEW MAIL POUCH TOBACCO!

"The answer is to attract new industry to the area," Jay Rockefeller was saying, and the old woman was nodding, agreeing, envision-
ing new industry coming to Sod. Across the street, in a sweater and
skirt and a purple wool coat with shiny silver buttons — no jewelry
other than her small emerald engagement ring, no visible makeup —
Sharon Percy Rockefeller was standing in the used-car lot next to
Mitchell's Esso station, listening with sympathy to a man who had had
an ear, an eye, and half of his face blown away in a mining accident.
That was over a year ago, he said, and he had still had no help from
welfare.

The contrast between the surroundings of the young Rockefellers
and their relatives in the North is almost grotesquely sharp. Five hundred miles away, back at Pocantico Hills, the Rockefeller family com-
pound in Tarrytown, New York (why was it so much a part of the old
style of the rich to cluster together in sealed-off family fiefdoms, one
wonders?) there is, among other things, the playhouse. This is the
playhouse where Jay Rockefeller and his sisters played when they
were children. The playhouse itself is three stories high, with an
indoor swimming pool (of course there is an outdoor one as well), a
four-lane bowling alley, a squash court, a gymnasium, and an embarrassment of other pleasures including a tennis court and a golf course.
The playhouse, in other words, is a private Rockefeller country club —
for the children.

All around, on the surrounding acres of the estate (collectively, the
Rockefellers are the biggest private propertyholders in Westchester),
each Rockefeller has his own house, each with its *own* pool, *own*
tennis courts. Jay Rockefeller's mother, the former Blanchette Ferry
Hooker, inherited two fortunes of her own — one from the Ferry Seed
Company, and another from the Hooker Electrochemical Company.
Her father was so keen on tennis for his four daughters that he hired
a private tennis professional to come and live on the Hookers' Green-
wich estate. Jay Rockefeller's father landscaped his share of Pocantico
Hills so that, even though there are other houses nearby — even a

fair-sized town — he can stand at any point on his property and have an uninterrupted view of woods, river, hills, and sky. He does not like to have other structures mar his vista, much less billboards that urge him to chew Mail Pouch Tobacco. Why, then — it is impossible not to ask — when they could have so much else, are the young Rockefellers *here,* in *this* godforsaken place? And, while here, why are they doing what they're doing? Even John D. Three doesn't seem quite to understand. At his son's Pocahontas County picnic, Jay asked his father, "Dad, what do you think of what I'm doing down here?" His father looked briefly bewildered, and then replied, "Well, I think what you're doing is very nice — but does it have to be in *politics?"*

Jay Rockefeller shrugs, and says, "My father represents a set of values that just don't have much meaning any more."

The Rockefellers have long had, as a family, a strong sense of mission. They have demonstrated a crusading spirit which — with the various Rockefeller foundations, grants, restorations, and other benefactions — has seemed aimed specifically at trying to set the ills of the world to rights. They have become America's arch-do-gooders. Whereas the Ford Foundation, for example, was unabashedly created as a mechanism to help the heirs of Henry Ford escape huge inheritance taxes, the Rockefeller family philanthropies have always seemed sincerely more high-minded, designed to help the needy and deserving. It has been said that the Rockefellers have approached philanthropy this way out of a sense of penance and a Protestant sense of guilt over the inequities dealt out by the first John D. Rockefeller in the process of making himself the richest man in the world. Though the first John D. enjoyed throwing shiny new dimes to poor children when they knelt begging in his path, there were a great many other people who crossed his life who met with nothing short of disaster. And, considering the respectability and eminence and lofty worthiness of today's Rockefellers, it is hard to believe that barely a generation ago Mrs. David Lion Gardiner, dowager of New York's venerable Gardiner clan, gathered her family about her and said — referring specifically to the five Rockefeller brothers — "No Gardiner will ever play with the grandchildren of a gangster." Today, of course, the Rockefeller name is associated with industrial and banking efficiency and integrity, with civic rectitude and duty, with the improvement of international relations and the human condition in general, and with vast patronage of the arts, medicine, and science.

At the same time, there is said to be another side to the Rockefeller coin — and coin is something the Rockefellers have much of — which is less apparent, yet far more concentrated, far less desirable, even sinister. There is a theory, more widely held than most people realize, that the Rockefellers want nothing more nor less than to divide up the entire world between various members of their family. They want in fact to be kings, controllers of all they survey, and are systematically nibbling away at this planet's real estate until one day it will all belong to them. One of the problems young Jay Rockefeller faced in his campaign for the governorship of West Virginia is that he has been cited as one of the key figures in the international Rockefeller conspiracy to rule the world. In fact, his opponents in the state actually circulated literature to this effect. To the easily frightened, this is a frightening notion.

Among the items supporting the conspiracy theory are these: Nelson Rockefeller, as governor of New York, has control of that state. Uncle Nelson, furthermore, has developed large landholdings in Venezuela, giving him more than a small amount of leverage in that country, and elsewhere in South America. Uncle Winthrop, in the meantime, was until recently governor of Arkansas, is still a political force there, and a large landholder.

Uncle Laurance has concentrated his efforts on developing large resort hotels occupying considerable acreage in the Virgin Islands, Puerto Rico, and Hawaii. New Rockefeller resort tentacles have been stretching out elsewhere in the South Pacific. Uncle David, the best friend one could possibly have at the Chase Manhattan Bank (since he's chairman of it), is not only an awesome power in Wall Street but one of the two or three most powerful commercial banking figures in the world. David has also spread his interests to include the film and entertainment industry. Father John D. Three, while his main thrust has been in the direction of philanthropy, has also been a key figure behind, in addition to other things, the restoration of Williamsburg, Virginia. And now with young Jay making a bid to take over

West Virginia — well, conspiracy or no, it is certainly true that Rocke-fellers have spread their activities across a great deal of the earth's ter-ritory.

But people who know young Jay Rockefeller merely laugh at this sort of talk. Jay, they point out, has always been an intensely public-spirited young man. He has also, from early boyhood, wanted des-perately to be something other than a rich man's son, the fourth-generation bearer of a celebrated name. He has wanted to succeed — indeed, to be famous — in his own right. "Anybody who goes into politics has to have a pretty big ego," says one of his friends, "and I'm sure Jay's is one of the biggest around. His ego gives him self-confidence, makes the guy positive he'll win at whatever he sets out to do. At the same time, his ego doesn't *show* — the way, for example, the Kennedy ego always showed and was vaguely offensive. He's a whole new kind of *today* politician."

This ego, and this ambition, Jay Rockefeller doubtless inherited from his mother. Even Jay's wife, who knows her mother-in-law well, admits that there is more of Blanchette Rockefeller in Jay than there is of John D. Three. Blanchette Rockefeller, for example, was the first distaff Rockefeller to merit her own paragraph in *Who's Who*, where she is listed as an "organization executive," in connection with her many trusteeships — of New York's Museum of Modern Art, the Community Service Society, the Brearley School, Vassar College, the Metropolitan Opera Guild, and the New York Philharmonic. It is from his mother, too, that Jay gets his hail-fellow personality, and his natural athletic ability — neither of which John D. Three possesses. Neither mother nor son is willing to sit back and just be a Rockefeller, a fat cat, and there are moments when Jay Rockefeller seems actually embarrassed by the name he bears. "Damn it, it's in *songs!*" he says. (". . . And if I never had a dime, I'd be rich as Rockefeller. . . .") And not long ago, caught short of cash in a Washington restaurant, Jay Rockefeller tried to pay his bill with a personal check. The waiter refused to believe he was who he said he was, and only a helpful friend with a credit card averted the possibility that the red-faced Jay might have been sent into the kitchen to wash dishes. As a bache-lor, living in Washington, he also developed a cynical approach to the girls he dated. "I'd always have to ask myself, with each new girl, is she going out with the name, the money, or the guy?" he says.

Jay Rockefeller had spent no more than three years as a Harvard undergraduate when the urge to make something special of himself overtook him and, without graduating, he took off for Japan for three years of study at the International Christian University in Tokyo. Here he worked as an English instructor and — a language whiz — became fluent in both reading and writing Japanese. He then returned to Harvard, graduated with a degree in Far Eastern affairs and languages, and went on to Yale to study Chinese.

Like many other young Americans during the early days of the Kennedy Administration, Jay Rockefeller became excited about the work the Peace Corps was doing. He joined the Corps in the summer of 1962, becoming a special assistant to the director, Sargent Shriver, and, appropriately, working as a recruiting officer for Peace Corps posts in the Far East. (Of all the Kennedy clan he is said still to admire Shriver the most, though Jay is too politic to say so.) A year later, he moved on to the State Department, again concentrating on Asian affairs. During these Washington years, Jay Rockefeller lived — with his friend Bill Wister (of the very proper Philadelphia Wisters) — in a handsome town house on Volta Place with a heated pool behind it and a park in front of it where Jay and Bill and their friends played tennis and touch football on weekends. While there, Jay himself gained something of a reputation. He was known as a fellow who would take one girl to a party, meet another one there, and — with no more than an offhand invitation to the second girl to visit "the family shack" — whip her off to Volta Place in his XK–E, after quickly phoning Bill Wister to tell him to get lost. "In those days," says one girl who dated him, "even though it was very clear that he knew a lot about the Orient, he was so cocky and vain and arrogant that — well, if he hadn't been so good-looking *and* a Rockefeller besides — I'd have hated him. In fact, I think I did hate him."

Inwardly, Jay Rockefeller still felt restless, unfulfilled. At one point, after meeting Maxwell Taylor and hearing about the Green Berets, Jay Rockefeller excitedly proposed to his friend and fellow Peace Corpsman Ray La Montaigne that they should both — since they had never been in the service — join the Marines. Both men marched down to the recruiting office to enlist, where they were promptly informed that La Montaigne, at twenty-seven, was too old, and that Jay Rockefeller, at six feet six inches, was too tall.

It was another friend of Jay's — Charlie Peters, now editor of the *Washington Monthly* — who first directed Jay's attention to West Virginia. Peters, who admits that he is a frustrated politician and would himself have liked to run for governor of his native state ("But I didn't have the money"), was an active worker in both the John and Bobby Kennedy campaigns. Peters had made Jay Rockefeller the godfather of his son, and had said to him, in effect, "If you ever want to go into politics, start in West Virginia because if you can accomplish anything in West Virginia you can do it anywhere." At that point, Jay Rockefeller's knowledge of West Virginia had been, like his father's, pretty much limited to the luxurious confines of the Greenbrier. He had never been treated to the desolate reaches of the northwestern part of the state, around such Appalachian communities as Morgantown. At Charlie Peters's suggestion, Jay Rockefeller took an aerial tour of West Virginia, where, among other shocks and surprises, he first witnessed the rape that has been committed upon much of the state by strip-mining.

Strip-mining is the cheapest and hence the most profitable — but not the only — way to extract coal from the West Virginia hills. Literally whole tops and sides of mountains are plowed aside by bulldozers to open up the coal veins. Once the coal has been removed, the slashes are abandoned. Strip-mining requires no particular engineering skill, and practically anybody capable of driving a tractor can do it. Leases to strip-mine from local property owners, who don't understand much about leases to begin with, are easily and cheaply obtained. The physical results to the countryside are, in the meantime, irreparable. Rains falling on the exposed mountainsides create mudslides that descend to clog and pollute the rivers. Attempts to reforest the stripped regions have proved failures; not enough soil is left for a tree to put down roots. As one ecologist succinctly put it, "It's a tough job to try to rebuild a mountain." The disastrous flood of early 1972 was not a direct result of strip-mining, but it dramatized the haste and ruthlessness, and lack of foresight, with which men have gone after coal in West Virginia.

Land after it has been strip-mined is virtually without value, and what has happened to much of West Virginia is that it has simply been lost beyond reclaiming. The idea of saving what was left of West Virginia immediately appealed to Jay Rockefeller's crusading spirit. This was in 1964, and Jay Rockefeller's first job in the state was with an antipoverty program called Action for Appalachian Youth, where he was assigned to remote Emmons County.

"One of the first things I discovered down here," Jay Rockefeller says, "is that there are two things rural West Virginia people really get excited about — high school sports and local politics." Democrats are in the majority in the state — though that doesn't mean the Democrats will always vote that way — and so Jay Rockefeller turned his back on his family's Republican tradition and became a Democrat. He also became a high school sports fan, and in his political campaigns — first for the West Virginia House of Delegates, next for secretary of state, then for governor — he has been known to take in as many as two high school basketball games an evening. At these games he appears, stands up, waves, and gets cheered (and of course sometimes booed), and makes a little joke about his height and the advantage it gives him in getting a ball into a basket.

One of the girls Jay Rockefeller had been more or less steadily dating was Sharon Percy, seven years younger than he and the daughter of a Republican senator. When Sharon Percy's twin sister, Valerie, was brutally murdered in a still-unsolved crime — while Sharon slept in the bedroom next door — Jay Rockefeller hurried to Sharon's side. His support during and after this tragedy is really what brought them together, and they were married in the spring of 1967. Sharon moved to West Virginia, became a Democrat, and began helping her husband stuff envelopes, lick stamps, and tack up posters on rural telephone poles.

The young Rockefellers' life style in West Virginia has been simple, folksy, and old-shoe. Both Rockefellers insist that they live simply by preference, and not for political reasons. Though beautiful and wealthy, both Rockefellers bend over backward not to be ticked

off as rich snobs. They have made a few mistakes. As any other
young society girl might do upon moving to a new city, Sharon Rockefeller joined the Charleston Junior League, traditional meeting place
for "nice" people. This drew some criticism and, at Jay's suggestion,
Sharon now underplays her membership in the League (though she
still maintains it). She has since preferred to concentrate her efforts
on an organization called Mountain Artisans which recruits women
from West Virginia hamlets and teaches them to stitch New York–
bought fabrics into countrified quilts and pillows and patchwork quilts
and bodices. Not long ago Sharon Rockefeller brought a fashion show
of mountain-made clothes to Bonwit Teller's in New York, where a
number of Manhattan's so-called Beautiful People snapped them up
eagerly. ("Just think, they're made by genuine poor people!" one
woman cooed.) Mountain Artisans boutiques have been set up in other
stores in other cities.

The young Rockefellers' life style has been called phony. "They're
just like two little plastic people," one acquaintance says, "little windup
Judy dolls programmed to turn on with their simplicity and sweetness
whenever you push a button. It's just done to get votes." Well, perhaps, but so far it has appeared to work, and what is the point of being
in politics if not to get votes? The Rockefellers' house is in the fashionable Loudon Heights section of Charleston, and is a traditional
ranch-style affair. Originally it had only two bedrooms. (Again, the
contrast with the Kennedy style is a marked one; Bobby Kennedy,
when he moved to New York to run for the Senate, established himself
in a posh apartment in the United Nations Plaza, probably the most
expensive address in Manhattan.) Since his marriage, Jay Rockefeller's
house has grown somewhat larger. "I've kept adding on," he explains.
"When I bought it, I didn't expect to get married, and when I got
married I didn't expect to have two children." But the Rockefellers
are quick to point out that their house in Loudon Heights is surrounded by many houses that are larger and more grand. Though comfortably staffed (two maids) and decorated (by Mrs. Henry "Sister"
Parrish), breakfast is in the kitchen with Sharon serving cornflakes
out of a box. When the Rockefellers entertain, it is nearly always
political ("We really never do any social entertaining at all," Sharon
says), and inevitably informal. Sharon Rockefeller herself is a fair

cook — her thick broccoli soup is a house favorite — and luncheons by the backyard pool usually consist of her soup and plates of home-made sandwiches, served with pitchers of lemonade and beer.

Even more wary of the political stigma that might be attached to his money and name ("I honestly don't think the name Rockefeller means that much down here"), Jay Rockefeller is concerned lest he be branded a Northern carpetbagger, using West Virginia merely as a stepping-stone to something bigger — namely Washington, D.C. For this reason he turned down a chance to run for the United States Senate from West Virginia, and chose the governorship as his target instead, promising, if elected, to serve two full terms, or the most that the state law allows. "I don't want that New York image," he says frankly. Both Rockefellers have been beseeched to appear on such talk shows as Dick Cavett's and David Frost's, but have refused "because I'm not running for a *national* office; I'm running for a *West Virginia* office." And, not long ago, a New York journalist was following one of the Rockefellers' exhausting campaigning trips through West Virginia (trips conducted in Chevy station wagons, not limousines). The journalist happened to be wearing a Bill Blass suit (slightly nipped waist, slightly flared trousers), and Gucci shoes. Jay Rockefeller suddenly turned to the journalist and said, "Look — don't take this personally, but would you mind not standing so close to me? I mean, you look just a little bit too New Yorky, if you know what I mean — and that could really hurt me here. It's what I'm trying to get *away* from, see?" Also, until recently, Jay and Sharon Rockefeller systematically turned down interviews from national magazines. Asked why the change of policy had come about, Sharon Rockefeller gave a disarmingly honest answer: "Well, perhaps if we're nice to reporters, they'll write nice things about us." She may be right, because the Rockefellers quickly got an affectionate national press.

The crucial point in Jay Rockefeller's campaign for governor — and the point that he knew could cost or win him the election — was his dramatic stand against strip-mining. If elected, he promised, he would see to it that strip-mining was abolished. Strip-mining, meanwhile, was a political issue in West Virginia only depending on where you happened to be. That is, if one inveighs against strip-mining in a county where it's being heavily done, one may find oneself in heavy trouble.

In non-bituminous areas of the state, nobody could care less. Strip-mining is accomplished by bulldozing, and also by blasting, and in the latter area West Virginia's explosives industry has much at stake. A telling message on the marquee of a Boone County motel said recently: "WELCOME STRIP-MINERS — THE WEST VIRGINIA EXPLOSIVE MANU-FACTURERS ASSN." Explosives manufacturers, it may not be necessary to point out, know how to make bombs, and during the Rockefeller campaign there were threats and unsettling moments such as an incident when two hundred angry strip-miners pressed in on Jay Rockefeller at a meeting and it was necessary to employ a bodyguard to hold the crowd back. Jay Rockefeller himself remained cool.

Men such as Washington's Charlie Peters who have worked hard for Rockefeller behind the scenes were convinced that his stand on strip-mining would win him the election. "It took a lot of guts to come out against that," Peters says, "and I think the people of West Virginia admire guts, and even those people who were profiting from strip mines privately admitted that what they were doing was ruining their state, making it unlivable. Deep well drilling does cost more, but it's still profitable, and it employs more people — which the state needs in order to get men off the relief rolls. Anyway, Jay has winning qualities that will take him a long way. He really likes meeting people, he likes being the center of the stage, and he gets a tremendous kick out of campaigning. Also, he has no impulses to be autocratic. I've never seen Jay be nasty. Bobby Kennedy could be nasty — shouting orders at people, telling them where to get off. But Jay is a persuader. He's more like Jack Kennedy than Bobby. I used to say that I'd never seen Jack Kennedy be nasty, but one afternoon one of Jack's aides said to me, 'You've never seen Jack blow up? You should be upstairs in the suite right now.' And Jay has a great asset in Sharon. She's enthusiastic, and bright, and pretty. If you compare Jay with Ted Kennedy, you have to admit that in that respect Joan is *not* a political asset. Oh, Joan is pretty — but she's so shy and standoffish and ill at ease. Wherever she is, Joan Kennedy looks as though she wished she weren't there."

Understandably, the greatest criticism leveled against the Rockefellers is that they are really not sincere about West Virginia, that they are using this forlorn state as a stepping-stone to some loftier position.

And Jay's and Sharon's glad-handing manner with the simple folk of the little towns has been called a practiced artifice. It is true that some of the things Jay Rockefeller says sound a bit manufactured. For example, to Mrs. Mitchell, proprietress of Mitchell's Esso Station, he inquired cheerily, "Who's your closest competition?" Mrs. Mitchell looked blank for a moment, and then said, "Don't got no competition." "Say, that's just *great!*" beamed the young Standard Oil (Esso) heir whom the opposition had already begun calling "Jay-Bird." At other times, though, his logic slips a gear and fails him, revealing his youth. At a gathering of school board officials, in Hamlin, West Virginia, Jay Rockefeller made a speech which included the puzzling statement, "I believe in spending money on educating children, which is what most children really are." Well, it had been a long day.

He can, on the other hand, be fast with a quip. When a reporter asked him not long ago whether or not he would someday like to live at 1600 Pennsylvania Avenue, Jay Rockefeller replied, "Route Ten doesn't go that far." To which Sharon added, "And at the rate we're going we'll never make it."

By those who consider themselves sophisticated politicians, Jay and Sharon Rockefeller have been labeled naïve and square. Perhaps they are — a bit. They hardly ever drink, don't smoke, and pop breath-sweetening lozenges into each other's mouths before each stop along a campaign route. In their car they carry packages of Oreo cookies for snacks and marshmallow-filled chocolate bars for quick energy, along with the boxes of campaign literature and buttons. When informed that ahead of them, in the sheriff's car that was leading their entourage, the sheriff and his men were amusing themselves listening to pornographic tapes on the car's tape deck, Sharon Rockefeller was shocked. "Why, I simply can't imagine such a thing!" she cried. Another Rockefeller aide was chatting casually about his personal trips with pot and LSD. "But don't ever mention that sort of thing in front of Jay and Sharon!" he warned. "I mean, man, they're *straight.*" And the Rockefellers seem sincerely to love what they are doing. When two-and-a-half-year-old Jamie (as John D. Rockefeller V is called) complained to his mother not long ago that she was never home, Sharon simply patted his head and said, "You'll just have to get used to it, that's all." Also, the Rockefellers do seem genuinely to love their adopted state.

Perhaps for the simple reason that it is so totally unlike the palaces and playhouses in which they grew up.

Jay's folksy manner, his friends insist, is *not* a put-on. He really *does* want to be liked for the guy he is, not for the money or the name. His friend Ray La Montaigne likes to tell the story of how, one day when Ray's father was visiting him from New Hampshire, Jay Rockefeller dropped by. Ray introduced Jay to his father, and then, after visiting for an hour or so, Jay announced that he had to be on his way. He started out the back door toward where the XK–E was parked. "Oh, Jay," said Ray La Montaigne. "If you're going out that way, would you mind dropping that bag of garbage in the can as you go by?" "Sure," Jay Rockefeller replied, scooped up the garbage, and was off.

"My father," says Ray La Montaigne, "was born in French Canada, of poor parents, and became a self-made man in the restaurant business, in a little New Hampshire town. To him and to others like him of his generation, the great symbol of American success was John D. Rockefeller. For weeks after that day Jay came by, all my father could do was shake his head and say, 'Can you *imagine?* John D. Rockefeller the Fourth takes out my son's garbage!' Now that's what *I* call beautiful people! If anybody can put West Virginia on the map, he can!"

Part Two

WHERE THE MONEY
IS QUIET

Photo by Bud Lee

The Albert Mosses in horsey Southern Pines

6

The North Carolina Pines:
"Sand in Our Shoes"

IF there are people in Kansas City, Central California, and West Virginia who are longing to get their places and their accomplishments on the map, there are others in other places who wish devoutly that the mapmaker would forget that they are there, where there is money that almost nobody knows about, which is just what those who have the money would prefer. "Please don't come here," these people say. "We have found what we want here, and there are enough of us already. We want what we have, and we want it to stay exactly as it is." This is getting harder and harder to do.

For example, to the average Florida-bound motorist in winter, the stretch of U.S. Highway 1 that cuts across the center of North Carolina — past towns with such unprepossessing names as Gupton, Method, Vass, Stem, Mamers, and Wagram, and across rivers called, ridiculously, the Pee Dee and the Haw — is a journey merely to be endured. Woebegone farmhouses, none far from surrender to the wind, spatter the landscape, derelicts adrift in the grass. There is even a quality of thinness in the sunlight slanting against red earth that speaks eloquently of hard times. One longs for the softness of Spanish moss and palm trees that will be encountered farther south, and emerges from this countryside speaking piously of the poverty of North Carolina. It is hard for the uninitiated to believe that in the middle of all this, not far from the main north-south route, lie two tiny towns, Pinehurst and Southern Pines, with a combined permanent population of a little more than six thousand (swelling considerably during the winter season) that are devoted to the quiet and gentle pleasures of the rich.

Here, for a few square miles, the mood is unhurried and peaceful. These are the Carolina sandhills, softly rolling country with tall stands of loblolly and long-leaf pine creating deep, uncluttered vistas that seem to stretch for miles, free of undergrowth except for scattered patches of scrub oak. The sandy earth, in dappled sunlight, is blanketed with needles and fallen cones, and the air is heady with the odor of the pines and bright with the scarlet wings of cardinals. There is an abundance of bird life. Thousands of the North's summer birds spend their winters here, and wild geese are protected on a huge preserve. Each tiny pond is dotted with ducks.

In the village of Pinehurst, narrow lanes without names twist in and around and back upon each other, in a plan calculated to befuddle the interloper, past all hedges and gates and drives that lead to large and sprawling houses shaded by magnolia and rhododendron, suffused with privacy. In early spring, the town's most beautiful moment, gardens explode with daffodils and tulips, and the little streets are aflower with azaleas and dogwood. Camellias blossom in midwinter. Farther out, in more countrified Southern Pines, the zigzag split-rail fences extend along unpaved roads for miles, past pastures and stables of elegantly bred horses, private paddocks and show rings and jumping and racecourses. "Here, for status, you don't build a swimming pool. You build a private racetrack," says one Southern Pines woman. Through the pines, on an average winter morning, you can catch a glimpse of hunters in their pinks, riding to the hounds. Houses here are spaced far apart, across this open country.

Together, the two little towns would seem to compose a kind of island. "In the five months I spend here each winter, I don't think I travel more than a radius of five miles," says one woman. At the same time, an invisible but quite tangible frontier separates Pinehurst from Southern Pines. "Officially," says another winter resident, "Southern Pines has nothing to do with Pinehurst, and Pinehurst has nothing to do with Southern Pines. At least that's the theory. Of course, in actual practice it doesn't work out that way, and there's a certain amount of mixing back and forth. But not too much. In Southern

Pines, we speak of being over *here,* and talk of Pinehurst as being over *there.* We talk of *we,* as opposed to *they.* We complain about having to go *all the way* to Pinehurst, and they grouse about coming *all the way* to Southern Pines." The two towns are scarcely more than four miles apart.

Such disparity, furthermore, within what would seem to be an enclave of general privilege, has nothing to do with nuances of social position — not outwardly, at least. It is not a question of one town being *better* than another — not exactly. It is a difference based on the divergence of two athletic pastimes. Pinehurst is devoted to golf, and Southern Pines is dedicated to horses. It is ironic, perhaps, that right next door to each other should exist a capital of a sport — golf — that in the last fifty years has truly become a game for the masses, and the capital of another sport — fox-hunting — that hardly anybody understands, much less indulges in, any more.

But of course golf and horses beget two entirely different life styles. When a horse person speaks of "walking around hitting golf balls," and a golfer speaks of "galloping around on horseback," it is clear that the two will never see eye to eye on anything. They are much further apart here in the pines than Democrats and Republicans, even blacks and whites. The charm of horseflesh eludes Pinehurst competely, and Southern Pines considers golf a thoroughly frivolous preoccupation, even a middle-class one (even though, originally, golf was a game played by the aristocracy). Golf has become democratized; fox-hunting has not, and is suffering for it as the older devotees pass on and leave few interested youngsters to replace them. Horse people *do* think of themselves as socially superior to golfers. When a golfer was declaiming enthusiastically about the delights of his sport to a horse person not long ago, the visitor listened patiently for a while and then said, "Well, perhaps — but golf isn't exactly what you'd call a *gentleman's* game." And there is the nub of the matter. Horses are owned and bred and ridden and hunted and shown by ladies and gentlemen. Golf is something played by cloddish conventioneers who come each year to Pinehurst's big, many-verandaed hotel, the Carolina.

Pinehurst takes its golf so seriously that in order to get so much as a starting time on one of the Pinehurst Country Club's five courses one must actually *live* in Pinehurst. In Southern Pines, the horse is worshipped even after death. The garden of Miss Betty Dumaine, an ardent horsewoman, encompasses the massive grave of Grey Fox, a great hunter in his day, and his resting place is marked with a huge flat stone monument, engraved with his name, dates, and lineage, set in the grass and surrounded by a planting of shrubbery and flowers. The stone is as large as most terraces, and is frequently used as such — set up with tables and garden chairs — and is a popular gathering-place for cocktails when Miss Dumaine entertains. Many a solemn toast has been raised to the memory of her noble animal.

Southern Pines, furthermore, concentrates its affection on one sort of horse only: the hunter. "There are a few trotting people over in Pinehurst, but they never come here, you never see them," says a Southern Pines man. As for racehorses, "Well, several people here have one or two — but we don't concentrate on them. We don't want to be like Lexington, Kentucky, which is the horse-*racing* capital. We don't want to attract the sort of people that go with horse racing — *jockeys,* you know, and that sort of crowd." At the same time, Southern Pines insists that it has "all the best hunters and show horses, the ones that will be shown at Madison Square Garden and all the best shows, all across the country." The horsey heart of Southern Pines is the Moore County Hunt, founded a number of years ago by the late James Boyd, who loved horses and wrote period novels, including *Drums* (1925) and *Marching On* (1927). Boyd's widow still lives in Southern Pines and, according to one resident, "still considers herself the grandest woman here." After Mr. Boyd's death, another man, Mr. W. Ozell Moss — and the Mosses are easily the grandest *couple* in Southern Pines — took over the Hunt and developed it until it has become by far the most exclusive club in the area, and one of the great hunts in the United States.

The Mosses themselves own the Hunt's pack of hounds, considered the "best-mannered" — in hunting parlance — of any pack anywhere. Three mornings a week — Tuesday, Thursday, and Saturday — during a season that extends from Thanksgiving to the end of March, the Moore County Hunt assembles, and fifty to a hundred hunters take off through the trees, across the fields, and over the fences of Southern Pines in pursuit of the fox.

Fox-hunting is heavily surrounded by rules and rituals. Earning your

"hunt buttons," or the right to wear pinks, is as difficult and as important as earning one's "H" at Harvard used to be, back in the days
when all such things were taken seriously. If not entitled to wear pink,
one must wear black. An elaborate set of regulations determines which
style of hat one must wear. Visitors from other hunts must wear their
identifying colors, but otherwise one is not supposed to be "conspicuous" in dress. Southern Pines was highly critical, not long ago, when
Mrs. Jacqueline Kennedy Onassis was photographed at a hunt in New
Jersey wearing wrap-around sunglasses (not only bad form, but dangerous in case of a fall), without her hair tied back in a little net bag or
snood (as good form dictates), and wearing entirely the wrong kind of
hat — guilty on three counts of being a parvenue. The strict tradition-
alism of fox-hunting takes in such lofty dicta as (from a manual on the
sport): "There is no class of person who gets the Hunt into disrepute
more than *grooms* [italics the manual's]. These, as a rule, are thought-
less and often leave gates open, causing damage by allowing livestock
to wander. Strictest orders should be given to them by their masters,
not once, but several times, during a season." In other words, surviving
in a tiny pocket of affluence in one of the poorest parts of the country
is an anachronistic stronghold of the Edwardian age.

Fox-hunting is supposed to be all *pour le sport,* and obviously there
is no wagering involved as there is in, say, golf. But there is a certain
amount of competitiveness and, when the hounds "speak" and it's off
at top speed over the fields and fences, there's more than a little jock-
eying for position — not to win, exactly, but to "ride up front" near
Mr. Thomas Morton, the Master of the Field. Men and women who
have been chatting cordially a few minutes earlier quickly become the
bitterest antagonists, struggling for this position and this honor which
carries a mysterious but distinct cachet. Less serious hunters — along
with older people who are just out for a brisk morning's ride — are
content to ride behind at an easier pace until the fox, if he's a gray
one, runs up a tree, or, if he's a red fox, "goes to earth," or into a hole.
Though there is supposed to be no shortage of foxes in Southern Pines,
the fox population is discreetly "encouraged" by food left out for the
vixens during the summer months.

The undulating sandhills of North Carolina are perfect for fox-
hunting because the soft, sandy soil is the perfect surface for horses'

feet. There are few holes, and no rocks, no steep climbs, no hazardous descents. The roads of Southern Pines are kept largely unpaved out of consideration for the horse population. This same sort of terrain is also perfect for golf courses, which helps explain why these two strange-bedfellow sports have collided here in North Carolina. The sandy soil was what Mr. James W. Tufts, a millionaire real estate man from Boston, first noticed when he came here in 1895. (Tufts was from the same Boston family that gave the land on which Tufts University now stands.) At that time, golf was a sport just beginning to be popular in America. It had been imported from Scotland; and, looking at the sandhills of Pinehurst (which were then known as the Barrens), Mr. Tufts envisioned a vast golf course, bigger than any that then existed in the world. From the Page family, local gentry — and Pages are still prominent in Pinehurst today — Mr. Tufts purchased some five thousand acres of land for a dollar an acre. Everybody thought he was crazy, and that the Pages had easily got the better of the deal.

"After he bought it," his grandson recalls, "everybody told him it wasn't worth but eighty-five cents an acre." In any case, with his new land Mr. Tufts went to work building what amounted to a private town. It included hotels, a library, churches, stables, stores, a post office, greenhouses, garages, and the Pinehurst Country Club, which today has five eighteen-hole golf courses — each with a first tee right at the clubhouse — along with a driving range, putting greens, a lawn bowling green, and tennis courts.

"Ninety holes of golf!" Mr. Tufts was able to advertise to a nine-teenth-century, golf-hungry nation. Ninety-*one* holes of golf became the local joke, with the Ninety-first Hole being the name of the club-house bar. Among the remarkable things about the remarkable Mr. Tufts and his enterprise was that he bought his land in June 1895 and was able to open his complete resort just six months later, in December. Builders today build slower, not faster, than they used to build. Also, for seventy-five years after its founding, the resort and the town re-mained firmly in the hands of Mr. Tufts's direct heirs and members of the Tufts family. Then, to everyone's distinct surprise, in 1970 the Tuftses sold their interests to something called the Diamondhead Cor-poration, which no one had ever heard of. There were mutterings about "Mafia connections." But, in recent months, residents have adopted a live-and-let-live attitude about the new proprietors, and all continues as peacefully as before.

Because Mr. Tufts was from Boston, Pinehurst became, and has remained, a resort particularly popular with New Englanders. The Victorian clubhouse of the Pinehurst Country Club and the Carolina Hotel remain very New England in flavor, and much of the architecture in Pinehurst follows suit. Driving along Pinehurst's shaded streets, one might easily be in a Massachusetts village. Modern houses are zoned out, though a few *almost*-modern ones have crept in behind the tall shrubbery. Even the name of the town has New England origins. While the village was taking shape, it was known locally as Tufftown, a name that did not strike Mr. Tufts as particularly appealing. He began casting about for another. The Tuftses had a summer place on Martha's Vineyard, where a local real estate outfit was conducting a name-the-development contest. "Pinehurst" was one of the names submitted in Martha's Vineyard, though it was not the name chosen, and Mr. Tufts liked it and took it for his town. It was prophetic. When Tufts first bought the land, heavy lumbering had bared the earth of all growth. But soon afterward the pines began to reappear. Now they are everywhere.

Today, those of the Tufts family who are still around think that "the charming sound" of the word Pinehurst had a lot to do with the town's quick success. At first, Mr. Tufts had planned it as a resort for consumptives — who, before development of drug treatment of the disease, were big business for woodsy hotel-builders. But when, lured by the splendid golf, nonconsumptives began clamoring to play the Pinehurst courses, Mr. Tufts saw that he had a tiger by the tail. Soon the consumptives were being politely but firmly asked to leave, and today all deeds of houses sold in Pinehurst specify that no one with tuberculosis may buy a house. Pinehurst is one of the few places in the world where discrimination based on state-of-health is actively practiced.

Led by the Tufts enterprises and the enormous popularity of the game over the past half-century, Pinehurst became golfdom's Mecca. Today you can get into a heated argument in Pinehurst over whether there are twelve or thirteen other golf courses in Pinehurst besides the Pinehurst Country Club. The fanciest new club is called the Country

Club of North Carolina. Though there is disagreement about the architecture (it employs a good bit of glass), its eighteen holes of golf are generally less crowded and pleasanter to play than those of the Pinehurst.

Golf in Pinehurst has, in the meantime, created its own social systems. The elite of the golfing world here are members of something called the Tin Whistle Club, an organization that derives its name, supposedly, from the fact that, years ago, a tin whistle hung from a tree near the approach to the ninth hole on one of the golf courses. When this whistle was blown, drinks were served. The Club, with a membership of about two hundred men, and sprinkled with Boston Saltonstalls and Standard Oil Bedfords, is today devoted almost entirely to bibulous pleasures. Ladies are rigorously excluded from all functions, and for its headquarters the Club uses a pleasant book-lined room off the main lobby of the Pinehurst Country Club.

Even more exclusive, since there are only about forty members, is the Wolves Club, also all-male, devoted to after-golf bridge-playing. The Wolves got *its* name from an old Webster cartoon showing Mr. Caspar Milquetoast, "the Timid Soul," cowering under the gaze of three vulpine creatures who are his partner and opponents at the bridge table. Bridge, at a quarter of a cent a point, is taken very seriously by the Wolves in their tiny clubhouse, which has room for only three bridge tables, a few chairs for passing kibitzers, and of course a bar. Liquor, though it is consumed with great enthusiasm, presents something of a problem in the Pines. Restaurants are allowed to sell nothing stronger than beer or wine, and customers are required to "brown bag" their harder liquor if they want to drink. Clubs serve liquor, but only from members' own bottles. There is no bar in the Carolina Hotel, a fact which has brought dismay to the face of many an arriving conventioneer. State liquor stores will sell no more than five bottles to a customer at a time, but, as one resident points out, "You can go right back in and buy five more bottles as many times as you want."

Perhaps the most unusual local club of all is the Dunes Club, which looks like a roadhouse from an old John Garfield movie and yet is, of all things, a quite fashionable and absolutely illegal gambling club. Right in the heart of the Baptist Bible Belt, where it's hard to turn on your radio without hearing part of a sermon on sin, the Dunes's green baize tables are active even on Sunday. Renowned for its food, the tables open up after the dinner hour. "Every now and then the Dunes gets raided, but the police always warn them ahead of time," one man says. "Oh, and they make them close it down every so often, but it opens up again right away. The Dunes is a real *institution* here. We couldn't get along without it." And so a pattern of Pinehurst life involves golf in the morning, drinks and lunch with the Tin Whistle crowd at midday, on to the Wolves for a rubber or two of bridge, and then home to pick up the wife for a steak at the Dunes and some gambling.

There are some unkind souls who have had the poor taste to call *both* Southern Pines and Pinehurst "stuffy" and anachronistic in their struggle to remain unchanged in the face of a changing world. And it is true that with their New England roots there is a certain amount of upper-class Yankee reserve about the towns. Both are resolutely Republican, even though Mrs. Ernest Ives, the late Adlai Stevenson's sister, is an enthusiastic resident — and an outspoken Democrat. One overhears some surprising things, such as, at a party recently, a woman saying, "When Eisenhower won the presidential election unanimously . . ." And a Boston-bred woman asking another of her ilk, "But how can you *know* anyone from Philadelphia well enough to stay with them?" Because of its proximity to Fort Bragg, Pinehurst can say, "We could make two baseball teams out of the retired generals who've moved here." The late General George Marshall was a long-time resident. Retired generals, as a group, tend to be a conservative lot. Fort Bragg is a training center for airborne troops, and it is no surprise to look up on a sunny afternoon and see thousands of little men dropping from the sky in parachutes. Throughout the Vietnam war, the Pines have remained hawkish, unreconstructed.

A great deal of time, in both Pinehurst and Southern Pines, is still spent discussing social nuances. How, for instance, should one treat the Raymond Firestones' head stable man, who goes to all the parties? Obviously, he is considerably above the ordinary stable-groom category, but where does one draw the line? The horsey Raymond Firestones, who have built a splendid house, are very much admired in Southern Pines. Not long ago, when the visiting lecturer at the Thursday night

"Forum" at the country club — a cultural series — arrived without his white tie, the management politely whispered to Mr. Firestone, asking if he might have an outfit at home that the lecturer could borrow. It was the assumption that Mr. Firestone alone in Pinehurst might possess a white tie and trimmings, and to be sure Mr. Firestone did — several, in fact, for the visitor to pick from. That visiting lecturers in Pinehurst-Southern Pines are required to dress in white tie is an indication of the degree to which local residents are willing to go in order to maintain links with a more formal past.

A few months ago, at a Southern Pines party, a guest from out of town was tasteless enough to begin a long harangue with Mr. Firestone about what he considered to be the poor quality of Firestone tires. The next day, the hostess called Mr. Firestone to apologize for her guest's behavior. Mr. Firestone murmured that it was quite all right, really, and then he added, almost timidly, "Is there anything else your friend would like to know about tires?"

Another glamorous figure in the area is Joe Bryan, a bachelor said to be "even richer than the Cannons" — the towel people — who has built a magnificent house-cum-stable on a high hilltop overlooking a man-made lake which he built "because I like to watch my horses drinking."

Perhaps the most striking quality of the area is the restful *slowness* of Southern life. Everything seems to take extra long to do, and there are some people who do find this restful. Others, more accustomed to a brisker Northern snap and efficiency, find the slow pace highly irritating, and inveigh against the fact that it takes so long, in Pinehurst and Southern Pines, to get anything done. Here, for example, is a bit of dialogue between a man from the North, wanting to buy a pocket comb, and a salesgirl, overheard at the Pinehurst Drug Store:

MAN: "Do you have any pocket combs?"

SALESGIRL: "We sure do!"

"May I have one please?"

"A pocket comb?"

"That's right."

"What color comb you-all want? A black one?"

"That'd be fine, yes."

"Black? You-all sure?"

"Yes, fine."

"Any special size?"

"Well, *pocket* size, I suppose — about so big."

"About *so* big?"

Etc., etc.

This is, of course, the American South, and another settlement, West Southern Pines, is the black neighborhood which visitors are rarely taken to see. It is, needless to say, less resplendent than Pinehurst and Southern Pines proper, and white people are advised that it is unsafe to travel there at night. On the other hand, it is considered more respectable than the black ghetto of Fort Lauderdale. One is also told that an "unwritten rule" prevents blacks from walking on the streets of Pinehurst or Southern Pines after dark. But one woman asks, with a certain logic, "Why would anyone, black or white, want to walk there anyway? There's no place to go, nothing to see, nothing to do."

But those who live here would live nowhere else, while the arguments about Pinehurst versus Southern Pines go on and on. "They get very dressy and chi-chi over *there*, in Pinehurst," one woman says, "but over here we're much more informal. Nobody here cares what you wear — but you'd better not be seen sitting on a bad-looking horse. Also, we're just enough off the beaten path so people let us alone. A lot of people don't know we exist, which is just fine with us. We're not easy to find, so we get lots of privacy. A reporter from *Playboy* came to do a story on this place. He fell off his horse, first thing! We were all delighted."

And Mrs. Donald Parson, who has had a house in the area for many years and whose comfortable life has bridged both towns, says, "It doesn't really matter which place you live in. It's the *feeling* of the place that counts, the mood. It's easy here, it's relaxed. We don't aspire to a Palm Beach, or a Camden. No one cares here if you have five cents or five million. We wander across each other's lawns and gardens at cocktail time, and we're always welcome wherever we end up. There's no effort that goes into it, no striving or ambition in that sense. It's known, you know, as 'getting sand in your shoes' — that's what happens when you fall in love with this place — sand in your shoes from these lovely old Carolina sandhills. We've all got sand in our shoes here. And once you get sand in your shoes, it never shakes out."

Photo by Murray Radin

The Villa Cornfeld, Geneva

7

The Alpine Set:
"You Can Live Forever Here"

THERE is a breed of wanderer that is forever seeking new and unspoiled paradises. In order to qualify as "unspoiled," a paradise must be cheap. Even though such places are increasingly hard to find, this kind of traveler is relentless in his quest.

But there is another sort of voyager whose approach is perhaps more sophisticated, whose pocketbook is certainly fatter, who has relented. He has settled for a paradise that is thoroughly spoiled. Tamed. Civilized. He has gone to live in Switzerland. Tiny Switzerland (though if it were flattened out, it might be as big as Texas) probably contains more quietly rich expatriates per mountainous square foot than anywhere else on earth. It has also become a haven for the jaded, the overpublicized, the world-weary — people who have been everywhere, met everybody, had everything, and who now wish only to be pampered and cosseted and waited upon by a discreet manservant. "Life here," says Sir Noel Coward, one of the Old Guard of what calls itself the Alpine Set, speaking from his pink-and-white villa high above the clouds, "really is terribly sweet."

And sweet it is — not so much in the *la dolce vita* sense as in the candy-box sense of the word. Consider what Switzerland offers to those who have settled here among never-never-land mountaintops like so many beautiful birds after a long flight. It offers a kind of perfection. Everything works. The trains arrive and depart on time, letters are delivered in a twinkling, telephones never produce wrong numbers,

Swiss plumbing never falters. In restaurants and hotels, when buttons are pushed, service appears — superb service.

To the overurbanized American, Switzerland offers a Walt Disney movie version of life, the kind with Fred MacMurray in the leading role, where all problems are happily resolved at the end. There is no crime rate because there is no crime. There are no race problems because there are no races; the Swiss are nearly all white and Protestant. There is no violence, no student unrest. An unescorted woman is quite safe in any park at any hour of night. There is no smog, no unemployment, no poverty, no garbage in the streets, no strikes. If you wish to cross the street, the traffic politely stops. If you take a taxi, the driver will not volunteer an opinion of Mayor Lindsay in New York or of Mayor Daley in Chicago, or of anyone else, unless it is specifically solicited. The Swiss police, who seem to have been hired for their good looks as much as anything, do no more than look mildly pained if you drive into a one-way street from the wrong direction. And this is hard to do because everything in Switzerland is carefully marked. Directions are clearly printed everywhere. It is impossible to get lost.

The Swiss are notably honest. "In all the years we've lived here, we've never gotten gypped," exults Irwin Shaw, a Swiss convert from many years back. The climate is benign. Palm trees grow in winter along the northern shores of Lake Geneva, and for skiers there is skiing in the high glaciers all summer long. There are no health hazards and, if one should get sick, the country is full of excellent doctors. Even old age seems to have disappeared here, where restorative baths and spas and cures and sanitariums abound, all dedicated to rejuvenation and longevity. "There's this wonderful little virility man . . ." murmurs James Mason. For the ailing psyche, Swiss psychiatrists are notably soothing. At Vevey, not far from Lausanne, is one of the most remarkable institutions devoted to the eternal youth of the human species. This is La Clinique Générale "La Prairie" of Dr. Paul Niehans, where such people as Somerset Maugham, Konrad Adenauer, Gloria Swanson, Bernard Baruch, and even Pope Pius XII have paid an average of $1,285 a week for treatments designed to restore the flagging vital organs and halt, or at least slow down, the normal aging process.

Dr. Niehans's theory, very broadly stated, is that as our bodily organs age, cells within them deteriorate and die. Niehans replaces these less-than-perky cells by injecting the patient with live cells taken from the embryos of animals — from the testicles of unborn bulls, for example. These new cells, it is claimed, prosper within the human patient's body and revive the ailing organ. The treatment at Vevey begins with a test that is designed to pinpoint the areas of the body most needful of the restorative new cells. In all, fourteen bodily organs are covered in the tests, and a separate injection may be required for each — at $150 and up per injection. (This, plus $300 a week for the clinic and $200 for the tests, makes up the cost of the treatment.) The commonest ailment at Vevey is cirrhosis of the liver, and it is perhaps significant that La Prairie insists that patients refrain from all alcoholic beverages for at least three months following their discharge.

The alumni of La Prairie speak ecstatically of their new youth and vigor, but medical opinion in the United States is much more guarded in its enthusiasm. "It's like the heart transplants," one doctor says. "It's much too early to say whether what Niehans is doing really works." "Nonsense," replies a recent Niehans patient. "Dr. Niehans has proved that it's no longer necessary to grow old!" Switzerland is Shangri-La.

Famously neutral and uncommitted, the Swiss are noncontroversial and apolitical. There is, of course, a Swiss government, but it is delightfully unobtrusive, even invisible. It sometimes seems possible that the country is run by elves and gnomes from a secret mountain workshop. "I know we have a government, but I couldn't tell you who is in it," says one Swiss gentleman with typically Swiss good cheer. Switzerland is a kind of Oz. Even its physical makeup seems contrived and artificial — lakes, mountains, hillsides covered with wild narcissus; a little bit of Germany, a little of Italy, and a bit of France. It is true that the waters of Lake Geneva may not be as pellucid as when Browning wrote of them. It is true that prices are high. But, as Irwin Shaw, who was born in Brooklyn, says, "The more civilized a country is, the higher the prices. Every time you go to a place that's cheap, you know the people are suffering. I don't like countries like that. Forget 'em." Best of all, Swiss taxes are very, very low — among the lowest in the world. Few Swiss pay more than ten to twelve per cent income tax. And the Swiss have a charming way of deciding what sort of tax you ought to pay. You sit down with the tax collector and *discuss* it. Yes, life can be sweet indeed, and private.

Consider the Charles Chaplins. Chaplin was among the first to expatriate himself to the high mountains in the narcissus-scented air, and he is now considered the paterfamilias of the Alpine Set. His château above Vevey has beautiful gardens, and the house is always filled with fresh flowers. In his eighties, Chaplin is somewhat slowed down, but he still takes short walks and suns himself on his terraces, attended by his secretary and servants and pretty wife. And he always appears at the annual Christmas eve gala given by Madame de Chevreux d'Antraigne, an Englishwoman who has a big house in Montreux. Her house has a hall of mirrors, and her party is a major event to which everyone in the Set turns out — Noel Coward, the David Nivens, James Mason, the William Holdens. Charles Chaplin rarely says much any more at parties, but he nods and beams and looks contented. "He seems to have removed himself from life a bit," says a friend. But isn't this what Switzerland is for? To escape from reality?

Consider Noel Coward in his pink-and-white chalet above the clouds, somewhere over the rainbow. "These little raspberries were flown in from Israel," says Mr. Coward, spooning them from a chilled silver bowl. "You must absolutely *submerge* them in this thick fresh cream, and then cover them with sugar." The road to the pink-and-white chalet is lined with tubs of pink-and-white petunias. Mr. Coward's bright purple lounging jacket matches the covering on his bright purple sofa, and his green slippers match the green baize covering of the coffee table. Like Switzerland, Mr. Coward is very floral, very coordinated, the epitome of elegant suavity. "When Gertie Lawrence and I danced, it was said that we were the *definition* of glamour," he says without a trace of modesty. A favorite footstool, in needlepoint, is designed with the opening bars of some of his songs — "Mad Dogs and Englishmen," "I'll Follow My Secret Heart," and so on — the labor of a friend. "Dorothy Hammerstein did a needlepoint pillow for me," he says, "Joan Sutherland did another. So did Mary Martin. Merle Oberon did me a pair of needlepoint slippers." He turns to his secretary: "Are the Lunts coming for drinks?" These are the sort of people who pass in and out of the Chalet Coward. Of all the things that his house contains, Mr. Coward is proudest of his blue-tile shower bath, which he designed himself, and which has jets of water that shoot out at the bather from all directions.

"The Swiss are terribly un-tiresome," Noel Coward says. "They aren't the least bit celebrity-conscious. They leave one at absolute peace. I've lived here since 1951, and the living is *bliss*fully easy. The air here makes one *sweet*ly lazy, which I adore. The most energetic thing I do is walk down to the village for a drink. Then I ring for the car to come and drive me back up. Joan Sutherland lives just above me, and the Nivens are just above her. Joanie's going to put in a swimming pool. I don't quite approve. It seems rather un-Swiss. And I suppose she'll make me trudge up to it. But I'm terribly lucky here. And of course there are the *lovely* taxes. Look — here comes the sun."

As if by command, the clouds in which his house has been drifting disappear, and the valley below is revealed, in Technicolor. The higher vineyards are a deep blue-green. Above, fat cows graze on pasturage so steep it seems miraculous that they don't topple over and come rolling down. Walt Disney could have done no better. To the south, the big-rock-candy-mountain silhouette of Mont Blanc rises and frames itself perfectly in Sir Noel's south-facing window. "Isn't it sweet?" he asks. And, "Shall we have some more of my delicious Jewish raspberries?"

Of all the beautiful escapees, those — like Noel Coward — who are British subjects find the Swiss taxes the loveliest. This group includes the Nivens, James Mason, Deborah Kerr, Peter Ustinov, the Chaplins. If these people lived at home in England, they would be taxed at murderous rates by Her Majesty's Inland Revenue. But, ever since an unfortunate experience in one of her colonies in 1776, Great Britain has refrained from taxing foreign-based Britons. By agreeing to remain outside of England for at least nine months a year, these British pay only the trifling Swiss tax. The rich from other countries have found similar shelter in Switzerland, which helps explain why the likes of Baron Edmond de Rothschild, Sadruddin Aga Khan, Lilli Palmer, Sophia Loren, Gunther Sachs, Maximilian Schell, Ingemar Johansson, Georges Simenon, Vladimir Nabokov, and a long list of other names are Swiss-based for at least part of the year. The Swiss tax system — or non-system — used to be equally attractive to Americans. Alas, it is no longer, and this is why at least one American woman speaks of the late President John F. Kennedy as "a worse tyrant than Hitler."

What happened was that, before World War II, Americans who lived *permanently* abroad were not required to pay tax on income from sources within the United States. Then, after the war, with Europe rebuilding and American businesses expanding into European cities, large numbers of Americans were going to Europe to work for short periods of time. For these people, the law was changed to apply not only to permanent nonresidents but to those who lived outside the country for as little as eighteen months' time. Immediately the rich — and their accountants — saw what was possible. By living eighteen months in a country such as Switzerland, where taxes were a pittance, they could escape U.S. taxes altogether. Immediately a very well-dressed migration began. At the same time, film companies were discovering the fiscal advantages of working in Europe, and suddenly — for Gary Cooper, William Holden, Orson Welles, Elizabeth Taylor, Richard Burton, Irwin Shaw, Audrey Hepburn, Mel Ferrer, Yul Brynner, and scores of others — Switzerland became the only place to live.

An example of what could be done was the technique employed by Elizabeth Taylor. With an income of roughly $1,000,000 a year, she established a Swiss residence and corporation into which all her money went. Of this she was required to pay a Swiss corporate tax, a minuscule two-tenths of one per cent, or about $2,000 a year. Her corporation then paid her a salary. If, by tightening her belt, she was able to get by on $10,000 a month — $120,000 a year — her Swiss income tax could not have come to much more than $15,000 annually. In other words, she was able to keep over $900,000 of her yearly million by living in Switzerland. At home in the United States, her tax bill might have run as high as $850,000. No wonder she could put enough money aside to buy an inch-and-a-half long diamond.

But in 1962 President Kennedy's tax reforms put a stop to all this. Today, only the first $25,000 of a non-U.S. resident's income is tax-free, and everything above that is fully taxable at U.S. rates. Obviously, to the super-rich, $25,000 tax-free is not an exciting figure. When the new laws went into effect, the allure of Switzerland rapidly evaporated for a number of Americans, including Miss Taylor, who gave up her Swiss residence, though not her Swiss bank accounts.

The 1962 law got to be known as the William Holden Law, and no one resents this more than Mr. Holden, who points out that he was a relative latecomer to Switzerland. "I didn't come here until 1959," he points out, "so I only got three years before they pulled up the ladder."

Furthermore, he has proved himself to be less fickle than Miss Taylor and has stayed on even though the tax advantage has gone. He owns a large villa on the lake outside Geneva which he calls "Beau Jardin," and he has remodeled it extensively — adding rooms, combining others by tearing down partitions, installing huge glass window-walls which "the Swiss builders don't understand — they want rooms like little caves." And now his Swiss villa would look right at home on Stone Canyon Road in Bel Air.

"I've stayed on for a variety of reasons," Holden says. "With my own lack of education, I wanted my sons to be bilingual, or perhaps trilingual." The two boys were teenagers when the Holdens arrived, and have since spent ten years at Swiss schools. "Also, Geneva is sort of halfway between New York, where I go frequently, and Kenya, in Africa, where I have interests. I'm a wildlife nut, you know. But what I like best is the way the Swiss respect the individual. They might be curious, but they're too civilized to invade your privacy. This is something we're losing in the United States, probably because of our bureaucratic form of life. The press here respects your privacy always. The press here wouldn't dream of asking a question about your private life. In the U.S., the press dwells on tragedy. If there's an accident, they can't wait to get to the poor victim to interview him on his experience. Americans seem to have become more watchers than doers. The Swiss believe in everybody attending to his own business. It gives life here this wonderful sense of peace and quiet."

Peter Viertel, the sportsman-novelist and husband of Deborah Kerr, who was first attracted to Switzerland by the skiing, as his wife was by its offer of a shelter from British taxes, is somewhat less generous in his appraisal of Swiss life. Perhaps he is simply too active a man to settle happily into an atmosphere of perpetual relaxation and avoidance of care. Viertel says, "It's an easy country to live in. It gives you a feeling of safety. But the stimulation of the conversation here is nil. You read the newspapers, you listen to the radio, and you talk to your friends, but you're not a part of a going community where you discuss things with people who have views other than yours. You *have* to get out from time to time. Otherwise you get rock-happy — like living on a magic island. But there's one good thing about living in an isolated cell like this. When you go to Paris or London or wherever, you're like the new boy coming to town. You get a bigger thrill when you see your friends again, and they're much happier to see you than if you'd been there all along."

Life in a never-never land can become a *tiny* bit boring. But the Alpine Set is, after all, a notably mobile one. They do get out from time to time. The Viertels, for instance, also spend a certain amount of time sunning themselves at Marbella, on the coast of Spain. To the less well-heeled, it is a different story. Stuart Dalrymple, an American businessman who was stationed for ten years in Switzerland before returning to the United States, says, "Actually, we retreated. Our life in Geneva made Zelda and Scott's existence look like a Cub Scout picnic. At the end of a decade, with two girls unable to articulate in English, a more than slightly jaded patina on our not-so-rosy cheeks, and no roots whatever, we opted to come home." The Dalrymples now find the good life in Massachusetts.

Imagine a movie starring David Niven, James Mason, Noel Coward, with the porcelain beauties of Deborah Kerr and Audrey Hepburn (who still keeps a chalet in the pines above Rolle), all set in a landscape where the real estate goes for about two hundred and fifty thousand dollars an acre. William Holden will play the handsome American. You can see what sort of gilded and mannered story would have to ensue. In a way, it is as though the members of the Alpine Set had written their own script, and were acting out their lives in a setting of their own devising. You can see why Elizabeth Taylor wouldn't stay. Switzerland is just not suited to her broad style. Neither was it to Van and Evie Johnson's, who hated it. "I suppose one can't expect people like that to come and sit by a lake and give little dinners," says Noel Coward, whose recent little dinner was for a visiting Sir Laurence Olivier.

Members of the Alpine Set see a lot of each other — English-speaking souls cluster together — and the titled and celebrated from all over the world are always passing through Switzerland (to visit their doctors or their banks), but life is not without controversy. The Old Guard — the Chaplins, Noel Coward, et al. — tend to think of William Holden's Hollywood-type house as a bit too much. "You approach it by boat," says Sir Noel with famous disdain, "through water that is absolutely *awash* with French letters. There's a walkie-talkie from the pier to the house, but it doesn't always work, and so the boatman has to announce you by shouting at the top of his lungs: 'Four people coming up for tea!' "

Then there is the somewhat mysterious presence of a young American named Bernard Cornfeld. Starting with brains, *chutzpah,* and very little else, Bernie Cornfeld built up a mutual-fund empire, Investors Overseas Services, Ltd., that at one point was estimated to be worth over two billion dollars. The Cornfeld empire has, of course, collapsed, dragging down all sorts of other people with it. But Cornfeld himself remains very much on the scene in Geneva where, it is assumed, he emerged from the tatters of his company with a sizable personal fortune.

He is a smallish man with a pixie face who wears his blond hair in a long and flowing style, and whose taste in clothes runs to belted silk jump suits with flaring lapels. A bachelor, he still lives in the vast stone castle he bought when he was at the height of his powers, and his house is still filled with miniskirted bunnies, tourists, and itinerant hippies whom he leads, Pied Piper fashion, on water-skiing parties by day and boisterous pub-crawling by night. His social behavior is outrageous. He shows up at formal dinner parties three hours late, often barefoot, with his colorful retinue in tow, and insists on sitting on the floor to eat. In the old days, when he was considered a financial force (it was once said he could buy all of Switzerland if he wished), this sort of behavior was tolerated, and when Bernie and his friends swung into such spots as Griffin's, a Geneva discotheque, the room would snap to attention. Now that he has fallen from financial grace, he is regarded as really nothing more than a semi-amusing curiosity.

Bernie Cornfeld doesn't seem to belong in such a quietly rich right place as Switzerland. He would seem a little out of place in our movie. But perhaps not. After all, Walt Disney often tossed a good-natured buffoon, a kind of village idiot, into the plot to addle the waters of his fantasy, pretty-pretty world. A little comedy relief is welcome, even in Munchkinland. And Switzerland, true to form, is allowing Bernie Cornfeld to settle slowly into the elegantly turned woodwork and perhaps, in a year or so, the slight blemish his presence creates will have disappeared, by hocus-pocus, altogether.

Photo by Slim Aarons

Fairfield County's contented commuters

8

Fairfield County:
Perilous Preserve

I T is probably harder to maintain anonymity and privacy of wealth in the United States than in a country like Switzerland, which virtually has privacy written into its constitution. It is difficult to tuck an American fortune behind a protective alp, much as one might like to try.

Not long ago a young woman was walking her two dogs along a shaded road in Greenwich, Connecticut, where she and her husband had just built a new house, and an automobile drew up beside her and the driver opened his window and inquired, "Can you tell me where the Rich family lives?" After a puzzled moment, the young Greenwich matron replied, "Well, I think that adjective would really apply to every family here." Obviously, the motorist was looking for a family *named* Rich. But the Greenwich lady's reply was not inappropriate to Greenwich, nor to other parts of Connecticut's Fairfield County. Here, according to the fond belief of many of the residents, in this roughly triangular piece of real estate in the southwestern corner of the state, is contained the greatest concentration of wealth — in many cases anonymous wealth — of any county in the United States. Here (again in Greenwich) was where a woman, when asked why she chose to live there, answered simply, "Because we're so rich."

Actually, by dollar-count, Fairfield is not the richest American county, but only the tenth richest. The richest, officially, is Montgomery County, Maryland, and Fairfield lags behind even Bergen

County, New Jersey. But, loyal Fairfieldians point out, Fairfield County in addition to such luxurious towns as Greenwich, Darien, New Canaan, Westport, Weston, Fairfield, and Southport, also includes the sprawling city of Bridgeport. Bridgeport, with its air redolent of brassworks, may qualify as one of America's least attractive cities, and is facing the problems — urban decay, racial disunion, poverty — of other industrial towns its size.

Fairfield County also includes such small industrial towns as Stamford, Danbury, and Norwalk, which have *their* share of similar woes. When one thinks, in Fairfield, of Fairfield County, one does one's best not to think of these places; one edits them out of the mind, as it were. When Dorothy Rodgers, wife of the composer, first moved to Fairfield County she volunteered to do some Red Cross work in Bridgeport. She was told, gently but firmly, that it would "not be appropriate" for her to work in Bridgeport, a short drive from her house, but in Greenwich instead, which lay a fair distance down the pike. As for Danbury, most Fairfield people seem unaware that it is even in the county, and look startled when reminded that it is.

When one has subtracted these cities and their immediate environs from the rest of Fairfield County, what is left can be described as one of the most beautiful residential areas in the country. The southern rim of the county faces Long Island Sound, a jagged, rocky coastline with hundreds of tiny coves and harbors, secluded beaches, and gently rocking deep-blue water dotted with diminutive offshore islands and, on any summer weekend, clouds of sailboats. Inland (there are two kinds of people in Fairfield County, "water people" and "backcountry people") the land rises in a series of wooded hills threaded by bright streams and narrow, winding roads. The terraced climbing of the hills means that it is possible, even from many miles inland, to catch, here and there, distant glimpses of the Sound. Across this whole terrain, behind rhododendron-shrouded gates, guardhouses, and even simple mailboxes on white posts, are spread some of the handsomest and best-cared-for houses to be found anywhere. "One wonders," someone said not long ago, "as one drives along these roads, whether there really *are* any poor people any more." On the Sound side of Fairfield County, the look of the place is more suburban. The Sound side is more built-up. The houses, though large and expensive-looking, stand closer together. This is because the prices for waterfront acreage have climbed to the stratosphere, and houses have been built on smaller lots. Back-country, the feeling is definitely rural. A number of people keep horses, and one passes jumping courses, paddocks, and handsome barns and stables. This is hunt country, much of it, and, as it does in Southern Pines, the sound of the hunting horn rings across autumn mornings. Wildlife here is in great variety — deer (a mixed blessing since they devour shrubs and flowers) and rabbits, raccoons, possums, squirrels, pheasant, partridge, and scores of other kinds of birds. Would it mar the pleasant picture of this place to remember that this is also a part of the country where one can encounter the particular problems which seem particularly to beset the affluent and ambitious — divorce, alco-holism, drug problems in the schools? Yes, but this is also part of Fairfield County, and residents shake their heads and ask, "But aren't these problems everywhere in the country?" The Kiwanis Club of Westport operates a rehabilitation center for drug addicts. Psychiatrists do a good business here.

But it would not be fair to think of Fairfield County as an entity. There are actually several Fairfields, and each town and village has a stamp and character all its own.

> *Here's to old Fairfield County,*
> *Society's uppermost shelf,*
> *Where Greenwich speaks only to Southport,*
> *And Southport just talks to itself.*

So goes an old bit of local doggerel, and it sums up with a good deal of accuracy the status of the two towns. Of all the addresses in Fairfield County, Southport, from a social-money standpoint, is decidedly the best. Located on a hilly point of land overlooking the Sound, very near the easternmost limits of Fairfield County and among the towns far-thest from New York City, Southport is a small, splendid town of hidden estates, private lanes, with many fine Colonial and Federal houses, and a few small, discreetly elegant shops. Greenwich, on the westernmost edge of the county, where Connecticut dips its geographic toe into New York State, has been called a "larger Southport." Though Greenwich's large houses and estates are not unlike Southport's, there are more of them in Greenwich and, while Southport is a village, Greenwich is a city of over fifty thousand population, with apartment houses, a hotel, restaurants, shopping centers, and a congested downtown business section — and, if one looks behind the scenes, even a bona fide slum.

Southport has remained very WASP-ish in character, and Jews have been made to feel unwelcome there. Greenwich, on the other hand, has a black population — many of whom are employed as domestics — and, though this was not always true, Jews have been allowed to buy houses in the best neighborhoods. Joseph Hirschhorn, for example, the multimillionaire art collector, has a vast Norman house on the top of Round Hill surrounded by a spectacular sculpture garden which contains, among other things, over sixty works by Henry Moore. Round Hill is one of Greenwich's most prestigious addresses, and the Hirschhorn estate stands opposite that of Mr. and Mrs. Joseph Verner Reed, who have been called "the grandest people in Greenwich." The Reed estate is a hundred acres, most of it untouched woodland. In an area where land has gone for as much as fifty thousand dollars an acre, some idea of the worth of the Reed holdings may be gained by a simple act of multiplication.

Mr. and Mrs. Reed were, incidentally, the developers of another exclusive enclave — Hobe Sound, Florida, an island restricted to 280 families. "In the nineteen-thirties, there was a need for a Hobe Sound," says Mr. Reed, "a place where people of a certain affluence could go for vacations and to relax, without the tulle hat and seventeen-piece orchestra sort of thing that was going on in Palm Beach." Apparently during the Depression not everyone was depressed. The Joseph Verner Reeds and the Joseph Hirschhorns are friendly, despite the anti-Semitic cast of Hobe Sound, and have entertained each other occasionally. This represents a great change, people say, from the old days when, if a Greenwich real estate man sold property to a Jew, he automatically lost his license. On the other hand, the Hirschhorns' names do not adorn the membership list of the Round Hill Club or the *Social Register,* whereas the Reeds' quite definitely do, in both places.

Just why restrictive policies against Jews have remained in Fairfield County's best clubs is a question difficult to understand or answer, and the reasons for their existence are hard to pinpoint. No particular member, or group of members, of any club can be accused of overt anti-Semitism. It is almost as though these policies had a life of their own, were self-generative, and have remained not out of specific prejudice so much as out of the vague excuse that "this is the way it has always been." Dorothy Rodgers recalls that when she and her husband first moved to Fairfield a friend suggested that the Rodgerses join the local beach club. "It was a perfectly simple little beach club, without any social pretensions at all," she says. "It was not one of the fancy clubs. We simply thought joining it would be fun for the children." A few days after suggesting it, the friend telephoned Mrs. Rodgers to say, "I'm just so embarrassed I don't know what to say! I simply had no idea that they felt this way, but it seems they don't accept Jewish members no matter *who* they are." Mrs. Rodgers, a humorous and successful woman in her own right, as an author and designer, says, "Of course we're entertained in Christian homes out here, but I always wonder if it isn't mostly because of who Dick is. Would we be invited if he weren't Richard Rodgers? And meanwhile, with the shortage of servants, a great deal of the entertaining out here takes place at the clubs. We have a very pleasant life in Fairfield, with friends here whom we treasure and others who come out for weekends from New York. We don't golf, and we don't play tennis. We do play mean croquet on our lawn all summer. So we don't miss the club life at all." Mrs. Rodgers also believes that restrictions in clubs are less the result of formal anti-Semitism than the expression of a kind of naïveté. "I sometimes think these clubs exclude Jews largely because they don't *know* any Jews. They'd like to make Jewish friends, perhaps, but they simply don't know how!"

Meanwhile, there is rather little social intercourse between towns like Greenwich and Southport and the other communities in the county. Bette Davis, who lives in Westport, explodes and says, "My God, I'd never be invited to a party in *Southport* — unless they wanted me there as some sort of curiosity, or freak. After all, I'm unmarried, a woman who works for a living, who makes her money in the entertainment industry, and who has the scarlet letter 'A' for Actress branded on her bosom! If I lived in Southport, I'd never be accepted. Here, of course, it's quite different."

Westport has always been a little different. Early in the nineteen-twenties, the town of Westport was discovered by a group of New York writers and artists who began coming to Westport for the summer. Soon they were buying and restoring old farmhouses and barns. *New Yorker* writers and cartoonists, a notably clubby lot, led the way, and people like Peter De Vries, Hamilton Basso, Jerome Weidman (who has since moved away) and Whitney Darrow, Jr., were among the early arrivals. They were joined by others from the theater and films such as June Havoc, Eileen Heckart, Ralph Alswang, and David Wayne. To this rich and bright brew were added infusions from the worlds of radio and, eventually, television, book publishing, and, to top it off, a large contribution to the population from the world of advertising.

Madison Avenue has, furthermore, contributed for the most part people who are from the so-called "creative" end of the business — copywriters and art directors. This has given the town of Westport the feeling of a bright, brash, assertive — somewhat raffish, middle-class-based, but still very well-heeled — artists' colony. Downtown Westport abounds with what are called "fun" shops. There are fun dress shops, men's shops, gourmet shops, gift shops, ice cream shops, cheese shops, delicatessens, bookshops, and grog shops. Collectively, the fun shops of Westport exude an aura of franticity, of desperation. The fun totters on the brink of hysteria, as though the shops were not at all sure how they were going to pay their bills for the fun merchandise on their shelves. One suspects the shops are as overextended as, indeed, many of their best customers doubtless are. All over Fairfield County, shopkeepers complain about slow bill-payers; some of the wealthiest, biggest-spending families pay bills only once a year. But one suspects that there are more shops in Westport than can be supported by even this high-living community. Compared with Westport's, the shopping district of the more sedate and quiet town of Fairfield is a dreary affair. It consists largely of Mercurio's Market, whose claim to fame is that it was here that the late Margaret Rudkin — who went on to make a fortune in Pepperidge Farm bakery products — brought her first few loaves of bread to sell.

Weston, in the backcountry, is sort of an extension, on a much more woodsy scale, of Westport. That is, the population of Weston also includes writers, artists, actresses, and actors. But Weston is much smaller, with only a handful of small stores at its center — stores which, on the tax rolls, are classified as residences because the town, officially, is zoned against businesses altogether. Westport has grown too large for it, but Weston is still small enough to operate on the old New England town-meeting system. To Weston residents, the town meetings are an important part of the town's charm. Understandably, the most heated arguments at town meetings are over issues which threaten to increase taxes.

Sonny Fox, the television personality, who lives in Weston and is typically active in local affairs, is particularly interested in matters dealing with the local schools. "Whenever there's a school bond issue that you think everybody's behind," he says, "you find at the town meetings, a lot of little old ladies in gray hair and sneakers who have crawled out of the hills somewhere to fight it. These little old ladies are always big taxpayers, and of course they don't have children in the schools — at least not any more. I remember one woman who got up in town meeting and made a long speech saying, 'Why are we spending all this money on schools? Why don't we use it to spray the trees? The hell with the children! Let's save our elms!' Somebody in the back row said, 'Great idea! Let's just spray the children.' Our town meetings really get pretty wild."

Compared with towns like Weston, Westport, Southport, Fairfield, and Greenwich, other Fairfield County towns such as Darien and New Canaan seem more predictable — very pretty, very cozy, but essentially bedroom towns of successful businessmen-commuters who work five days a week in Manhattan.

One reason for the distinctive character of so many Fairfield communities involves zoning. If you don't count school bonds and other tax issues, zoning is easily the number one topic of conversation in Fairfield County. If you want to get a heated conversation going at a Fairfield County dinner table, simply mention that inflammatory six-letter word. In a particularly excited state about zoning is Greenwich. One of the factors that has permitted Greenwich to retain its precious "rural character" has been the extensive amount — close to ten thousand acres — of privately held vacant land which has been left, as in the Joseph Verner Reed estate, to Nature's green thumb. Slightly more than half this land, or about five thousand acres, lies in the backcountry, and for more than forty years, this land has been zoned to a minimum of four acres per family. An additional twenty-five hundred acres is zoned so as to require that each family occupy no less than two acres. These high-acre zoning laws apply to just about a quarter of Greenwich's thirty thousand total acreage. Meanwhile, Greenwich has been caught in a press between an exploding population, an increased migration from city to suburb, and pressure from developers who have sought to persuade large landholders that there are fortunes to be made if their property can be down-zoned, broken up, and sold. Few property-owners are immune to the temptations of large sums of money, and few rich people seriously resist the chance to become richer. But so far the attempts to invade the historic four-acre zone have been met with public outcry and defeat.

The sociological argument for breaking up the larger landholdings has been the claim that the rich on the big plots of land must now, in the 1970's, make way for the billowing upper middle class, that enclaves of power and property no longer make sense in a society where any man who prospers deserves to live in as pleasant surroundings as he can find. In Greenwich, this argument has pitted Mr. Lewis S. Rosenstiel, the eighty-one-year-old chairman of Schenley Industries, against the conservatives and traditionalists of the town. For several years, Mr. Rosenstiel — a Greenwich summer resident for thirty-six years — has been making a determined effort to have eighty-three acres of land which his Rosenstiel Foundation owns — in the four-acre zone — reduced to half-acre lots which would then be sold at less than a thousand dollars a lot. Mr. Rosenstiel's arguments are sociological, he insists, not economic. He has called Greenwich's four-acre zoning laws *"de facto* economic discrimination," and those who support his view point out that it is also *de facto* racial discrimination. Mr. Rosenstiel and his foundation would like to open part of Greenwich to middle-income families, some of whom would most certainly be black families. Not long ago, a hearing on this matter took up a total of thirty hours stretched over seven nights, and produced more than a thousand pages of testimony. Tempers ran high, and insults were shouted by, and at, some of America's most prominent and — as a rule — quietest families. The matter, still unresolved, has divided Greenwich into two angry camps, while others, who agree with Mr. Rosenstiel's point of view but who still like Greenwich the way it is — and don't want to see it changed — find themselves ambivalent on the subject. Underneath it all, unspoken but still there, is the knowledge that Lewis Rosenstiel, the champion of integration (economic and racial), the foe of discrimination, is also an outsider — a Jew.

Similar zoning arguments go on in other Fairfield County communities, and committees are forever being formed to look into other uses to which vacant, high-zoned land can be put. As property taxes rise, and the larger landholders feel the squeeze, there is increased pressure on them to break up their estates, and there has been much talk of putting residential land to discreet commercial use. If, say, a company bought twenty-five wooded acres and built a well-designed research center in the middle of the tract, no one would know it was there. A number of two-to-four-acre-zoned lots would go off the market, and the town would gain a rich taxpayer. Weston has talked of attracting this sort of business, but one man who lives there says wryly, "What they want is a company that will build a factory in the middle of the woods where no one will see it. When you do see it, it should look like a beautiful house. The factory should produce something that doesn't create any smoke or smells or noise, and deliveries should be made at night — preferably by Cadillac limousines. It would be better if this factory could be run by computers, because computers don't have kids that have to go to school and add to the tax load. But if it has to have employees, they should all live far away, in another county. And the factory should not require any town services — police, fire department, or garbage pickup. Not surprisingly, this sort of ideal company and factory has been a little bit hard to find."

On the question of commercializing vacant property, Greenwich possesses a certain psychological advantage. It has been able to keep its city taxes comparatively low. Greenwich has done this by limiting city services, which, in turn, has helped the town preserve its treasured rural look. Though it has excellent police and fire departments, many miles of roads have neither streetlights or sidewalks. A large part of the town is without sewer service. (In these sections, septic tanks, sump pumps, and the rising water table — rising higher with the construction of so many swimming pools because pools impede natural drainage of ground water — are topics of conversation almost as popular as zoning.) Parts of the town must use private garbage collectors. Many roads are unpaved, which means that they are inexpensive to maintain, and that they also discourage sightseers and others who don't belong. The public schools are excellent, but the rich of Greenwich send their children to private schools — to Greenwich Academy or Greenwich Country Day — so the schools have not been under undue pressures. Greenwich has a population ceiling of 86,820 people, which it expects to reach by 1985 — unless, of course, the zoning laws are changed.

The second great force that has shaped the character of Fairfield's towns, perhaps even equal in importance to zoning, lies in the towns' means of access. Three major arteries of transport thread their way east and west, running roughly parallel to each other, across the breadth of Fairfield County, from the New York line to Fairfield's outer limits: the Merritt Parkway, the Connecticut Turnpike and the New Haven Railroad. The Parkway, with a beautifully landscaped center mall, winds gracefully through the backyards of largely invisible estates; it is the traditional dividing line between shore-country and backcountry real estate, with everything to the north of the Parkway being backcountry. In the spring, the Parkway's length is aglow with flowering dogwood. For all its beauty, there were eyebrows raised in the 1930's when it was built. Why, for example, did the Merritt thread its way so artfully around the Rockefeller estate (the Greenwich Rockefellers, that is, first cousins of the Tarrytown ones) when a more logical route would have been straight through it? Perhaps, if you are a Rockefeller, you can detour a parkway. The newer Connecticut Turnpike, which runs along the shore, is largely a truck route (trucks are not permitted on the higher-class Merritt). The oldest route, and the most important in terms of the social makeup of Fairfield towns, is the New Haven branch of the Penn Central Railroad.

Greenwich is the first of the fashionable Fairfield stops as the railroad makes its uncertain way from Grand Central Station in Manhattan. The oneway trip takes about an hour, and for years, Greenwich has attracted a certain kind of commuter — the man who, for all his success and affluence, nonetheless needs to maintain a regular schedule at a place of business in New York City. Thus you find living in Greenwich men like G. Keith Funston, former president of the New York Stock Exchange; James A. Linen, of Time, Inc.; and IBM's Thomas J. Watson, Jr. The towns of Southport and Fairfield, on the opposite side of the county and farthest from New York, have attracted quite a different sort of resident. They are beyond the commuting range, except to the most indefatigable commuter, and they are also suburbs of Bridgeport. Many wealthy Bridgeport manufacturers have built houses here. These towns have also drawn well-heeled retirees and others whose needs to go to New York are infrequent. In Southport, you find people like the industrialist Charles Sherwood Munson; Standard Oil heiress Ruth Bedford, and retired advertising tycoon Chester J. La Roche. The area is also popular with people who use it primarily for weekend visits and summer vacations, such as Mr. and Mrs. Rodgers and the Leonard Bernsteins. Westport, which is just about the longest practical commuter distance from New York, has attracted those whose commuting hours are irregular — the actors and painters and writers — as well as those businessmen who are so secure in their positions that they need not arrive at their desks before ten-thirty or so, the Madison Avenue men.

Commuting in and out of Fairfield County has developed into something very close to an art form, and each train has a character, and conveys a status, that is all its own. The 7:37 A.M. out of Westport, for example — or, even more so, the one before it, the 6:59 — is the sort of train for the bright, aggressive, ambitious young man on his way up, doing well and bucking for a promotion he will very likely soon get. He rushes to the front of the train each morning — in order to be the first one to get off — busies himself with briefcase work at his seat, and will be at his desk by eight-thirty. The mood on these early trains is tense, absorbed, unsociable. A little later on, on the 9:13, the passengers are quite a different lot. Here are the bankers, the lawyers, the heads of companies whose first engagements of importance on any given day occur not much before lunchtime. These men will stroll into their offices around ten or a little after, and secretaries and staff will have coped with their day until then. On this train, populated with decision-makers, the atmosphere is more relaxed, serene. In the smoker, bridge-players quietly play for gentlemanly stakes. There is another class of man on this train, though, who tries very hard to seem relaxed — the man who is for the moment unemployed, and who is on his way into town for an interview.

Still another commuter type is the man who belongs to a private car association. He sits grandly in the last car on the train, window shades lowered to screen him from the gaze of common mortals, served by a white-coated steward. The grandest of the private cars is the Southport Car, which also picks up a few select passengers in Westport and Darien. Though it costs only about two hundred dollars a year plus commutation to belong to a private car club, it is said that "someone has to die" before you can join one, and even then rigorous tests must be passed. One Southport man, for example, moved away not long ago in disgrace when he was blackballed by the Southport Car. A similar car, and association, serves Greenwich and Rye (just over the New York state line in Westchester County), while another serves New Canaan.

Wednesday is ladies' day on the New Haven branch of the Penn Central, and by eleven in the morning the coaches are bright with female chatter — women bound into town for lunch, a bit of shopping, and a matinee. By three o'clock in the afternoon the trains fill up with commuting schoolchildren armed with transistor radios. And of course the most déclassé trains of all are those departing for New York around five in the afternoon. These are filled with cleaning ladies and handymen returning home to Harlem and the Bronx.

Returning home to a Fairfield County town presents its own set of problems — in particular, how to get out of the commuter parking lot as fast as possible, ahead of all the other commuters. Wives wait tensely at the wheels of cars, motors racing, while their menfolk sprint across the tarmac to meet them. In Westport, a shortcut to the parking lot has been discovered which involves scaling a fence. To those who don't understand commuting, its rules and rituals and handicaps, the sight of well-dressed men in Brooks Brothers suits, with Gucci attaché cases, scrambling over a fence to get to their cars is a bewildering one. There are other commuting techniques. One type of commuter has his wife meet him at, say, the train arriving at 7:51 P.M. The man himself will then take the train which arrives at 6:02, and will spend the intervening time at the station tavern.

A new arrival in Fairfield County not long ago was surprised by what he took to be the rudeness of his fellow passengers on the train. "I'd meet guys socially, at parties on weekends," he says, "and then I'd run into them again on the train, and they'd look right through me as though they'd never met me." Eventually, he learned that rudeness was not the cause of this behavior. "I discovered that each man has his own commuting pattern," he says. "He reads his paper, does some work, takes a nap, or has a drink in the club car — but the important thing is that it's *his* pattern. He's used to it, and he isn't going to change it. He tries to sit in the same seat in the same car of the same train every day. He either wants conversation or not — usually not. In order to cope with the commuting, you have to defend your personal pattern. So if you see someone you know, who might want to talk to you or sit with you, or who threatens to break the pattern, you have to ignore him. Everybody ends up doing this."

The good life in Fairfield County — the good schools, the pleasant clubs, the green grass, the lakes, the wooded hills — has its drawbacks as well as its rewards. Many parents feel that the celebrated "rural character," so carefully preserved, does not make for a particularly good place to raise children. It has been said, albeit facetiously, that if all the students in Westport's luxurious Staples High School who are using marijuana and other drugs were expelled, there would be no school to run. In towns like Weston, where specific businesses are zoned out, there are no movie theaters, no bowling alleys, no pizza parlors or other traditional places of teenage enjoyment. All these must be sought elsewhere. On the streets of Westport in the afternoon, after school, a group very much resembling Greenwich Village hippies hangs out, looking bored, listless and disaffected. There have been incidents of vandalism and breaking and entering — all laid to teenage idleness and boredom. Being a teenager in Fairfield County can also be lonely. With two- and four-acre zoning, one's best friends frequently live far away. After school, the kids monopolize the telephone, calling up each other. The easiest solution is to give the children their own telephone line. There are no buses or other public transportation through the best neighborhoods. If the children are to visit friends, someone must supply a ride. A solution, when they're old enough: get them their own car. Until then, if Mother and Father are too busy to do the driving, kids are given charge accounts with taxi companies. Taxi charge accounts are also required by Fairfield County maids.

Out of boredom, kids do stupid things. They steal things they don't need, or that their parents would probably buy for them if they asked, from local shops, and when this happens, the parents themselves are no help at all. A Westport shopowner says, "I saw a sixteen-year-old girl take a twenty-dollar cocktail ring from a counter and drop it in her bag. I knew the girl, and I called her mother. Her mother began screaming at me, saying, 'My daughter would never do a thing like that! You're a liar, and I'll never set foot inside your store again.' " Shop-owners are reluctant to call in the police on matters like these, for fear of offending and losing customers. And the police are faced with a special problem. Darien, not long ago, got its name unpleasantly spread across newspaper headlines in connection with a matter that involved teenage drug-taking and drinking. A Darien girl was killed in a car driven by a drunken boy. This gave Darien a bad name which it has not yet lived down, and it is said that local real estate values were damaged. Nobody in Fairfield County wants what happened in Darien to happen in *their* town, certainly not the property-owners or the public servants or the police. To avoid the publicity and scandal of "another Darien," the police departments of other villages admit that they play down, and hush up as quickly as possible, matters of youthful delinquency. Alas, the youth know all this and behave accordingly.

There are other difficulties involved in being a parent in an affluent community. Sonny Fox, who describes himself as "a kid from Brooklyn," moved to Fairfield County partly so that his children could have some of the much-touted "advantages" which he himself never had. But sometimes he feels that the youth of Fairfield are overprivileged. He was startled when his son asked for a motorcycle and explained, "All the other kids have them." On another occasion, he excitedly told his children that they had been invited to swim in a friend's pool. One of his children asked, "Is it heated?" The Fox house is situated by a pretty stream. The children complain that the water is nearly always too chilly for swimming.

But for all its shortcomings, Fairfield County is, to those who love it, a very special sort of place. They regard it with a special affection very close to love. Bette Davis, who has been coming to Westport for over twenty years, has now made the town her permanent home. She lives in a comfortable Colonial house on the banks of a lively river, a house with large airy rooms done in bright colors — splashes of purple, yellow, and pink. Nearby, in Weston, her daughter lives with her husband and their child. Not long ago Miss Davis was having a drink and smoking in her emphatic way, and said, "I'm a Yankee. I was born in New England. Oh, I know a Connecticut Yankee is supposed not to be a *real* Yankee — not the kind of Yankee who comes from Maine and talks about his farm 'down East.' But there's still a Yankee thing here, and it rubs off, some of it, on everybody who comes here. The Yankee doesn't care *what* you are. It's *who* you are, as a person, that he cares about. All kinds of people have moved here, and they've learned that lesson. If you want to be left alone they'll leave you alone. If you want friends they'll be friendly. They'll give you anything you want. Also, I admit I'm a conservative. I like Fairfield County *exactly* as it is. I don't want to see it change a smidgeon — ever!"

Others are more realistic, more accommodating. They see that Fairfield County cannot be kept under a bell jar, not even by zoning laws, as a preserve for rich and private people. They see not only the new rich changing the face of Fairfield, but the old rich changing their ways too, willing to make way for changing times and faces, creating an inevitable blending of the social classes — creating a place, perhaps, where white and black, Jew and Christian, wealthy and not-so-wealthy, can live and enjoy the beauty of Fairfield's hills and streams and beaches. One woman who appreciates Fairfield's changing role, and who intends to make the best of it, is Barbara W. Tuchman, the historian, who lives most of each year in Greenwich. Barbara and Lester Tuchman also have a large antique-filled Park Avenue apartment, but living on a lavish scale is not Barbara Tuchman's style — though it was her father's style, and very much so. Her father, Maurice Wertheim, was a super-millionaire investment banker who headed Wertheim & Company on Wall Street. *His* Greenwich estate originally consisted of a hundred and twenty acres with a huge main house, stables, a jumping course, and a great many outbuildings. The place was tended by French maids, German governesses, stable boys, and a staff of gardeners.

Now the estate has been broken up — the Tuchmans have forty of the original acres, and Barbara Tuchman's sister has the remaining eighty — and the Tuchmans' Greenwich house is simplicity itself.

Low and rambling, all on one floor, it makes use of a lot of glass and consists, really, of one large living-dining room, a small kitchen, and, beyond an open breezeway, three bedrooms. Barbara Tuchman does her own cooking. Her car, one of the lower-priced three, is used to pick up her commuter husband, a New York physician, at the Greenwich station. It is not that the Tuchmans are poor — far from it. Barbara Tuchman inherited a sizable fortune from her father. It is just that their scale of living has been reduced to something more in keeping with the times.

"I do my writing in a little one-room house I built on top of the hill up there," Mrs. Tuchman says. "It has no telephone, and up there I'm completely alone, cut off. When I'm ready to join my family, I come down out of my tiny little ivory tower, back to this house. Do you notice something architecturally a little *odd* about this house? It's really a double house, you see, two buildings joined by the breezeway — and I'm someday going to close that breezeway in, so I won't have to put on a coat to walk to bed on chilly nights. But the fact is that these two buildings, on my father's estate, were the henhouse and the potting shed. As you can see, in my father's day even the hens lived very well, and there must have been a lot of potting done because it was a lot of shed. I love to remind myself of what these buildings used to be. Nobody, of course, can live the way my parents and my grandparents lived — in that great, grand, *vast* manner. I think that if my father, or my grandfather — who was a Morgenthau, and the Morgenthaus were even grander than the Wertheims — knew that I am now living in the old henhouse and the potting shed, thrown together, why, I'm sure they'd be spinning in their graves."

Part Three

THE SIMPLE PLAYGROUNDS

Those were the days in Sun Valley: (from left) "Rocky" Cooper,
Jack Hemingway, Ingrid Bergman, Gary Cooper, Clark Gable

9

Sun Valley:

"Mr. Harriman's Private Train Doesn't Stop Here Any More"

THE late Mrs. Edward MacMullan, who for many years more or less ruled the social seas of Philadelphia, once complained: "It's getting so difficult these days to find places where one can be sure of meeting one's own kind." She was referring to the no-longer-exclusive nature of such social institutions as private schools and private clubs, as well as to neighborhoods, committees, coming-out parties, and even churches. (Being an Episcopalian, Mrs. MacMullan pointed out, no longer seemed to carry much weight — not even in Philadelphia.) The same today is true of what were once the private playgrounds of the rich. As Mrs. MacMullan liked to put it, rolling back her eyes in dismay, "The camel has gotten into the tent."

Sun Valley, Idaho, for example, was designed to be next to impossible to get to. That was the whole point: it was not a resort for "most people." For years it sat there, shining and serene, aloof and inaccessible, like a queen at a command performance — very much *there,* and yet very much removed from the general audience. No stranger would have dreamt of approaching her without the proper introduction. This is not to say that Sun Valley was stuffy. On the contrary. She was merely self-assured. After all, she was America's original ski resort. the first resort in the world to be created purely for winter sports, and created in a day when only a very special breed of the very rich could get away in winter. As a queen, Sun Valley was proud and, as a queen, she regally bestowed lavish favors upon her most loyal subjects.

Most great resorts have been built within so-called "resort areas" — the Adirondacks, the mountains of northern New England, the Florida coastland. Not Sun Valley. She was special, and above all that. She was built as herself, pure and simple, and she was all there was for miles and miles. For years, her only neighbors were the harshly soaring peaks of the Sawtooth Range which guarded and enclosed her sunny, Shangri-La-like glen — a formidable spite fence. As a queen, Sun Valley was not to be easily wooed by commoners.

From the beginning, Sun Valley's fate was guided by large sums of money. Young Averell Harriman had inherited some one hundred million dollars from his father, E. H. Harriman (the "little giant of Wall Street") and had, by the early Thirties, become board chairman of his father's Union Pacific Railroad. Harriman the younger, and his second wife, Marie, had also become avid skiers, but had to journey to Austria or to Switzerland in order to enjoy their sport, since skiing was then almost unheard of in America. The Harrimans were regarded as very exotic types, and Sun Valley was the exotic brainchild of Marie Harriman — who simply wanted a stateside place to ski. Sun Valley was the money child of Averell Harriman, who agreed to pay for what his wife wanted. At her suggestion, he hired an Austrian Alpine expert named Count Felix Schaffgotsch to go into the American West and find a perfect spot for a ski resort.

Count Felix spent months looking at mountains. He visited Mount Rainier, Mount Hood, Yosemite, and any number of mountains of the San Bernardino range. He scouted the areas around Salt Lake City and around Lake Tahoe. He also spent considerable time in Colorado and crossed the Teton Pass in winter to get a view of Jackson Hole. None of these places — where numerous ski resorts now exist — struck his fancy. The mountains were either too high, too windy, too near a large city or too far from a railhead. Then someone suggested that he look at Ketchum, Idaho. Ketchum — once a mining boomtown of two thousand people — had shrunk to a hamlet of two hundred and seventy, nearly half of whom left the valley in wintertime. Soon after the count's arrival, little Ketchum buzzed with the news that an Austrian nobleman was out there in the snow, climbing mountains and going down them on skis, of all things, and talking of building a million-dollar hotel. "Heck, we'd tied boards on our feet to go out across the snow and get our mail, if you call that skiing," recalls old Jack Lane, a prominent sheepman of the area. After one look at the crazy-acting foreigner, Jack Lane cautioned his fellow businessmen, "Don't cash any of his checks."

A mile north of Ketchum the count skied into a windless basin surrounded by totally treeless slopes, and with pine-covered Baldy Mountain towering at the valley's western mouth, seeming to close the valley off from all intruders. The topography of the place was immediately striking, for hills in this region all have two features in common. Their north-facing flanks, shielded from the sun, remain cool and moist and therefore are covered with thick stands of pine. But the south-facing slopes, drained of moisture by the sun's heat, are bare of vegetation and smooth as a baby's cheek. This, the count figured, meant unimpeded skiing. It also eliminated the need for cutting trails. The count wired Harriman that he had found his spot. Within ten days, Harriman was at Ketchum with his private railroad car, and a Union Pacific check was written to pay for an initial forty-three hundred acres.

When the Union Pacific began building the resort — which still had no name — it chose as an architectural scheme something very close to the design it had used for the cars on its first streamliner. The earliest Sun Valley buildings have a railroad-station look. Jim Curran was the bridge engineer for the railroad. He knew nothing about skiing. But he had helped build tramways for loading bananas onto freight cars in the tropics, and saw that lifting a skier to a mountaintop and hoisting a bunch of bananas to the deck of a ship presented much the same sort of engineering problem. In place of the hook that carried the bananas, he put a chair, and the world's first skiing chair lift was born. The Harrimans had estimated that the cost of the original installation would be "about a million." By the time the place was nearing completion, in 1935, almost three million Depression dollars had been spent.

Next, the late Steve Hannagan — the colorful publicity man who had been able to drumbeat a desolate Florida sandbar into something called Miami Beach — was hired to put Harriman's purchase on the map. Hannagan knew nothing about skiing either, and when he first visited the area he pronounced it a "godforsaken field of snow." The day was overcast. Then suddenly the clouds rolled back, the sun came out, and Mr. Hannagan noticed an astonishing thing happen. The temperature of the air shot abruptly up to ninety degrees. Immediately he announced that the place must be named Sun Valley. Both Harrimans objected to the name, but because Hannagan was assumed to be a genius in such matters they reluctantly agreed to it.

It turned out to be a brilliant choice. Both Averell and Marie Harriman, as skiers, felt that the word "sun" had unfortunate connotations. In Europe too much sunshine on a slope can produce the slush that skiers call "mashed potatoes." When the temperature drops the result is an unskiable icy crust. But Hannagan knew that most Americans were *not* skiers and, furthermore, that Americans were a pampered lot who disliked the cold. The first Hannagan poster for Sun Valley showed a happy, handsome youth skiing down the mountainside stripped to the waist. Close behind him came a pretty girl skiing in a bathing suit. The two models must have had a chilly time of it despite their larky smiles, for Sun Valley's famous winter warmth is available for the most part on south-facing verandas that are protected from the frosty breezes. But it didn't matter. Hannagan seemed to have brought skiing to the tropics, and Sun Valley was on its way.

From the moment the resort opened its doors in 1936, it was apparent that Sun Valley was capable of exerting a strong emotional pull on those who visited it. The list of people who became smitten with Sun Valley at first sight is long indeed. At first, Sun Valley's fans consisted mostly of the Harrimans and their friends. But soon well-heeled skiers and would-be skiers were pouring in from all over the country. It is hard to explain, but those who took a head-over-heels tumble for Sun Valley became her amorous slaves for life, and the relationships formed were deep, sentimental, difficult to express in human language. As one woman wrote of her beloved, "How can I express what this place means to me? My whole *soul* is wrapped up in these mountains!" Wills were written with instructions that burials be at the foot of Baldy Mountain, or that the deceased's ashes be scattered across a favorite trail. Strong men have been known to make absolute fools of themselves in their efforts to stay in touch with Sun Valley. For years, one Sun Valley lover periodically telephoned the Lodge whenever he was away. First he would chat with the room clerk, then with

Frederick, the former captain in the dining room, then with the pool attendant, then with a favorite ski instructor. At last he would ask to be transferred to the bartender in the Duchin Room where he would want to know who was sitting at the bar, and what they were talking about. His final request on these long distance ventures would be that the receiver be placed on the bar so that he could listen and enjoy, vicariously, the simple murmur of Sun Valley talk. His calls would come from as far away as London, Paris, Palm Beach, wherever he might be.

Another man for years made regular calls from New York with requests for selections from Hap Miller's Orchestra (called "the Lester Lanins of the West"), the band that to this very day plays sweet and stately music from an older and more naïve time — "All the Things You Are," "The Way You Look Tonight," "Just One of Those Things" — society dance tunes, as they used to be called.

In its isolation, reachable only by Pullman, Sun Valley was intended not only for the wealthy but for the *dedicated* skier. It wanted nothing to do with the duffer, or even the average skier. At the same time it attracted a few outdoorsy movie stars — Ty Power on his wooden skis, Sonja Henie on her flashing skates, along with the society dowagers from Boston and Philadelphia who enjoyed doing nothing more than snowshoe through the pines. There, on their skis, were the lanky figures of the Gary Coopers and there, coming in for lunch, was the plump but still recognizable bundle of Ann Sothern, who built her own baby-blue stucco house in the Valley and lived there for years. There was Norma Shearer stepping out of an elevator in the Lodge ("Norma's too cheap to build her own house," Miss Sothern used to sniff) with her husband, a ski instructor, Marti Arrouge.

Naturally, nobody wanted anything about Sun Valley to change. As Sun Valley gradually aged, so much more vociferous did its original fans become about seeing to it that nothing must be altered. The two main hotels, the slightly more "swell" Lodge, and the somewhat more modest Challenger Inn, began, in time, to reflect a bygone era, and this was just fine with everyone from the Harrimans on down. The interiors had been done in what might be called Depression Moderne, a style that relied heavily on indirect lighting, mirrors, copper, and whatever may have been the earliest ancestor of Naugahyde. The

famous heated swimming pools — among the first in the United States
— were "free-form" in shape, predating the now-common kidney and
oval shapes. A number of the public rooms began to wear a faded,
even seedy air, and it was not hard to forget that the Lodge's main
cocktail lounge, the Duchin Room, had been named not for Peter but
for his late father, Eddie Duchin. Into this comfortable and familiar
mold, even the guests at Sun Valley seemed to settle for a while.
Through the nineteen-forties, the Fifties, and even into the Sixties,
most of the people who arrived annually at Sun Valley were families
who had known and skied with each other "forever" — Mellons,
Goulds, Pierreponts, with their children and their children's nannies.
Then, not very long ago, a strange thing happened.

Sun Valley had been "fashionable" from the beginning. But overnight (or so it seemed) it started becoming chic, which is quite a different thing. Suddenly Andy Williams and his wife were helping turn
a cavernous below-stairs boiler room into a noisy discotheque, along
with the Henry Mancinis and Janet Leigh. Art Linkletter was there,
and so were William Wyler and his wife, plus Van Williams — television's Green Hornet — and Charles Schulz (of *Peanuts*), along with
the wife of Austria's ambassador to the United States, the Leonard
Bernsteins, Ray Milland, Claudette Colbert, the Jimmy Stewarts, and
the Robert S. McNamaras. Then came the Kennedys — all of them.
Robert and Ethel Kennedy arrived first with what appeared to be
dozens of their children, in their own jet, barely making it into the
tiny Hailey airport. Next a suite of rooms was being hastily flung together to accommodate Mrs. Jacqueline Kennedy and her children,
their two nurses, her two secretaries, and their accompanying Secret
Service people. In other words, Sun Valley's old-shoe dowdiness was
being discovered by what were already being called the Beautiful People, that heady mixture of the powerful and celebrated from the
world's politics, society, the arts, and just plain money. With them,
or just a panting step behind them, came such familiar institutions as
the ubiquitous photographers from *Women's Wear Daily* to report
on what they wore and what they did. ("I'd never even heard of
Women's Wear Daily before this happened," said one Sun Valley
regular.)

How did it all happen? The answer has less to do with the vagaries of fashion or sport or resort life than with sheer economics. From the outset, the emphasis at Sun Valley had been on luxury, and splendid food and service had been the rule in all the resort's restaurants and public rooms. Under the Harriman regime, a what-the-hell attitude toward expense had been encouraged. Among other things, the resort maintained its own private hospital with a highly paid staff which specialized, understandably enough, in repairing bone fractures. In a casual way, as the years went by, Sun Valley kept adding more chair lifts, opening new trails — all at great cost. Through these years, furthermore, Sun Valley had been managed by an affable man called "Pappy" Rogers whom guests held dear to their hearts for his lovable habit of saying, whenever they were about to check out, "Oh, why don't you stay on? It'll be on the house!" Rogers was forever treating guests to elaborate parties, and buying them expensive dinners. While all this freehanded spending was going on, labor costs were rising. Railroad travel, at the same time, was declining. Sun Valley had been conceived as a railhead resort, and in the great postwar air traffic boom, Sun Valley was suddenly awfully far away — particularly to a young and impatient new breed of American skier who had never heard of Norma Shearer. Skiing as a sport was sky-rocketing to mass popularity, and among the new breed of skiers, certain mystiques developed. One of these was that the newer the resort, the better it must therefore be. Also, skiers no longer demanded opulent service, nor were they particularly willing to pay for it. Skiing had become a family sport, and skiers looked for kitchenettes or even hotplates and cafeterias rather than hotels with maids' dining rooms. As these new skiers hopped from resort to resort, looking for the best skiing at the lowest prices, Sun Valley found itself in a kind of social backwater, a resort for skiing's Old Guard, the grayheads.

While all this was going on, with railroads in deepening trouble, Averell Harriman was becoming a figure of international importance. His interests were turning from skiing to public life, with several ambassadorships, a cabinet post, and the governorship of New York. Suddenly someone noticed that the Harrimans had not visited their Sun Valley house for years, and by the time Sun Valley was celebrating its mere twenty-fifth birthday in 1961, it was clear that the place was suffering from a sorry case of middle-age slump. The Union Pacific had, from the beginning, treated Sun Valley as a fiscal write-off. But, by the 1960's the question most often asked at the railroad's board meeting in New York was, "Well, how much did Sun Valley lose *this* year?" At each successive meeting, the question became less and less a joke.

In 1964, the Union Pacific called in the Janss Corporation, land developers in Southern California, and asked them what could be done. The Janss brothers, William and Edwin, are more than just developers. They are city-builders, having created, among other things, Westwood Village in Los Angeles. The brothers surveyed the property and reported that an additional investment of at least ten to fifteen million dollars was required to pull Sun Valley out of its doldrums. With this news, the railroad threw up its hands. Arthur Stoddard, then the president, announced that "running a railroad and running a ski resort have little in common" and agreed to sell the resort to the Janss brothers for an unpublished price that is said to have been rock-bottom.

There was instant dismay among the faithful. Ann Sothern flew to her telephone, called Bill Janss personally, and accused him of wanting to build a "slum" next to her baby-blue cottage. Letters of indignant protest — and advice — poured in from across the country. But the Janss brothers proceeded with all deliberate speed to facelift Sun Valley and to give it a whole new image with a heroic injection of youth and spirit. An extensive building program was begun. A new competition-size pool was added, new tennis courts, and a new shopping mall, with a ski shop, a pastry shop, a mod dress shop, a delicatessen, a barbershop, a drugstore, a gift shop, a bookshop, a decorator's shop, a jewelry shop, and a steak house slyly named the Ore House, featuring a mining-days decor. "Now get me *today's* people," commanded Bill Janss. In 1965, today's people consisted largely of the Kennedy family. The days of "Pappy" Rogers were over, but all the Kennedys were given an invitation to ski gratis at Sun Valley. Needless to say, they accepted it.

The Janss Corporation feels that the days of big resort hotels are over, and so there are no plans to enlarge the hotel facilities as such, though the lobbies, dining room and a number of the rooms in the Lodge have been redecorated. Janss has, however, been busily turning

Sun Valley from a sleepy ski village into a bustling city for the new American middle class. This has meant condominiums, apartments, light housekeeping units, and hundreds of new single-family dwellings, which are attached row-house fashion in clusters of four to eight. Janss's idea has been to broaden Sun Valley's appeal as much as possible without, of course, permitting it to be anything like a slum. In newly opened areas throughout Sun Valley, private houses are going up which will sell for anywhere from twenty-five thousand dollars to four hundred thousand dollars. Some twenty million dollars has been spent already, and the end is nowhere near in sight. To make Sun Valley more accessible, a new jet strip has been opened just minutes from the foot of Baldy Mountain for private and charter planes, and Janss has seen to it that commercial air service has been improved to Hailey, Idaho, just thirteen miles away.

Obviously not all the old-timers were happy with these developments, and there was some grumbling here and there. Ann Sothern has sold her little house, but not, they say, because of pique, but because she needed the money. Nonetheless, those who love Sun Valley have one thing to be thankful for in William C. Janss; he is a dedicated and accomplished skier. An ex-Olympian, he has spent millions of his corporation's money in improving Sun Valley's existing trails, adding new ones, and building new lift facilities. He has taken over Sun Valley personally, no longer in partnership with his brother. And of course what Bill Janss saw there all along was what anyone who has skied there soon finds — that Sun Valley offers some of the most superb skiing in the United States and perhaps in the world. Skiing aficionados claim that Sun Valley skiing is better than anything to be found in Europe. The occasional warm winds from the Mediterranean (which are the real villains, not sunshine, that cause mashed-potato skiing) never occur in Sun Valley. The normal skiing condition is deep — sometimes ten to twenty feet — powder. The weather averages three days of storm to twenty days of sunshine and, when storms occur, they have a unique habit of happening either on one face of Baldy or the other, never on both at once. This means that while one side of the mountain may become unskiable, the other is fine. Only rarely, when abnormally high winds cause the descending empty chairs to swing too violently, have Sun Valley's lifts been closed.

There is also another, somewhat subtler reason for Sun Valley's allure — Idaho's divorce laws, which require only six weeks' residence. This is the same as Nevada but, because Idaho does not permit gambling, Sun Valley likes to think that it attracts the "carriage trade" of the divorce-bound, while the run-of-the-mill go to Reno or Las Vegas. Such carriage-trade types as Mrs. William Rockefeller, Mrs. Patricia Lawford, Mrs. Merriweather Post, Ralph Bellamy, Mrs. James Murphy (now Mrs. Nelson Rockefeller), and Mrs. Henry Ford have all gotten Sun Valley divorces. (Mrs. Ford's daughter Charlotte, who was married to Greek shipowner Stavros Niarchos, did a strange thing: she came to Sun Valley, stayed for a little more than five weeks, then flew off to New York — thereby canceling her residence credit — and a little later went to Mexico for her divorce. No one knows why.) Many divorcées fill their Sun Valley time by learning to ski. A number, while learning, have fallen in love with their ski instructors, most of whom are imported from Austria and are chosen, it sometimes seems, for their bronzed good looks as well as their skiing skill. There have been quite a few Sun Valley marriages in the little chalet-style church that stands hard by the Lodge. Love, or at least deep emotional change, is always in the air. Small wonder so many people have become addicted to the place.

But it was really the Kennedys who were multi-handedly responsible for Sun Valley's renaissance in the world of skiing. They came like fairy god-people with magic wands that conjured up instant publicity. All Joseph Kennedy's children had skied Sun Valley when they were youngsters, and nostalgia, as much as anything else, may have urged Robert and Ethel Kennedy to accept Bill Janss's invitation. The former First Lady's arrival was something else, and no one was quite prepared for that. It was preceded by a flurry of telegrams which issued conflicting instructions and plunged the Sun Valley staff into a frenzy of disjointed activity. Originally, the entire Kennedy party was to be housed in Averell Harriman's cottage, with children placed three to four to a room. This is in keeping with Jacqueline Kennedy Onassis's technique of surrounding her own children with hordes of others, thereby making her two less conspicuous. But at the last moment, Jacqueline Kennedy's secretary telephoned to say that Mrs. Kennedy would prefer a suite of her own. By working all night long, a decorating crew put one of the new condominiums in order for her group.

She arrived, according to Pete Lane, who operates the ski shop, "looking all wrong. She had been dressed by Seventh Avenue," Lane says, "and she turned up the first day wearing bell-bottom ski pants. Can you imagine that? Bell-bottom ski pants!" Soon, however, she saw the unwisdom of her ways and, after a visit to Lane's store, made herself look more presentable. Mrs. Kennedy had only recently taken up skiing and, when she arrived at Sun Valley, she had really not quite mastered it. "Let's face it," says one who watched her the first day on the mountain, "she couldn't ski at all." She had tried skiing before, both at Stowe, Vermont, and at Aspen, Colorado, and had found little to admire at either place. "I was so cold at Stowe I could hardly stand it," she has said. But she was determined to give it one more try. In New York, her friend Leonard Bernstein had told her to look up his friend Sigi Engl, the celebrated director of skiing at Sun Valley. Engl avoids giving private lessons whenever possible — he hasn't the time — and tried to turn Mrs. Kennedy over to one of his large staff of instructors (so popular for private lessons that they have been nicknamed "Sigi's Rent-a-Kraut Service"). But Mrs. Kennedy begged for the great Sigi himself. Sigi agreed — if she would agree to adjust her schedule to his. She agreed.

"I want to learn to ski just a little bit," she explained, "I'm going to Gstaad and I don't want to look too silly." "*Gstaad!*" cried the ebullient Engl. "Why, if you go to Gstaad skiing the way you do now, you'll spend your whole time in the lounge waiting for the others to come down off the mountain!" Engl started her out on Dollar Mountain, his mountain for beginners. Before starting down the hill for her first run, Jackie said, "I'm warning you — if I fall this is my last time!" "If I'm going to be your last ski instructor take a good look at me," Engl called back. After four days of lessons, Engl had Jackie nine thousand feet up on the top of Baldy Mountain, and she made it safely, if a little slowly, down without a fall.

"She just hadn't been having any fun at it," Engl says. "Also at first she was a little lazy about certain exercises I wanted her to do, but she snapped out of that." Engl modestly refuses to claim that he taught the present Mrs. Onassis how to ski, but he does feel that he helped her learn to enjoy the sport, which, along with overcoming fear, is more than half the skiing battle.

Engl is prouder of results he has had with others of his rarely accepted private students. Though it is little known, the late Gary Cooper had a leg injured in an automobile accident (when he rode horseback in his Westerns, he could be photographed only from one side because he could maneuver only one foot into a stirrup; the other foot dangled). Sigi Engl taught Cooper to execute difficult skiing turns despite this handicap. Engl has had several one-legged skiers as students, and even once taught a blind man to ski, "by telling him which way to turn as we went down the mountain, and by letting him get the feel of the mountain under his skis. I taught him to read that mountain like Braille." Sigi had less luck with the Shah of Iran, who has visited Sun Valley twice. The Shah is a good skier, but likes to ski dangerously fast. "Your Majesty, I wouldn't want you to hurt yourself," said Engl politely. "If I should hurt myself, I would be a great hero to my people," replied the Shah, and went on skiing as fast as ever.

Sun Valley took Jacqueline Kennedy to its heart, and she took the resort to hers. Even the press and *Women's Wear Daily* photographers gave her more privacy there and spent most of their time squabbling among themselves or sabotaging each other's cameras. After the fourth day of lessons Engl tried once more to turn her over to one of his instructors. "Oh, but you and I have so much *fun*, Sigi," she murmured, and he relented. She had so much fun that one night in the Duchin Room she asked Hap Miller to play some Russian music. He obliged by playing the Fifth Hungarian Dance for her, and she rose to her feet and performed a Russian dance for the room at large. "She did it beautifully, too," says Miller.

Sun Valley was less sure how it felt about her late brother-in-law, the Senator from New York. Things got off to a bad start when the Senator appeared tieless at dinnertime in the dining room, and was politely told that gentlemen were required to wear neckties. He came back with a tie, but out of a spirit of revenge — or fun — he had removed his shoes and was wearing bedroom slippers. The crowd in the Harriman cottage was a loud and boisterous one, and the Kennedy children are a particularly energetic lot. Bobby and Ethel Kennedy, along with the Andy Williamses, preferred late, noisy evenings in the boiler-room discotheque. Jackie Kennedy had quiet dinners with her children in the cafeteria of the Challenger Inn (recently rechristened the Sun Valley Inn, on the public-relations theory that the old name suggested that skiing was a challenge, and not a right sport for everyone.) Some of the complaints about the Senator are directed not so much at him as at overzealous members of his staff. One young man, about to start down Baldy Mountain on his skis, was approached by an officious Kennedy aide and told, "Get out of the way. Bobby Kennedy wants to ski through here." When the young man demurred, the aide opened his parka to reveal a shoulder holster with the handle of a pistol emerging from it, patted it significantly, and said, "I told you to move." The young man is a well-muscled Westerner, full of grit, and he replied, "Well, I reckon if I don't have as much right to ski down this mountain as he does, you're going to have to shoot me to prove it, mister." He was allowed to continue on his way.

There was disgruntled talk that the Bobby Kennedy party was staying in the Harriman house simply because, as Averell Harriman's friends, they could stay there free, and after the Kennedys left, there was a puzzling discovery. The several pairs of expensive Head skis which the Kennedy party had been renting from Pete Lane's ski shop had been, without a word, packed up and taken home. The rented Heads have never been returned.

Though the Kennedys and their friends may have helped publicize Sun Valley and make it chic, Bill Janss and his staff insist that this is not the image that they wish to cultivate — in fact, that this would be a dangerous image for a resort of Sun Valley's new size and scope to maintain. That sort of thing could frighten trade away. "Sun Valley *isn't* for the Beautiful People," Bill Janss insists. "It's a *family* resort, and always will be. We want people to come here with their families, for long stays. We've made this a wonderful place for children — they can be on their own, and there's no place for them to wander off to. That's why the condominiums and the new houses are selling so well. People who like to ski are coming with their families. We'll never be like Acapulco."

If Beautiful People come, he adds, they will have to learn to ski well if they are going to have any fun at all. Towering over the resort, and at its very heart, is the massive Baldy Mountain — "a very disciplinary mountain," in Sigi Engl's phrase. Baldy's trails — such as the one called Exhibition, which is about as steep as a trail can be without being vertical — are not to be undertaken lightly, or by those who take skiing lightly. Skiers who have skied only Eastern mountains are overwhelmed, breathtaken, when the lift deposits them at the top of Baldy. The view of white peaks and green pines stretches out horizontally, for three hundred and sixty degrees, and for miles. One might be balancing on tiptoes on the top of the world. Some, less used to being up so high, go to pieces completely at the view and have to be carried down, blindfolded, to the base. Experienced skiers, though, gasp at the view and start down the mountain on their skis with wild cries of joy.

Baldy and the Baldy pin — a badge given to skiers who have made it all the way down without a fall — are essentially what Sun Valley is all about. The new owner knows this, as he continues to expand the skiing facilities, adding new lifts, building new trails. "The possibilities of this mountain are limitless," Sigi Engl says. "Already you could ski down this mountain over a hundred times, trying one series of trails after another, and never repeat yourself." The facilities for teaching skiing continue to improve. One of many innovations is the use of videotape; a skier is photographed going down a slope and, immediately, the tape can be played back to him showing him his mistakes. At the same time, the slopes will never be crowded, nor will there be lines at the lifts, because the capacity of the mountain is equal to the capacity of Sun Valley's Lodge, Inn, and outbuildings. It will remain so, because Sun Valley is a pocket of land locked within thousands of square miles of National Forest. No competitors will ever remotely encroach upon it. Carl Gray, a wealthily retired electronics manufacturer who has been skiing at Sun Valley for years, says, "I'm a businessman. I ski at Sun Valley because the cost per mile is cheaper — there's no waiting."

Sun Valley is still not all that easy to get to. From the East Coast, for example, one must fly via Chicago or Denver to Salt Lake City, and then north, by twin-engine plane (unless you own your own jet) to Hailey; and then there is a half-hour drive into the Valley. But still the Valley burgeons. The late Ernest Hemingway came to Sun Valley a number of years and, like so many people before and after him, began a lifelong romance with the place. He built a sturdy house in Ketchum, facing Sun Valley, and it was in Ketchum that he took his own life. He is buried in the shadow of Baldy, and a small monument to him has been erected nearby. Hemingway was regarded with great affection in the Valley — he wrote *For Whom the Bell Tolls* in a suite he rented in the Lodge — though there is still some disagreement about the manner in which Hemingway hunted game. Northern Idaho hunters are selective, they say, about what they hunt, but Hemingway, with a gun in hand, fired at every beast in sight, large or small, indifferent as to what he killed as long as he killed it. After a while, there were a number of his Ketchum friends who refused to go out with him.

Still, Hemingway belonged to Sun Valley and so does his widow, Mary Hemingway, a diminutive and gingery lady, seldom at a loss for an opinion, who still lives most of each year in the house her husband built. Mary Hemingway and her best friend, Clara Spiegel, another widow, entertain frequently at cocktail parties, and Mary Hemingway complains, "The cocktail parties here get bigger and bigger. There are just so many people coming here, people you have to ask or they'll be hurt — it's endless. I lead a much busier social life out here in the mountains. *Everybody* comes here now." It used to be, she says, "sort of exclusive — I'm no snob, Lord knows, but it was a little *set* out here of people you knew. *Them* days is gone forever! Look at the beautiful float trips people used to take on the rivers up in our primitive areas, further north. They were for real explorers, aficionados. You'd be on the river for a week and never see another soul besides your own party and your guide. Now it's like Broadway and Forty-second Street up there. You look down the river and there's your dentist from Larchmont! Well, I suppose there's nothing wrong with dentists. . . ."

Every year, on her late husband's birthday, which falls on July 21, Mary Hemingway gives a big birthday party for him at Sun Valley's Trail Creek Lodge. The Sun Valley chefs cater the meal for her, but she likes to provide some small culinary touch herself — she will make her own curry powder, for example, if there is to be an Eastern dish. Each year, Mary Hemingway's party is bigger than the last. At the most recent one she suddenly looked around the gathering and asked,

"Who *are* these people? New Sun Valley people, I suppose — and plain gate-crashers. Everyone I see here is a total stranger! Well, Ernest was a gregarious man. He was always terribly cordial to strangers, to *total* strangers — sometimes even a little *too* cordial, it used to seem to some of us. This isn't at all like what it used to be. But it *is* Ernest's birthday, and I really think Ernest would have approved."

The beach at Zihuatenejo

10

Mexico:
In Search of What Acapulco Used to Be

TRAVELERS have become as restless and changeful of their ways as resorts and small suburban towns — endlessly searching out new and *just right* places. The new breed of new rich, thirsting to find itself in the new social scheme of things, keeps looking for new oases of pleasure and peace.

And so, when American travelers say that a resort is ruined, they mean that it has been improved. Conveniences — such as the mixed blessing of air conditioning — have been installed. When Americans say that a resort is ruined, they mean that its prices have risen to equal those of other resorts. On both these counts, Acapulco certainly qualifies for the ruined, or at least considerably damaged, label, and so for several years the search has been on for the perfect little beach resort that is "just like what Acapulco used to be" — cheap, inconvenient, somewhat squalid, but with miles of white sand and turquoise ocean, where palm leaves click in sunny breezes, and where fat fish leap onto the line.

Excited reports have come back from this or that little-jewel port — reports which announce that *this is it; this is what Acapulco was.* All these reports have had the heavy support of local chambers of commerce, needless to say. And, needless to say, they have been contradictory, confusing.

The west coast of Mexico is favored (or afflicted, depending on your point of view) with a particular topography along nearly its entire length: stern and abrupt ranges of the Sierra Madre Occidental rise steeply from the ocean's edge, leaving the towns and villages of the coast cut off from the interior. Such roads as exist frequently turn into surging rivers in the rainy season, and a number of places are accessible only from the sea or by air. (This was once true of Acapulco, before a superhighway made it an easy drive from Mexico City.) The same terrain is repeated along the skinny peninsula of Baja California. Indeed, the mountains of Baja are so brave, rock-strewn, and arid — spiky with cactus, wild with jaguar, deer and bright parrots — that most of the peninsula is still an unpopulated wilderness. There are stretches where Baja California is scarcely more than thirty miles across, and yet those thirty miles from ocean to gulf are next to impossible to travel by land. Las Cruces, a hamlet in Baja, is in one of these remote regions. Though only forty miles from La Paz, Baja's capital city, Las Cruces does not appear on most maps of Mexico and, making use of a bumpy landing strip, can only be reached by privately chartered plane.

Las Cruces got its name, according to the local legend, when Cortes first sailed into the Gulf of California in 1535 and put ashore in the tiny harbor — before sailing north to discover the larger, more protected harbor at La Paz. Upon landing, there was a skirmish with the Indians, and three of Cortes's men were killed. Years later, three stone crosses — one larger than the others, possibly to indicate that one was an officer and the others enlisted men — were found lying on their sides in the undergrowth. These crosses, one is told, were carried to the top of a hill overlooking the harbor and erected there, though they hardly look to be over four hundred years old.

In the late 1940's, a dashing young Mexican named Abelardo Rodríguez — whose wife, the former Lucille Bremer, once danced in a film opposite Fred Astaire — came to Las Cruces and decided to build a hotel there. (Sr. Rodríguez's father had been president of Mexico, then governor of Baja California, and had, in the process, collected considerable wealth and Baja real estate.) Serving as his own architect and interior decorator, Rodríguez built a low, sprawling building in the villa style with wide terraces, airy loggias, fountains, a swimming pool, tennis courts, a trapshooting range, and a putting green. The rooms — there are only twenty — have stone fireplaces, and all face the sea and the harsh profile of the deserted island of Cerralvo, twenty miles offshore, which seems to hang in the sky. The mood here is of quiet elegance. In the bathrooms, fresh cakes of Guerlain soap are placed daily (though the chilling sight of a scorpion scrambling up the wall reminds one that one is, after all, in the tropics); all fruits and vegetables are flown in from Los Angeles. Still, the place *is* remote. The hotel has a radio that can reach La Paz, but there is no telephone or telegraph service (a gasoline-driven generator provides electricity) and, when one is a guest there, one literally cannot be reached.

Rodríguez also built himself a large house at Las Cruces and, because there was none in the area, he built a handsome church (a priest flies in every other week to say Mass). Then, flushed with the success of his first resort, he went on to build two others — Palmilla, some distance to the south near the little town of San José del Cabo, and the Hacienda Cabo San Lucas, practically on the top of the peninsula. (At each of these places he also built churches, and Rodríguez today sees a symbolic connection between his three churches and the three original crosses at Las Cruces, and with the Trinity, and now says that having built his churches, he no longer worries about getting into heaven.) From a business standpoint, however, the two new hotels — both larger than Las Cruces — put Rodríguez into serious competition with himself. Guests were abandoning Las Cruces for the other places, and Rodríguez hit upon the idea of turning Las Cruces into a private club, "for members only," which charged annual dues — a gimmick, needless to say, to insure Las Cruces a fixed income. Rodríguez dressed up his membership list with a number of movie stars, including Bing Crosby, who built a villa of his own and spends several months a year there, fishing and snorkeling, and Bob Hope, who has never been there at all.

The new status of Las Cruces as a club has had an off-putting effect upon prospective guests. Some people have got the notion that Las Cruces is now some sort of private estate belonging to Bing Crosby, and others, afraid of being turned away, no longer try to stay there. Their fears are unfounded. While it is "up to the discretion of the manager" whether or not a nonmember may stay at Las Cruces, the place is, after all, in business to make money; if rooms are available, the manager never says no. Also, though membership is "frozen" at a hundred and eighty members, there are plenty of vacancies. Dues are two hundred and forty dollars a year, and they entitle a member to stay at Las Cruces for ten days a year free of charge.

On the other hand, Americans who suffer from either the There's-Nothing-to-Do or the There's-No-Place-to-Go syndrome, should be discouraged from visiting Las Cruces. There *is* no place to go. Of the two kinds of fishermen — those who are serious fishermen and those whose wives *think* they are serious fishermen — Las Cruces is for the former. Some of the richest waters in the world lie offshore, teeming with sailfish, marlin, albacore, roosterfish, and dorado.

At regular intervals, pods of whales swim into the gulf to mate, and manta rays the size of grand pianos flip their preposterous bodies in the air. But night life is nonexistent. There is excitement, of sorts — a bitter feud between Crosby and Desi Arnaz, another member (Crosby, they say, wants Arnaz expelled from the club), is always worth a few minutes' gossip and speculation. Las Cruces is popular with men who fly their own planes because that remote landing strip is an excellent means for getting illegal goods from the United States into Mexico (the planes unload quickly at Las Cruces, then fly on to La Paz to complete their flight plans), and the clandestine flights arriving and departing are fine fodder for conversation. (Materials brought in this way — such as firearms for hunting trips — are generally for their owners' use, and so the Mexican government, aware of the practice, looks the other way.) But the greatest asset of the place, for those who fancy it, is the isolation, that splendid quiet.

Outside the hotel door, not long ago, a local wren had built a nest in a hanging lantern and was attending to three hatchlings there. She thoroughly disapproved of the occupancy of the nearby room which she clearly regarded as her own. Each time the guest forgot her busy presence and let his screen door slam shut, she registered her displeasure by flying at his face, making provoked noises. One evening two guests sat on the terrace near her nest playing a quiet — very quiet — game of dominoes. Once they shuffled their dominoes too noisily, once more incurring one of her testy demonstrations. That quick-tempered little bird could symbolize how very, very hushed the life at Las Cruces is supposed to be.

Mazatlán — almost directly across the Gulf of California on the

Mexican mainland — is something else again. The changes that have taken place in Mazatlán in recent years are awesome. The old harbor, which used to remind many people of a smaller Rio de Janeiro, has been decorated with advertising billboards; the water of the bay has achieved an evil color and, as the city has grown, something that looks and acts very much like smog hangs stubbornly in the air. Tourism — and Mazatlán's reputation as a sport-fishing capital — has done this. The downtown section of the city has undergone a sad decay and, meanwhile, along the beach to the north of town a gaudy "strip" of hotels, motels, and "boatlets" — not unreminiscent of Las Vegas — threads its neon-flashing way. The "piano bar" is a device that is apparently much favored in Mazatlán, and each new hotel announces its piano bar in tones more strident than the last. In Mazatlán, too, it is possible to see, with great clarity, how very Americanized much of tourist Mexico is becoming. That new language which some have called "Spanglish" is widely in evidence; ask a question in Spanish, and you are answered in English, and vice versa. Prices for articles in shops are now quoted simultaneously in pesos and in dollars, which never used to be the case, and in all the restaurants the food — lamb chops in brown gravy, ham with pineapple slices — has become determinedly "American." Where tortillas used to be served with meals, hard rolls are now offered. When asked for tortillas recently, the waiter looked dismayed, and the fiery *salsa picante* — sauce of green and red chilis — has disappeared from the table in favor of American catsup. At the same time, one observes Mexicans being served appetizing-looking dishes and suspects that the natives may be eating far better than the tourists who gaze glumly at their pallid potatoes.

Meanwhile, though Mazatlán itself may lack charm, there does exist a charming way of getting — and leaving — there, if one is not rushed and can take the time. A ferry makes leisurely and regular crossings between Mazatlán and La Paz, taking overnight to cross the Gulf of California. On a night that is clear and full of stars, with a sea crowded with phosphorescents — and followed by leaping porpoises all the way — this is a lovely trip. The boat leaves Mazatlán on Tuesday and Saturday nights, arriving in La Paz the following morning. From La Paz, sailings are Thursday and Sunday nights. The boat, owned by Balsa Hotels (who operate the sumptuous Presidente

Hotel chain in Mexico), offers two classes of passage, and first class is luxurious — all staterooms with private bath — and the dining room and bar are so appealing that many passengers stay right there all the way across the Gulf, never visiting their staterooms at all.

Puerto Vallarta — as the crow flies, some two hundred miles south of Mazatlán — is another resort widely said to be "ruined." It was the "new Acapulco" of ten years ago and, since then, has achieved international fame as the location used for the film *Night of the Iguana,* and as the place where none other than Richard Burton and Elizabeth Taylor have bought a house. If, however, Vallarta has been ruined, it has been ruined in a delightful way. It has grown, but it has grown — so far, at least — in an orderly fashion. The architecture has been kept simple and provincial, in keeping with the red-tile-roof feeling of the place. Though there is a new Hilton hotel, as well as a Presidente, there are still none of the monolithic, high-rise buildings that have marred the horizon of Acapulco. A new "Gold Coast" — a stretch of big, sprawling houses (built for costs of a hundred and fifty thousand dollars and up) — has been carved out of what, four years ago, was virgin jungle, but this development blends pleasantly into the landscape. There is a new road running south to the fishing village (and pretty beach) of Mismaloya, which, mountainside, has now become overgrown and softened with natural green. Signs of growth are everywhere, and everyone is building — demonstrating the Mexican builders' ingenuity when it comes to tacking new rooms, even whole apartments, on to existing structures; where there was one house, now there are four or five. The foresighted Rosita Hotel, still only three stories high, has four floor-buttons in its elevator. The bar of the Oceano Hotel, the "in" meeting place at the cocktail hour, is a-rustle with unfolding blueprints and architects' sketches. Suddenly, all the taxis in Vallarta are a citified yellow, and what the other day was a native cantina is now a discotheque ("A-Go-Go") with psychedelic light and air conditioning. The old man who used to sell fresh peanuts on foot now rides about in a motorized cart. Big Greyhound buses lumber into town, and jets from Los Angeles land at the airport. And, though prices have climbed somewhat, Puerto Vallarta is still a tourist bargain. A room in a good hotel can be got for as little as eight to ten dollars a night, which is in pleasant contrast to Acapulco, where forty-five dollars a night is no surprise.

A great and continuing drawing card for Puerto Vallarta has been the possibility of the Burtons' presence there. "They're due in any day now — perhaps tomorrow," one hears, almost daily. The rumor that the Burtons are due in momentarily has been responsible for any number of two-week vacations being extended to four or six, and every day or so, with predictable regularity, the false news that the pair have, in fact, arrived spreads up and down the beach. Actually, Mr. and Mrs. Burton visit Puerto Vallarta only rarely. Still, their big white stucco house, the Casa Kimberly (named after a brand of Mexican gin) remains a major tourist attraction.

Meanwhile, despite its rapid growth and a certain amount of commercialism that has crept in — to the distress of old Vallarta's fans — Vallarta remains a cozy resort. Las Muertas beach is still the town's communications center — there are no telephones — and all information is exchanged, plans are made, and invitations are issued from here. An hour's speedboat ride away lies Yelapa, a grass-shack settlement, populated with colorful escapees from Greenwich Village and Haight-Ashbury, that offers a splendid white sand beach beyond which lies a freshwater lagoon, fed by a cascading river. And Vallarta continues to offer a number of small, intimate cafés and restaurants where everybody, very quickly, gets to know everybody else. One of the pleasantest of these is called Chez Elena. It requires a stiff climb up a steep hill to get to, but offers such delicious specialties as cactus and tortilla soup and other culinary inventions of the proprietress, a half-Mexican-half-American woman named Elena Cortes. Doña Elena, as she is called, is every bit as extraordinary as the food she prepares. A plump and forthright lady with salty opinions on nearly everything, and no shyness about expressing them, she sees to it that all her guests immediately get acquainted with one another, and then she regales them with stories — all of them hilarious, many of them ribald — of her own unusual past. "Her restaurant is a Happening," someone has said, and that is as good a description of it as any. Drinks at Chez are free with dinner — a nice touch. And if the hostess takes a particular fancy to you, she may treat you to a dollop of a special aphrodisiac liqueur she keeps handy. The label on the bottle advertises that it "gives you that volcano feeling." It does, too. No, Vallarta has not become another Acapulco yet — not quite.

Manzanillo, further down the coast, is too busy being a bustling commercial seaport to make any concessions to tourism whatever (the opposite of Vallarta, where almost everything seems designed to please the tourist), and its pretty harbor is marred by large oil-storage tanks, and not long ago, a rusty tanker spewed black smoke over the city night and day. Beyond the harbor lies the extensive *Zona de Tolerancia* (or "Zone of Tolerance"), as Manzanillo quaintly calls its red-light district, and when the ships come in, this is a very busy part of town. A number of miles outside town, two resorts — Las Hadas and La Playa de Santiago — have been built, and these have both found favor with Americans. These are, however, very *American* places which, if they didn't happen to be in Mexico, could just as well be found on a sunny beach in Florida. Both are very self-contained places, dozens of miles physically — and many more emotionally — from any city. "It's a place to come and relax and do nothing," said a Las Hadas guest. "Go out in the evening? There just isn't any place to go."

One man's paradise is another man's anathema, but if one were asked to pick a favorite small, still-unspoiled beach resort in all of Mexico, one might choose Zihuatenejo, the little town whose name cannot be pronounced without sounding something like a sneeze. Zihuatenejo is nothing at all like what Acapulco used to be, either — nor could it ever become *another* Acapulco. It lacks Acapulco's scale — that great bay, for instance (the best natural harbor in Mexico), the array of rocky hills, and the violent rocks of the Quebrada where the famous divers leap into the sea. Zihuatenejo's landscape is subtler, more delicate and rounded. The beach is there, a sweeping arc of sand brushed by a gentle surf — and so is a degree of isolation. There are no telephones in Zihuatenejo and, though it is physically no farther from Mexico City than Acapulco is, there is no direct road — nor, one is assured, will there ever be one. (The city fathers of Zihuatenejo have tempered their cupidity with reason, and have decided to take advantage of the town's remoteness.) One flight a day enters Zihuatenejo from Mexico City, and one flight a day returns — making use of a horrific airstrip which seems to be composed of jagged boulders. (The head of the airlines office in Zihuatenejo explained recently that because of the strip's terrain he cannot let planes land or take off with a full-weight load of passengers. Once, however, when an unusually large number of people had to leave on the same morning, he did, against his better judgment, sell every seat on the plane. "I went to the beach with a bottle of rum and my pistol," he said. "I drank the rum and waited for the plane to make it into the air. If that plane had crashed, I was going to shoot myself" — a noble gesture and very Mexican *macho,* if cold comfort to the passengers.

In Zihuatenejo, too, there *is* some place to go. One can go across the bay — by waving for a passing boat and persuading its driver to take you — to a little beach settlement called Los Gatos, where several small restaurants serve oysters, lobster, and clams pulled fresh from the ocean. (The restaurants are in friendly competition with one another, and if one restaurant doesn't have the dish you happen to want, your waiter will run down the beach to another restaurant to find it for you.) After lunch at Los Gatos, there is swimming and snorkeling in the still-water beach — created, according to the local tale, by a Zapotec king for his favorite mistress; he built a barrier reef of huge rocks beyond the beach to give her a gentle pool to swim in. (One believes this story more readily than the one about the crosses at Las Cruces.) Also, in the town of Zihuatenejo itself there are several good restaurants, cafés and cantinas — and a handful of little shops.

There are a number of good hotels — intimate (none of them is large) rather than luxurious — tucked against the mountainside, overlooking the bay, in a natural garden of cactus, Judas flower, hibiscus, bougainvillea, and jacaranda trees, with large green parrots, which are quite tame, fluttering about. In return for reasonable rates, the hotels offer reasonably good food, service and conveniences. In one hotel, however, there was a plumbing novelty. Though the hotel had both hot and cold water, on one side of the corridor there was cold water only, and on the other side there was nothing but hot. The mischief — a crossing of pipes — was committed long ago, and has resisted correction since it is buried no one knows where under the tile and masonry. The irony was that the more expensive rooms, facing the sea, had guests complaining of icy showers; the less costly rooms, in the back, had an embarrassment of hot water — too hot, in fact, to shower in at all.

But it is not for plumbing perfection that one seeks out a place such as Zihuatenejo. It is, in fact, for the opposite — for a sense, real or imagined, of the undiscovered, the unexploited, the "untouristy." And this, of course, is the quality which those who have found Zihuatenejo consider most precious and are trying hardest to protect. "I literally refuse to tell people where I go in winter," one woman says. "Not even our dearest friends know about this place." "I just couldn't bear to see this place ruined," another said, "another Acapulco. I'm just afraid that if people find out about this it will be simply *overrun!*" Well, for the time being, it can't be. With only those few small hotels — and that airstrip — there is just no way for an overrunning throng of tourists to get there, and no place for them to stay. There are no Sun Valley condominiums, as yet.

Zihuatenejo offers a sense of the primitive, along with certain amenities, but for the intrepid tourist who insists on the elemental, with only the barest of comforts provided, two other small towns on Mexico's west coast ought also to be mentioned. They are Puerto Escondido and Puerto Angel, both in the state of Oaxaca, about halfway between Acapulco and the Guatemala border. Though the map indicates a road from Oaxaca City into each port, these roads are also for the intrepid; the trepid are hereby warned. (Local car-rental agencies will not rent you a car if they suspect you plan to drive to either of these places.) In both Puerto Escondido and Puerto Angel (the latter is a slightly larger town), there are fishing boats for hire — fishing and the beaches are the towns' main attractions — but there are no hotels as such. There are, however, small *posadas* which are actually little more than rooming houses. Advance reservations at these hostelries are next to impossible to get (Puerto Angel installed its first electric lights only a year or so ago), and the best advice for an arriving visitor comes from a Mexican: "Whenever you arrive in a new town in Mexico, and are looking for help to find a place to stay, just go to the main *zocalo* in the center of town, and sit on a bench there. Pretty soon, within half an hour or so, someone will come along who will be able to help you." Like so many odd facts about this smiling, improbable country, this one turns out to be absolutely true.

From the west coast of Mexico one can fly east to Cozumel and Isla Mujeres, two of Mexico's Caribbean islands that are promoted as still "unruined." Cozumel, the larger of the two, is where Jackie Kennedy Onassis has stayed, and this gives one an immediate idea of the decorous gentility of the place, quite a different mood from that of Puerto Vallarta (a raunchy mood set by Elizabeth Taylor). Everyone is very *dressy* in Cozumel. Men wear jackets and ties at dinner, and the women, in pearls and cashmere sweaters from Peck and Peck, sit about conversing in low, cultivated voices over bloody marys. The hotels — there are several, all large, modern, and expensive — are marbled, air-conditioned, and antiseptic. The east coast also lacks the landscape of the west coast — all those plunging mountains — and is flat for almost its entire length. On the other hand, the water of the Caribbean is calmer, bluer, and clearer — with excellent snorkeling and skin-diving. From Cozumel, too, there are side trips into the Yucatán wilderness. There are the *cenotes,* curious geological features of the area — wide, circular wells, often so symmetrical that they look man-made, which suddenly open up in the jungle floor, and which contain deep, sunken pools of black water. A *cenote* was first an underground cavern, or dome, formed by water erosion of the limestone which forms most of Yucatán's substructure. Eventually, after enough erosion, the top of the dome collapses, leaving a mysterious-looking round hole. The Mayans believed that these eerie holes were sacred to the rain god, and when he seemed to need appeasing, virgins were dropped into the *cenotes* until rain came. Also, a few air miles down the coast and across the Yucatán Channel from Cozumel, the ruins of the ancient Mayan city of Tulum can be visited. The tombs, temples, and pyramids here are interesting because they are among the few remaining in Mexico that have not been restored. They lie untouched, just as they have lain for hundreds of years, high on a bluff overlooking the sea with the green and steamy jungle pressing around them.

At Cozumel, too, the conversation tends to run to how long it will be before this is "another Acapulco," and "ruined." Everyone has his favorite estimate — two years, three years, and so on. Heads shake and

tongues cluck as prices inch higher. There has been a small exodus of
sorts from Cozumel to Isla Mujeres, a twenty-minute plane ride to the
north. But Isla Mujeres (which means "Island of the Women"; Cortés,
they say, landed there and found only women on it, but no explanation for their presence there) is merely a smaller version of Cozumel,
and so a number have returned — taking comfort, perhaps, in the fact
that an island favored by Mrs. Onassis cannot — not this season at
least — be completely vulgarized.

But in the meantime, where is the Acapulco that was? Perhaps the
curious combination of elements that is responsible for what is present-
day Acapulco cannot exist anywhere else — the combination of the
beaches, that magnificent bay, the sheltering mountains, the soft,
warm, still, moist air that has made Acapulco from the time tourists first
started going there a particularly — there's no other word for it — a
particularly sexy place. That has always been Acapulco's special quality — brown-skinned young men and women half-naked in a pool that
has underwater bar stools, couples embracing each other on the sand,
clinging to each other on the dance floor. Acapulco is like a large, very
classy bordello, with the atmosphere of sex so thick you could cut it
with a butter knife and spread it, like caviar, on canapés. Sex and
personal indulgence — a place where, you are sulkily told, Merle
Oberon — the town's leading hostess, as everyone in the world must
know by now — has a dressing room bigger than her husband's bedroom, and where somebody else has perfumed water in all the toilet
bowls. It is the hot, damp air that helps do it — air trapped and
pocketed by the green encircling mountains and floating steamily from
heated swimming pools and saxophones.

But there is something else that may be what Acapulco was. It is a
great stretch of beach that lies about sixty miles to the north of
Acapulco, just south of the little town of Petatlán. The mountains
come to a thundering point here, then cascade down. The Pacific
comes thundering in, dashes against rocks, then subsides against miles
of sand. Flying fish flash against the sky. It is a long climb down the
rocks from the road to the beach, but worth it. The place is called
Playa del Calvario — perhaps because the promontory of rock that
addresses the beach reminded someone of Calvary. In any case, in the

amphitheater between the sea and the outlying arms of rock there is the same warm, moist, *sexy* air. There is no town here, no buildings — nothing. But perhaps some such lovely, lickerish Eden as this was what Acapulco was before anyone came there — anyone at all.

Photo by the New York Times. *Courtesy of P. J. Clarke's*

A quiet night at P.J.'s

11

New York, N.Y. 10022: Indestructible P.J.'s

MEANWHILE, in thoroughly spoiled New York City, as every-one knows, it is no longer chic to be elegant. The wrong places of yesteryear are becoming the right ones of today. That is, anything that is not somewhat disreputable is presumed to be somehow imper-tinent, and this supposedly accounts for the decline of, among other things, New York's "pretty" restaurants — the closing of the Colony, Le Chauveron, the sudden abysmal emptiness of the Four Seasons, the rapid fall from grace of Raffles. Consider, on the other hand, the saloon at the corner of Fifty-fifth and Third which has just completed the most successful year in its eighty-year history, and is a happy gold mine for all concerned. "This place," confides the slender young man with the over-the-ears hair to his blond ladyfriend in the knitted skull-cap, "is perhaps *the* place in New York. You won't find anything like this in Altoona. Down there, that guy in the blue sweater is what's-his-name of the New York Knicks."

What's-his-name of the Knicks, seated in display position at the corner of the bar, is surrounded by kids, many of whom cannot be of legal drinking age but who are drinking beer nonetheless. He displays the easy grace and confidence of a star among fans, grinning at the kids' questions and shrugging off their "oh, wows." What's-his-name is not a regular, but drops in occasionally because he's sure to be recog-nized. Down at the other end of the bar, near the garbage cans, sit two regulars, a pair of ladies whose favorite topic of conversation is

New York under Mayor Fiorello H. La Guardia. Tonight, they are discussing what has happened to the subway fare since La Guardia's day. The regulars sit at this somewhat less appetizing end because there is a better chance of seats here. It is five o'clock, and the place is filling up again after the brief post-luncheon slump. Outside, the city is a mixture of rain and unsatisfactory air, and the Third Avenue bus stop on the corner is disgorging passengers headed for the swinging doors with the cut-glass panes. Inside, against mirrored walls that are not only flyspecked but in desperate need of resilvering, the decor consists largely of signs which warn against the danger of overcrowding, the management's lack of responsibility for lost articles, the fact that minors will not be served, that tax is included in the price of each drink, that gentlemen without escorts might think twice before coming here to meet other gentlemen without escorts. Over the bar hangs a sign that says, "BEER — THE BREAKFAST OF CHAMPIONS." A vase of plastic lilacs blooms among the bottles. "This is really New York," says over-the-ears-hair solemnly.

He may be right. As the hour approaches six, the noise level reaches din proportions, with Joan Baez contributing lustily from the jukebox. Rocky Graziano — a regular — has just arrived with Jake Javits, and is moving along the bar greeting friends with "Hi, guy!" (They call him "the Thespian" here.) At one of the corner tables, Bobby Short is showing off his new fur-lined overcoat. "Something gorgeous happens when I put this on — watch!" he burbles, putting on the coat and briefly parading the gorgeousness. A blond young woman enters carrying an ocelot on a leash. The place frowns on pets, but the young woman explains prettily, "He's just like a little putty-tat," and is allowed to stay. What at first appears to be a tiny child has just pushed through the cut-glass door, but it is quickly clear that she is a midget with a five-year-old's body and a rather pretty fortyish face. She is apparently known here, for a chivalrous male patron hoists her by the armpits onto a bar stool, a position she could not achieve unaided.

But the clientele is not composed just of oddities and celebrities and put-ons. There are also intense young men in J. Press suits with skinny briefcases, silver ID bracelets and gold wedding bands, waiting for wives or girl friends and discussing parking places. Hairy, bearded types in denim jackets and beads and boots glare truculently at one another and talk sporadically of Film. A very pretty airline stewardess wearing a diamond wedding band flanked by sapphire guards is explaining to three very interested young men the availability of free passes to exotic ports on her carrier. She seems to suggest that these passes could be theirs for the asking. Behind a counter in the corner, a short-order cook is setting up his grill for hamburgers, lining up his bags of buns, bottles of catsup, and plates of onion slices in neat rows. Behind the bar, the two bartenders are shouting jovial obscenities to one another as they work, epithets accompanied by appropriately indelicate gestures. Two off-duty patrolmen are in earnest conversation (this is, after all, an Irish bar, and the Irish have always had the Police Department in the family), interrupted by a drunk who keeps tugging at their sleeves, trying to tell them something. The drunk speaks in syllables, but the syllables do not form words in any recognizable language. ("There's a medical term for that," one of the bartenders explains to a customer. "Brendan Behan used to get that way in here after he'd had a few.") The policemen shuffle their feet in the sawdust on the floor, in embarrassment or perhaps to keep warm; this saloon, perhaps because it encourages the consumption of alcohol, is drafty and underheated. Through it all, via another swinging door, there is a frank and unlimited view of the men's room that opens, closes, and opens up again. To anyone who giggles over this circumstance — or who, heaven forbid, protests — the bartender's reply is "Them that's proud never complains!" It is, in other words, a typical evening at P. J. Clarke's, the pub where the primary rule is never be surprised at anything.

There are one or two other rules — unwritten, of course. For example, one is not supposed to enter P.J.'s expecting such a queer reward as solitude, or even privacy. P.J.'s is a determinedly social saloon, and anyone standing at the bar is expected to engage in lively conversation with whomever he is standing next to. Nontalkers are frowned upon, sometimes even asked to leave. Not long ago an uninitiated customer had the poor taste to bring out a paperback book and start to read it at the bar. The bartender's reaction was swift and decisive. "If you're going to read," he announced, "go on down to Tim Costello's. That's where all the goddamned *intellectuals* hang out!"

At the same time, P. J. Clarke's customers are expected to take the

unexpected in their stride. One is not supposed to react to the sight of
the famous blue eyes of Paul Newman across the room, or to Mr. and
Mrs. Aristotle S. Onassis dining quietly at a corner table. Arlene Francis and Martin Gabel are regular customers, as are Artie Shaw, John
Huston, and Mayor John Lindsay. Nor was anyone particularly surprised to read, among the 1971 findings of the Knapp Commission,
that P. J. Clarke's was the payoff spot where two men — one of them
a police officer — negotiated the price that would allow a lady with
the unlikely name of Xaviera Hollander to continue operating one of
the neighborhood's glossier brothels (specializing in kinky sex) free
of police harassment. (Mrs. Hollander's price for peace, according to
tapes from the bugged P.J.'s bar, was twenty-one hundred dollars in
three installments.) This was regarded as simply another aspect of
P.J.'s raffish charm. "They always did get a lot of gamblers and rack-
eteers and crooks up there," sniffs Fred Percudani, bartender at the
rival Tim Costello's down the street. "Here, we attract more of an
executive-type crowd."

P. J. Clarke's is possibly the only saloon in town where the jukebox
offers the latest hit by Melanie as well as "Paper Moon" as selections.
(Tim Costello's provides discreet radio music from WPAT.) When,
for reasons that have never been quite clear, a definitely non-executive
type named Lawrence Tierney found his head involved with one of
Clarke's old-fashioned ceiling fans, nobody thought a thing about it,
not even Mr. Tierney, who not only announced that he would not
sue anybody for the lacerations incurred in the encounter, but apolo-
gized, and offered to have the fan repaired. When, after a particularly
bibulous evening, a well-dressed young couple lay down on the dining
room floor and went to sleep, no one paid them any heed except for
Eddie Fay, one of Clarke's ex-wrestler bouncers, who gently tried to
coax the pair back to consciousness with cups of strong coffee. About
a year ago, two men wanted by the FBI on narcotics charges were
arrested while relaxing at P. J. Clarke's. A few months later, Clarke's
became the first Third Avenue saloon to be the subject of a snooty
New Yorker cover. And through all these varied goings-on P. J.
Clarke's customers rejoiced in the knowledge that their favorite water-
ing hole has achieved something of the status of a New York monument, that it will now in all likelihood remain at the corner of Third

and Fifty-fifth for as long as the Statue of Liberty remains in New York Harbor. As the sole holdout in the block otherwise occupied by a new forty-five-story Tishman tower, Clarke's is a nineteenth-century anachronism, a dowdy oasis in a street of tall steel and glass. Clearly, shabbiness is not only chic but offers a kind of passport to immortality.

The success and survival of P. J. Clarke's make, as the Irish say, a tale to tell, and from the beginning involved an uncommon combination of fiscal wizardry and Old World witchcraft. Patrick Joseph Clarke was a dead ringer for Admiral Bull Halsey, and his conversation consisted mostly of grunts. Apprenticed in the old country, he was a strict saloonkeeper and when he opened his place in 1892 there was no nonsense allowed. Woe betided the waiter who failed to put his tips in the kitty, or the bartender who tippled from Paddy Clarke's stock. It was he who established the anti-intellectual cast of P. J. Clarke's. Some said this was simply because his chief rival, Tim Costello, courted the writers and artists — Hemingway, Thurber, Steinbeck, Robert Ruark, and John McNulty. "Pansies and willie-boys!" Paddy Clarke called them, and that was that. A bachelor, he was pious and churchgoing, and also strongly superstitious. During Prohibition ("It's like a bad cold, it will go away," he used to say) he was once badly beaten by thugs, and his relatives began urging him to write a will. But Paddy Clarke was convinced that if he wrote a will he would surely die the next day. And so, with his fingers still crossed against the morrow, he died intestate in 1948.

It was this single fact, ironically enough, that set the course of Clarke's saloon toward becoming an unofficial city landmark. (A spokesman for the Landmarks Commission has said that Clarke's architecture is not sufficiently distinguished to warrant making it an *official* landmark, as though Clarke's customers could possibly care.) Because when Paddy Clarke died with neither direct heirs nor a will, all his relatives — brothers, sisters, nieces, nephews, both here and abroad — fell to wrangling over who should receive which share of Paddy Clarke's estate, the most important part of which was the building with the bar downstairs and three floors of cold-water flats above. Visions of wealth and the easy life danced in the eyes of all the relatives, particularly those back home in County Longford where exaggerated reports of Paddy's wealth had filtered. But when the relatives could not agree — and there is bad feeling between a number of Clarkes today over the matter — the court ordered that the building be sold. Thus it was acquired in 1949 for thirty-three thousand dollars by a young man named Daniel H. Lavezzo who, with his father, had been running a business importing Italian antiques, but who had also made a profitable sideline out of dabbling in real estate properties, particularly those in somewhat rundown neighborhoods.

From the beginning, Dan Lavezzo admits that he had no consuming interest in being a saloonkeeper. But he was interested in making money and so, since he was now running a saloon, he decided to run a profitable one. Clarke's had already acquired a reputation as a popular spot for society and show folk, in a day when debutantes and Park Avenue blades considered it fun to go "slumming" in the slightly dangerous shadows of the old Third Avenue El. Two movies — *The Lost Weekend* and *Portrait of Jennie* — had used Clarke's, or a reproduction of it, as settings. And it had become increasingly a place where out-of-towners headed when they wanted the feeling of rubbing shoulders with the greats of Manhattan, even though, in most cases, the out-of-towners just rubbed shoulders with one another. Because it was also a popular bar with the police force, Clarke's customers also enjoyed the feeling that they were rubbing shoulders with men whose exciting task it was to deal with crime. The occasional presence of a lady no better than she should be was merely titillating, particularly when she was balanced with a diamond-encrusted Hope Hampton or a Barbara Hutton. Lavezzo determined to change as little of this ambiance and clientele as possible, and went about the task of preserving Clarke's special Irish flavor with a fine Italian hand.

He installed Charlie Clarke — P.J.'s favorite nephew — as his general manager. Charlie, who had been born in one of the flats upstairs, and who had been a popular waiter and bartender for his uncle, gave the place a valuable aura of family continuity that kept the old trade from straying elsewhere. When Glennon's Bar & Grill, competition from across the street, was forced to close by a landlord who wanted to sell the building, Dan Lavezzo hired Jimmy Glennon, the popular bartender, and brought him — and his customers — over.

(For years, Glennon has been writing a book: *How to Be an Irish Mother.*)

By the mid-1950's the El was down, and Third Avenue had begun its renaissance as a street of glittery skyscrapers. Advertising agencies and publishers and film companies abandoned Madison and moved to Third, bringing with them new customers for P. J. Clarke's. In 1955, Dan Lavezzo bought three small two-story rooming houses behind Clarke's on Fifty-fifth Street, broke through into them, and added the back dining room, which, because it was darker, cozier, and slightly less noisy than up front in the bar, quickly became the most "exclusive" dining area.

Lavezzo had been living in Greenwich, but when the State of Connecticut gobbled up his property to make way for the New England Thruway he needed, for tax reasons, to spend the money realized from the sale of the Greenwich house on another residence. At the time, the flats in the two top floors above Clarke's had been condemned, and so Lavezzo decided to throw these tiny flats together into two large apartments, one to a floor. The third floor thus became bachelor quarters for Dan Lavezzo, who is divorced, and the top floor became an elegant pad for Michael Butler, the millionaire sportsman and producer (*Hair* and *Lenny*). The second floor, meanwhile, housed the Lavezzo antique business, which was taking increasingly less time than the real estate and restaurant business. This was the state of affairs when the Tishman Realty and Construction Company, which has been responsible for some of the city's more monolithic structures, announced plans to build 919 Third Avenue, which was to occupy the entire east side blockfront between Fifty-fifth and Fifty-sixth streets, including P. J. Clarke's. The interests of the Tishman brothers and Daniel H. Lavezzo were about to collide.

Robert Tishman, who heads the construction company, has a reputation of driving a hard bargain. "He is one tough cookie to deal with," says Lavezzo, with more than a touch of respect in his voice. So, though on a smaller scale, is Danny Lavezzo. "He is a very sophisticated trader," say the Tishmans. Lavezzo, a compact, wary-eyed man in his early fifties, has the air of a man not easily persuaded to do anything he doesn't want to do. Though he has been known to consume as many as fifty beers a night at P.J.'s — "I never drink the hard stuff on the job" — Dan Lavezzo is known as a hard man to catch off guard. He was not at all anxious to sell his building to the Tishmans, nor to lose the one-to-two-million-dollar-a-year business which his building was then providing. "There's a lot of superstition in this business," Lavezzo says, "and most guys who run a successful joint believe that it's bad luck to move. If things are going good, you don't even fire a busboy — much less go to a new address." Clarke's to be Clarke's, *had* to be at the northwest corner of Fifty-fifth and Third.

Dan Lavezzo also owned a building in the middle of the block that the Tishmans wanted and which, because of its central position, was even more pivotal to their plan. This gave Lavezzo the upper hand. And so, after a battle of nearly two years' duration, during which negotiations broke down several times, Lavezzo and the Tishmans reached an agreement. Lavezzo would sell both Clarke's and the second building to the Tishmans. The mid-block building would be razed to make room for the tower, but Clarke's would be permitted to stand untouched and, as a guarantee, Dan Lavezzo was given a ninety-nine-year lease on the property as part of his price. In the deal, a figure of somewhere in the neighborhood of one million dollars went to Lavezzo for the air rights above his store — or not a bad appreciation on his original thirty-three-thousand-dollar investment. Other restaurateurs in the city turn positively glassy-eyed with jealous admiration of Lavezzo and his feat. "The monumental *chutzpah* of the man!" cries Vincent Sardi. Lavezzo, typically, just shrugs it off. "Air rights? Air rights?" he asks innocently. "I don't remember anybody talking to me about air rights." "He's putting you on!" snorts Jerry Speyer, a Tishman vice president and Robert Tishman's son-in-law. "He knows goddamn well what he got for the air rights." Also as part of the deal, because of a complicated zoning conflict between commercial and residential properties, the top two floors of Clarke's had to be lopped off, forcing both Messrs. Lavezzo and Butler to find new apartments elsewhere.

It was not the first time that an old-shoe neighborhood bar had had a modern tower built around it. Hurley's, for example, has been contained within the Rockefeller Center complex, and just down the street on Third Avenue, Joe & Rose's Restaurant is presently being encased in a huge new office building. But, because the architects at

Skidmore, Owings & Merrill felt that Clarke's was something of a special place, they designed a handsome courtyard around it, to set it off a bit, and then placed 919 Third Avenue several yards behind the regular building line to even *further* set it off. The Tishmans offered to lease part of this new plaza to Lavezzo for an outdoor café, but Lavezzo turned them down. The Tishmans are still somewhat disgruntled about that. After all, what realtor likes to see some of his property untenanted? But Dan Lavezzo thinks little of outdoor cafés in New York. "You get dust and soot in your potatoes," he says, "and some bum can spit at you or try to panhandle you, or make a remark. Listen, if I was up on Fifth Avenue with a view of the Park, that would be something else. But I'm on Third with a view of the back door of the Post Office." Michael's Pub — in a new location in the Tishmans' building — has set out umbrellas and tables and chairs in front of its share of the new plaza. Lavezzo doesn't think they add much. "Clarke's has always been an indoor sort of place," he says. "People come here to get away from the streets and the traffic and the crummy people." Lavezzo is prouder of the hospitable new bike rack that he has set up behind his saloon, and of the handsome new row of globe lights along his outside wall. The other night, while customers stood in line for tables at P.J.'s, Michael's Pub next door was achingly empty, its bartender engrossed in the *Racing Form*.

In Paddy Clarke's day, Irish bars like his along Third Avenue served free meals, usually a thick soup or a stew, with their drinks, but Dan Lavezzo brought in a simple but reasonably varied menu of dishes for which the best adjective would be honest. What was formerly the free lunch counter next to the bar is now set up to serve what Clarke's regulars agree are some of the best hamburgers and chili in town, and the food in the dining room is — considering the tiny kitchen from which it emerges — very good indeed. Chalked on a blackboard, the bill of fare includes such items as steak Diane, meatballs with chili, and zucchini Benedict, which means with hollandaise sauce. Not long ago, Dan Lavezzo was tickled to receive, from a friend returning from France, a menu from a fashionable Paris restaurant which listed "spinach salad à la P. J. Clarke's" — a salad of tossed spinach greens and fresh white mushrooms — and he is still proud of the fact that in 1966 Craig Claiborne of the New York

Times gave his restaurant a rating of three stars. ("Not bad for a corner saloon," he says.) There is also an extensive and reasonably priced wine list. Dinner for two, with drinks, can be had for under ten dollars.

There are other Lavezzo touches — such as the fact that virtually the only advertising he has ever done has been to print the name of the place on matchbooks and sugar cubes. (As a favor to his friend George Plimpton, Lavezzo runs an ad in the *Paris Review* consisting only of P.J.'s telephone number.) Also, his is one of the few remaining bars in New York that still serve real ice cubes in the drinks, and not the slivered machine-made wafers that have melted almost before the drink reaches the table. Then there are the huge, old-fashioned porcelain stanchions in what is the town's most public men's room — nicknamed "the Cathedral" because it is surmounted by a vaulted Tiffany glass ceiling — into each of which is placed, each evening, a block of icehouse ice. One customer, apparently unused to such amenities, emerged from the Cathedral not long ago carrying one of these blocks of ice and asked the bartender for "some Scotch for this rock." Then there is Dan Lavezzo's standard of service, which he likes to be prompt, polite, but informal and unfussy. To help achieve this he pays his waiters, who work in white shirtsleeves and aprons, on the scale of bartenders.

Dan Lavezzo is distrustful of publicity, and such as P. J. Clarke's has had has been self-generated, with no assistance from its proprietor. He reacted "with resignation" to the printed reports from the Knapp Commission hearing about Clarke's being a police payoff station. "What the hell can you do?" he asks wearily. "Everything goes on at a bar." And why, he wonders, did the D.A.'s office wait until the two men it wanted had wandered into P. J. Clarke's for a drink before making their arrests? The officers, it turned out, had been following the pair for weeks. Was there a touch of press-agentry in the federal agents' decision to make their big move in a famous and conspicuous place? And Lavezzo is cynical about the press itself. "If something bad happens here, the papers are always sure to spell your name right," he says. But if the *Daily News* runs a picture of Ari and Jackie Onassis coming out of here, the caption will say they're leaving 'a Third Avenue saloon.'"

Too much publicity of any kind, Lavezzo feels, can be bad for a place like his, particularly in a city like New York where things go out of fashion almost before they're in. "Look at the places that were big a few years back," he says, "the places that were all over the papers like the Peppermint Lounge, Arthur, Le Club, Hippopotamus — they're all dead or half dead now. Look at Elaine's. Nobody gets more publicity than she does these days. She's got friends feeding items about her into the columns every night. But the trouble is she's attracting all the sorts of people she didn't want to have. And I've heard reports of rude treatment and bad service. There used to be a place up the street called Stella's. Stella's was the *in* place for a while, and Stella used to insult the women and grope the men. She got away with it for a while because people thought it was cute. But she closed up and moved to Florida a long time ago. If I were Elaine, I'd be *very careful.*"

Getting and keeping the right kind of clientele is, one gathers, something like performing a tightrope act. "I don't want this to become a singles joint, like Maxwell's Plum or those places up on Second," Lavezzo says. Single girls in New York have long been aware that P. J. Clarke's is not a promising hunting ground for men. Two pretty young magazine editors who had stopped by Clarke's for beers during the evening rush hour were told, somewhat abruptly, by the bartender, "Look, if you two girls just came in to get out of the rain, don't take up room at the bar." And when, several years ago, Clarke's began to get a reputation as a rendezvous for the gay crowd, Dan Lavezzo put up a sign saying that men unescorted by ladies can only be served at the far end of the bar. This sign hangs face to the wall on most "normal" evenings, but can be flipped around so as to state its business should the occasion demand. Lavezzo says, "We don't want people to have *too* good a time here. We don't want people singing or banging on the table, or getting too noisy or getting into fights. I have my two bouncers, Eddie and Mark, to take care of that sort of thing. The trouble is, you can't rough people up the way you used to — if you do, they'll sue. What we want is to keep this a nice, friendly place where people can eat and drink in a relaxed, homey atmosphere."

For the most part, Lavezzo gets his wish, though there are occasional bad moments. There is one man, the bane of Third Avenue saloonkeepers, who goes from bar to bar trying to engage the customers in arguments. He will argue, it seems, about almost anything. When he appears, and becomes too belligerent, he is gently but firmly ejected from Clarke's. Also — and members of the Women's Liberation Front should take note — Clarke's bartenders insist that they have much more trouble with disorderly women than they do with men. "A drunk woman is impossible," Lavezzo says, "and you really have to be careful throwing *them* out." For some reason, there is a curious witching hour in bars like Clarke's. It occurs around ten P.M., and is the moment when trouble starts. No one knows quite why, but bartenders heave a sigh of relief when ten-thirty comes, knowing that if a saloon can make it peacefully through that moment it will probably make it through the night.

And Lavezzo must be doing something right, because Clarke's is nearly always thronged with people from the time it opens at ten in the morning until three or four the next, when it closes, seven days a week. If there are any complaints they are of crowds at the bar and long lines waiting for tables in the dining room. Business has never been better, and Dan Lavezzo admits, "Now that we're stuck out here like a sore thumb, people notice us who never did before. It's the best advertising we could have." He has been gradually phasing out his upstairs antiques business, and would like to open another dining room on the second floor. The new dining room would be, according to Lavezzo, "a little more elegant, maybe, but still P. J. Clarke's, still the nineteenth-century feeling. I'd have no trouble filling it." His plan, however, has presently run afoul of his new landlords, the Tishmans. To accomplish it, Lavezzo feels that he would have to expand his kitchen facilities in the basement, including some space that belongs to the Tishman tower. Because of an existing contract with another restaurant owner in the building, the Tishmans say they cannot legally rent Lavezzo the space. At the moment, matters are at a standstill.

Paddy Clarke was a great lover of animals, and in his day, there was always a dog, or sometimes two, around P. J. Clarke's. (Even today, dogs have a better chance of getting into Clarke's than ocelots.) One of Paddy's dogs was a habitual wanderer, and became well known around the East Side — so well known that cab drivers, spotting him on his rounds, would pick him up and drive him home to Clarke's, always certain that they would be paid their fare. Another dog, patently female, was named Bobo Rockefeller, after a favorite Clarke's customer. All these dogs were known and loved by Clarke's regulars, but the old-timers agree that there was never a dog quite like the one Paddy Clarke named Jessie. Jessie, according to Paddy, was a "Mexican fox terrier," but whatever she was she was an extraordinary person. If you gave Jessie a nickel she would trot across the street to Bernard's drugstore and buy a chocolate bar. She would return to Clarke's with the chocolate bar and nudge you to unwrap it for her. If you gave her a quarter, she would go in the other direction to a meat market, and there she would purchase a bag of dog scraps. Paddy Clarke used to insist that at the end of the day she collected his bar receipts and helped him check them against the chits. She was the official screener of Clarke's customers. If Jessie growled when you came through the door, you could not be served.

When Jessie died, Paddy Clarke had Jessie stuffed and placed in a position of honor, on a shelf just above the entrance to the ladies' room. Only slightly the worse for time and dust and smoke and a few moths, she is still there, as immortal as Clarke's itself, a mascot and a symbol. She still wears a savvy expression, keeping a beady eye on things. Isn't it pleasant to think, in this age of instant self-destruct mechanisms, that thanks to Danny Lavezzo's ninety-nine-year lease, Jessie will still be there in the year 2066, by which time there will surely be saloons on the moon. So will P. J. Clarke's still be there, indestructibly dowdy, triumphantly tacky. If Patrick Joseph Clarke had made a will, the way everybody had wanted him to, who knows what might have happened to his bar and grill? As it is, it would seem that only an act of God could remove P. J. Clarke's from the corner of Fifty-fifth and Third. And God, in most cases, was on Paddy Clarke's side.

Photo by Erich Hartmann, Magnum

Andrew Goodman inspects a model at Bergdorf's

12

New York, N. Y. 10019:
What Are They Doing to
Bergdorf Goodman?

ARE there no more absolute strongholds of the super-rich? Well,
there are places that have tried to be. But they too are changing
fast, and turning into something else.

At Bergdorf Goodman, for example, it used to be that nothing was
done that was not done with elegant flourishes. When Andrew Goodman, the president and owner of the store that confers New York's
most prestigious fashion label, once brought in a urine sample to be
sent over to his doctor, his secretary in the Christmas confusion had
it gift-wrapped and sent to the doctor's house. It was under the tree on
Christmas morning. And they tell the tale of how once in the Bridal
Salon the bride-to-be was hesitant about buying a white wedding gown
because, as she put it, she was still in mourning for her first husband.
A hasty conference was called among Bergdorf's brass, and the bride
wore gray. At the same time, during the recent craze for women wearing cartridge belts slung around their hips, Bergdorf's would not stock
the belts because Andrew Goodman found the fashion personally dis-
tasteful.

It was, therefore, something of a shock to the business, social, and
shopping communities of New York when Andrew Goodman announced in 1971 that one of the last family-run stores in America
would pass out of his family and, pending FTC approval, become a
part of the Broadway-Hale department store chain — the conglomerate
that also recently gobbled up *another* of the last family-run stores in

America, Neiman-Marcus. What will become of the Bergdorf touch?

Bergdorf's has also always been a store that is nothing if not cozy. It has been, as they say in the motel business, a "Ma and Pa operation," and quite literally Andrew Goodman's father, Edwin Goodman, who founded the store (with a Herman Bergdorf who long ago departed) and his wife were known by all the store's employees as "Dad" and "Mom." There are still old-time Bergdorf's people who refer to the present president as "young Andrew," and to his son, who is thirty-one, as "little Eddie." The Goodman fiefdom on Fifth Avenue has been run with such an air of benevolent paternalism that not only the staff but many of the longtime customers treat the place as they would a second home. After all, what other New York specialty store has on its top floor a vast apartment for the Goodman family where, when the lights go out, the storekeeper can sleep right on top of his merchandise. The third elevator in the main bank serves the apartment (which also has its own entrance on Fifty-eighth Street), and through the years customers and salespeople have grown used to the Goodmans, and their children and grandchildren with their nurses, going up and down that elevator. The rule — up until the time the elevators finally went automatic — was that if any member of the Goodman family got into the car, he or she was taken to his chosen floor, reversing directions if need be, regardless of where the other passengers were headed, and the passengers were expected to be understanding. Most were, but one woman wrote crossly, "Why don't you Goodmans wait until 5:30 when the store is closed — then you can ride up and down that elevator all night as far as I'm concerned!"

"The Apartment," indeed, has over the years developed its own mystique. It has become a sort of sacred place, since only a few of the elect have been invited into it. To be asked to the Apartment has awesome significance, though whether for good or evil one never knows until one *gets* there. It is as though, from the Apartment, a Big Brother of Bergdorf's watches over all. And perhaps he does. In the dining room of the Apartment hangs a portrait of the founder, Edwin the Elder, and not long ago Andrew Goodman, gulping down his breakfast coffee and realizing that he was going to be late for his office on the floor below, looked nervously up at the portrait and said, "Don't worry, Papa, I'll stay an extra fifteen minutes tonight."

The Goodman family has always indulged itself at Bergdorf's. Several years ago, for reasons which to the outside world seemed odd and whimsical, an antiques department was opened on the third floor where ten-thousand-dollar French clocks were sold hard by ten-thousand-dollar Russian sables. It was because Andrew Goodman's sister, Ann Goodman Farber, was married to a man who liked fine old furniture. Nena Goodman, Andrew's wife, collects paintings and is herself a painter of some talent, and so she has been given her own art gallery in the store — a boutique called Nena's Choice. One of their daughters, Minky (her name is Mary Ann but she had a governess who used to call her "a little minx") makes pottery, and it has occurred to her to ask for a corner of the store. But Bergdorf Goodman has also been indulgent to its staff, particularly those who have long demonstrated their loyalty to the Goodmans, and the store has many pensioners as well as people who have been kept on the payroll long after their usefulness has ended. Andrew Goodman takes pride in the fact that with a thousand-odd employees he knows nearly every one by name, and in most cases knows their children's names and ages, and their sizes. The faithful are granted special privileges. Mrs. William Fine, wife of the president of Bonwit Teller but who, as Susan Payson, used to work for Bergdorf's, once got a last-minute invitation to a formal party. First she murmured that she had nothing to wear, but then added that she thought she could work it out. She "borrowed" an eighteen-hundred-dollar designer dress from her stock, went to the party, and the first person she encountered there was Andrew Goodman. He merely winked, said he admired her taste in dresses, and all was forgiven. When Liberty Bandine, now the store's personnel director, first went to work for Bergdorf's she earned seventy-five dollars a week, and her boss became curious about the decidedly expensive way she dressed. Miss Bandine coolly explained that she earned a comfortable second income by playing the horses, and that she had a bookie named Whitey who drove a Bond Bread truck. Thereafter Whitey was permitted to park his truck at the store's Fifth Avenue entrance while Miss Bandine placed her bets.

Adding to this coziness and feeling of one big happy (and rich) family was the fact that Bergdorf's, now in its second generation of Goodman family control, had a third Goodman generation in the persons of a fine-looking son, young Eddie, and two fine sons-in-law, Harry Malloy and Gary Taylor.

That is, it did until recently. One by one, each of these men has left the store — first Harry, then Eddie, then Gary. The story along Seventh Avenue is that Gary Taylor, who had become Bergdorf's general manager, was sitting one day in a meeting where the subject under discussion was whether hemlines would stay up or go down. Suddenly Taylor rose and said, "Gentlemen, I have just come to the conclusion that this business is not my cup of tea," walked out of the store, and has never come back. This of course is not what really happened, though even Taylor admits that it makes a good story. But the fact is that Taylor, now twenty pounds trimmer — "no more of those rich lunches" — now packs his lunch in a brown paper bag and drives off every day to New Haven, where he is enrolled at the Yale School of Forestry, in the process of making the switch from high fashion to tall timber. Harry Malloy has became an insurance broker. And son Eddie Goodman goes to work every day down a dark flight of steps, past a row of rusted garbage cans, into the basement of an old church to an office marked "Broom Closet." The youngest of the three Goodman daughters, meanwhile, Pammy, whom the family calls "our hippie," is married to a man who does no work at all and is living in the New Mexican desert, building her own little adobe hacienda. Now Andrew has been left to mind his store alone. How did it all happen — and happen so fast?

From the beginning, a very special sort of store like Bergdorf's required a very special sort of man to run it. In 1878, Goodman's Store at 54 Main Street in Lockport, New York ("Next to Niagara Co. Nat'l Bank") was running small ads for such items as "25 doz. ladies' wrappers at 37½ cts." By 1919, Adele Simpson, the designer, recalls, her husband's grandmother ran a millinery shop on Fifth Avenue, opposite where Saks now stands, called Ufland's. The second floor of this building was rented to a small outfit of dressmakers and furriers called Bergdorf Goodman. When the troops were returning home from World War I, the Simpson children were told that it was all right to watch the parade from the Goodmans' upstairs window, since Bergdorf Goodman were merely tenants. Mrs. Simpson's husband, Wesley, remembers that among the onlookers was little Andrew Goodman. The man responsible for the long journey from Lockport that ended opposite the Pulitzer Fountain of Abundance on the Plaza, on the site of the old Cornelius Vanderbilt château, was Andrew's father.

There were some who called the senior Edwin Goodman austere. Others said that underneath the austere façade there breathed a warm and humorous man. Whatever the case, he was a man with determination and an ability to take the risks who, though he was one, did not look like a canny trader but like an Old World diplomat. And he had both an idea and the luck to have had the idea at just the right place and time. To begin with, Edwin Goodman was frankly only interested in the carriage trade, and his furs and custom-made suits and coats and dresses were made and priced for that market. He was an early fan of Beautiful People, and liked to surround himself with actresses, models, debutantes, and other society or purely ornamental types. He had a great weakness for titles, but his principal requirement in a woman was that she be rich. And, in fitting out rich ladies in coats and suits and furs and dresses, he felt he had learned something about the rich woman's psyche. Up until 1920, nearly every important dress a rich woman wore was made to order — slowly, with extensive sessions for measurements and fitting. But in the Twenties the pace of a woman's life was speeding up, and this gave Goodman his Idea: why not sell expensive and elegant dresses that could be bought right off the rack? The notion of ready-to-wear clothes at custom prices was unheard of, and indeed the prophets of doom in the trade were cheerfully on hand to tell Edwin Goodman that it would never work. But when word got around New York that dresses from Bergdorf Goodman which used to take weeks to have made could be bought and worn the same day, sales skyrocketed. By 1927 he was doing three million dollars' worth of business from the rented rooms over Ufland's, and a year later sales had jumped to five million dollars. In 1928, Edwin Goodman announced his plans to move to the Vanderbilt site at Fifty-eighth and Fifth, and once more there were enthusiastic Cassandras to point out that no merchant had ever been successful north of Fifty-seventh Street. The year of the move, sales hit six million dollars and the Goodman family installed itself in the gorgeousness of the top-floor apartment where, it was noticed, Mr. and Mrs. Goodman were listed as "janitor" and "janitress," since building codes prohibited anyone other than a janitor to live in a building where manufacturing took place.

The move to the south end of the Plaza, with its view of the park and upper Fifth Avenue that is unique in the city, was not made rashly or without certain precautionary measures. As shoppers at Bergdorf's have noticed, the store is not laid out like other stores, with a main shopping area on each floor. Instead, each floor is cut up into a series of small rooms. These rooms were Edwin Goodman's insurance. If the store did not work as a whole, he could wall off the passageways between these rooms and rent the rooms to other tenants. Fortunately, though there were one or two uneasy years at the beginning of the Depression, the Goodman carriage trade proved indefatigable, and Bergdorf's has never had to take in roomers.

In his new store, Edwin Goodman was able to indulge his own taste for European nobility as well as the snobbishness of his customers. He hired, for example, a grand duchess as a saleslady, and he found a good perfume man who happened, not entirely coincidentally, to be a Georgian nobleman named Prince Matchabelli. His publicity lady was the Countess de Forceville, and the publicity that the store received was appropriately high-toned. Edwin Goodman's son has carried on in his father's tradition, bringing to the store such luminaries as the great Jo Hughes and Dr. Erno Laszlo. Though not titled, exactly, these are something very close to the Blood Royal when one realizes that the likes of the Duchess of Windsor and Mrs. Cornelius Vanderbilt Whitney will practically not get dressed in the morning without consulting Miss Hughes. And without Dr. Laszlo's skin treatments and products, according to Leonard Hankin, Bergdorf's vice president, "Anita Colby would do a Shangri-La act right before our eyes." In the Mallett antique shop, meanwhile, it seemed right that the man in charge be a dashing London bachelor named Sir Humphrey Wakefield.

Personal service for the best "clients" — never "customers" — was another of Edwin Goodman's fetishes, and when the likes of the late Mrs. Thelma Chrysler Foy (a storekeeper's delight, so much did she love to shop, often buying twenty dozen pairs of gloves and eighty hats of an afternoon) stepped through his doors, the master himself descended from his fifth-floor office to help wait on her. Today, Andrew Goodman will often ask a prime client up to his big corner office for a drink, or to the apartment for lunch, where salesgirls troop up with armfuls of merchandise. This has led to a few embarrassing moments, as happened not long ago when rumor flew through the store that "one of the Bronfmans" was in Bergdorf's and buying heavily. The Bronfmans, of course, control a vast distillery fortune, and the shopping Bronfman was politely asked upstairs. There, all sorts of treasures were brought forth, including an eighteen-thousand-dollar antique spinet that, perhaps understandably, had gone unsold for some time. The Bronfman bought and bought — including the spinet — but while store executives were rubbing their hands, Nena Goodman became suspicious. She excused herself and made a few telephone calls. The "Bronfman" was an impostor, and was thrown out of the store empty-handed.

Nena Goodman's role in running to earth the ersatz Bronfman is typical of an operation that has always considered itself more of a family than a business. In times of crisis, all the Goodmans have pitched in to do their share. In his growing-up years and through Choate and Yale, young Eddie Goodman was not "groomed" for retailing, exactly, but it was always more or less understood, in conversations with his father and grandfather, that Eddie would follow their footsteps into Bergdorf's. When Andrew Goodman's daughters reached the age when they wanted summer jobs, they went to work at Bergdorf's. More recently, in Jo Hughes's fashion shows, which always close with a wedding scene, Andrew Goodman's eleven grandchildren provide Miss Hughes with a prime source for flower girls and pages. Just as the brooding influence of the Apartment overhead has shaped the attitude of every Bergdorf salesgirl, so has the Store loomed over the lives of three generations of Goodmans. And so it has been a shock to everyone connected with Bergdorf Goodman to realize that in a very few years there will be no more Goodmans there.

What is less well known is that Edwin Goodman, Sr.'s dynastic dream for his son and grandson very nearly collapsed a generation ago, not long after his white marble temple was completed on Fifty-eighth Street and the Plaza. And though the family has always conveyed an impression of cozy unity, there have, for many years, been rumblings from within. Andrew Goodman, for example, did not join his father's

enterprise without certain misgivings, and most people today who cite
Andrew Goodman as one of New York's great merchants are unaware
that he didn't really want to be one. He was of a generation in which
dutiful Jewish sons did what their patriarchal Jewish fathers told
them to, and perhaps, in the end, he would have *had* to go with the
store even though there was a time when he wanted desperately not
to. In his youth, Andrew Goodman showed certain signs of enjoying
the good life of a rich young man around town, and when his father
decided that Andrew was being frivolous about his studies he was
plucked out of the University of Michigan and sent off to Paris to be
apprenticed to the fashion house of Jean Patou. In Paris, there was
more frivolity and more parental displeasure.

There was consternation in the Goodman family, however, in 1935
when Andrew announced that he wanted to marry a beautiful Cuban
girl named Nena Manach. Not only was Nena a "foreigner," but
she had been married before and had a daughter by her previous husband (Vivien Goodman Malloy is only a half-sister to Andrew Goodman's other children). She was also a Roman Catholic. Nena's first
meeting with the senior Goodmans was hardly auspicious. At dinner,
served in the stiff and formal Old World style that Mr. Goodman
preferred, Mr. Goodman asked Nena where she had bought her dress.
She mentioned some shop on Madison Avenue, and there was a thundering silence. When she and Andrew continued to make plans for
their marriage despite Mr. Goodman's objections, Mr. Goodman sum-
moned Nena to his office. He handed her a legal document and told
her to sign it. It was a premarital contract in which Nena was asked
to promise that in the event of a divorce, she would not ask more than
one hundred dollars a month alimony from Andrew. In tears, Nena
signed the agreement, and she and Andrew were married in September of that year.

True, Mr. Goodman's attitude toward Nena gradually softened.
On their first wedding anniversary, he gave her a fur piece. It wasn't
much fur — only four skins — but in the box containing it were
scraps of paper which Nena realized was the torn-up marriage contract. And so Andrew Goodman took up his duties at the store only
as a sort of compromise. Having caused his father so much displeasure,
he could not cause him more.

Andrew Goodman today is a cheerful, handsome man who dresses with quiet conservatism — he refuses to join the swing to wider neckties and prison-stripe shirts — who talks easily on almost any subject and who actually has a stream-of-consciousness speaking style, leaping gracefully from subject to subject — from the impressive business done by Julie Trissell, Bergdorf's coat and suit lady (six million dollars a year in her department alone) to his irritation with New York's Landmarks Commission for attempting to get Bergdorf's building declared a landmark ("It's barely forty years old, for God's sake!") to his cautious optimism that the FTC will rule favorably on the Broadway-Hale takeover — despite grumbling from Ralph Nader's Raiders that by acquiring Bergdorf's Broadway-Hale will have some sort of monopoly on American high fashion ("Ridiculous!"). To help him with his flow of conversation, Andrew Goodman has an executive-type telephone setup in his office that lets him talk, and that talks back to him, as he moves about his office, and a wide variety of calls can thus be managed at the same time. "Of course it was a disappointment to have the boys leave," he said recently, between pushing buttons and juggling calls, "I wanted them to stay, and in each case there were long conversations with Harry, Eddie, and Gary. But I respect their wish to do their own thing. And with this merger I think I've accomplished several things — found a good marriage partner whose stock is excellent. They've promised to give us complete autonomy — as they've done with Neiman-Marcus, which has worked out very happily for all concerned. Under the terms of the deal, the family keeps the property and the apartment — Broadway-Hale will lease the store. In view of the family situation, I think I've set it up pretty well."

It is certainly true that all the Goodmans have been set up so that they are very well off. During the week in the apartment Andrew and Nena Goodman entertain frequently at small luncheons and dinners that are part business, part social. Because business takes Andrew Goodman into the fashion worlds of Paris, New York, and Los Angeles, their friends tend to reflect those worlds too, and so at a Goodman dinner party it would be no surprise to find Jimmy Galanos, just in from the Coast, or "the whole Dior gang," as Nena Goodman calls them, in town from Paris. The Goodmans' best friends are Mr. and

Mrs. Vincent Draddy (of David Crystal, the dress manufacturer) who
are their pop-in-on neighbors in the country. Nena Goodman prefers
eight to ten at a seated dinner (often black tie), but the apartment
is perfectly capable of handling two to three hundred people for a
cocktail buffet, such as the one tossed for the Duke of Windsor, and
another given for Count and Countess Hubert D'Ornanon, the
French perfumer and entrepreneur. The country house in Rye is a
large and rambling frame affair with airy, antique-filled rooms that
seem to open onto each other endlessly and stretch the length of a
football field. Here there is a pool and tennis court, and weekend
afternoons are spent with friends dropping over for a game or a swim
— the Draddys, or the George Berlingers, or financier Leon Mandel,
in from Palm Beach with his also-Cuban-born wife, Carola.

There are those who say that Andrew Goodman doesn't really run
the store, and hasn't for a number of years — that the real power behind the Bergdorf throne is non-family Leonard Hankin, Bergdorf's
vice president. One who voices this view is designer-manufacturer
Malcolm Starr, who says, "Leonard makes all the decisions — he just
brings them to Andrew for an okay." There is a certain amount of
truth in this, although Goodman and Hankin actually operate as a
curiously effective team in which Andrew Goodman is the charming
and kindly father-figure in the store, and Leonard Hankin is the man
called in whenever unpleasant tasks must be performed. As a result,
everybody who works at Bergdorf's loves "Mr. Andrew" unabashedly,
while "Mr. Leonard" is regarded with less enthusiasm by many people. The formidable Jo Hughes, because she is perhaps the foremost
woman in high fashion in America, can speak from an impregnable
position of power in the store, and can say whatever she thinks, and
usually does. She once asked Mr. Hankin, "Leonard, how can you
work in a place where you are so thoroughly hated?" His answer, with
a shrug, was, "Somebody has to do the dirty work — the needling, the
hiring and firing."

Hankin himself is a rosy-faced man with bright eyes and a fine mane
of white hair who, in contrast to Andrew Goodman, comes to work
in windowpane-checked suits and patent leather Gucci shoes. As an
ambitious young man, a number of years ago, working in Bergdorf's
fur department, he wrote a long memorandum to Mr. Edwin Good-

man which contained Hankin's suggestions for "goosing up" the store and its profits — including a department for less expensive dresses for younger and less rich women. Weeks passed, and there was no reply to the memo. Then it came: a summons to the Apartment. Mr. Goodman's terse comment, when Hankin arrived, was: "I like many of your ideas, but I don't want to see them carried out in my lifetime. After I'm gone, you and Andrew can do what you like." And that is more or less what has happened, including the addition of the very successful Miss Bergdorf department where under-one-hundred-dollar dresses can be bought.

A rumor that persists at Bergdorf is that Leonard Hankin once had the temerity to say to Andrew Goodman, "Andrew, why don't you stick to your charities and committees, and I'll run the store." Whether or not Hankin actually said this or not, it is true that in recent years Andrew Goodman has devoted more and more time to speechmaking and fund-raising for such causes as the United Jewish Appeal, the National Jewish Hospital, and the American Jewish Committee. Though his children are all baptized Catholics, he has remained a "conscious Jew," but not a practicing one. He also toils for a number of other causes and sits on boards such as the Fifth Avenue Association, the New York City Better Business Bureau and the Manufacturers Hanover Trust. Many of his activities are non-Bergdorf-oriented, though no matter where he is — even on a yacht in the Aegean — he telephones daily for the sales figures.

An inability to get along with Leonard Hankin has been cited as the chief reason why, one by one, Harry Malloy, Eddie Goodman, and Gary Taylor left the fold of family and store. All three men smile and say that this is not so, but it probably was a factor in each case. A while ago, another rumor circulated that the Goodman family, in order to keep the boys in the store, was considering firing Hankin, and it is true that Hankin became extremely exercised at one point when a Florida newspaper referred to him as "formerly of Bergdorf Goodman," and wanted a retraction printed. The three young men, meanwhile, have mentioned the difficulties inherent in being "a son in the business"— any business. Relations between themselves and their associates, they claimed, always seemed strained and unnatural. It is always hard for lower-echelon personnel to speak honestly to the boss's son; there is always the chance that he'll carry it up to his father's office. And so, one by one, they went.

Harry Malloy went first, after ten years in the store, and went into partnership in the insurance business. He thrives and is happy in it. Next went Eddie Goodman, after four and a half years with the store. "I majored in English Lit at Yale," he says, "and I toyed with the idea of teaching. But teaching is too pastoral for me. I like to see the input and output of what I do. I went with the store with misgivings — just as my father did, with ambivalent feelings about it, thinking that it was what I was supposed to do, remembering my grandfather. He was a great presence, a personage — there was a great scurrying about when he was coming to call, and you had to be scrubbed raw, before being ushered into the presence. And it's not that I don't like retailing, and fashion is the most interesting *part* of retailing, much more interesting than selling cars. But the point is, to be good at retailing, you have to adore it. You have a six-day-a-week job. You have to make it your life. I helped organize the Bigi department, and that was fun. But 1967, you may remember, was a bad year for the cities — I wanted to do something, to get involved. After leaving the store, I worked in Bedford-Stuyvesant as a member of a nine-man team that was trying to develop a college in Bed-Stuy, and also to bring new businesses into the area."

Eddie Goodman has since joined Pacifica Radio's station WBAI–FM, a free-wheeling listener-supported station that operates from a converted East Side church, as the station's general manager. Here he appears to be in sharp contrast with his surroundings — a tall, slim man whose suits and ties are even more conservative than his father's, and whose hair is unfashionably short, he works in a studio where intense and flowing-haired young men work in beads and cut-off jeans, taping programs of Ukrainian folk music or discussing the travels and teachings of Baba Ram Dass. A bowl of catfood for the studio cat, a fat yellow tiger, sits in the center of the cluttered room. "I'm sure they think me the squarest of the squares," Eddie Goodman says. "I've recognized that sartorial and tonsorial politics is a real thing, but I don't believe in it — nor do I believe in changing my life style to suit my new career." Eddie Goodman, his wife, and two little girls have a large Park Avenue apartment, a maid, and a nurse for the children, and take a house for the summer on the North Shore. He does, however, go to work by subway, getting off at Fifty-ninth Street, and says, "I guess there's some retailing still in my blood, because I always cut through Bloomingdale's to see how they're doing." He also says, "I often think nowadays that if the feminine liberation movement had started twenty years earlier, there might still be Goodmans at Bergdorf's. The pressure was always on me, the son, to go into the business. Nobody ever considered my three sisters. Who knows? They might have been great."

Minky and Gary Taylor, meanwhile, live in a big Victorian house with fourteen-foot ceilings on Long Island Sound, from which Gary Taylor commutes to the Yale School of Forestry. "I don't really consider myself a dropout from the rat race," he says, "and I'm not really going to become Smoky the Bear." Taylor, who is in his mid-thirties, admits that he has been a man slow to "find" himself. Originally from Denver, he was a Dartmouth dropout who wanted to be a writer, and for a while he lived in the Village writing poetry and trying to sell it. He worked for a while for various magazines, but never for the one he wanted to, the *New Yorker,* which turned him down. "I went to Bergdorf's because I was told that Leonard had spread himself too thin, and needed someone." When he left, he had the title of the store's general manager. "It wasn't that Leonard Hankin and I didn't get along, but it was a little strange. Before I went to the store, we used to know the Hankins socially and go to their house a lot. The minute I joined Bergdorf's, the invitations stopped. With Leonard, you're either a friend or a business associate — never both."

Along with other young Americans, Gary Taylor had become increasingly concerned about ecology — "Do you know that there is more tin above the ground in this country than there is *under* the ground in the entire world? We've got to begin to think of garbage as a new kind of natural resource." And so, it grew "in the back of my mind, as a child of my time, I had to get out and do something. And believe me, there's more to what I'm taking at Yale than just trees. I don't know what direction I'll be taking yet, but I'm at Yale to find out." After a few days of classes at Yale, Taylor wailed to his wife, whom he met while she was an undergraduate at Smith, "My concentration span has left me!" Said she, "You never had any."

The Taylors were packing for a trip to Portugal, and their four little boys, their nurse, and a big Dalmatian dog named Gypsy were all, in certain ways, underfoot. "I'm all with Gary for what he's doing," Minky Taylor said. "And I'm afraid I think Bergdorf's is a frivolous business — and the store *has* changed." When Eddie Goodman was getting married, for example, his future wife's mother brought a dress to the store to find matching shoes. A claustrophobic woman, she decided to leave the store by way of a staircase rather than the elevator and, going out, a fire door slammed. Immediately, alarms went off and the poor woman was tackled by guards in the street who threatened to carry her off to precinct headquarters. Though she kept screaming, "My daughter is going to marry Eddie Goodman!" it was a while before she was released. And not long ago Minky Taylor herself, making a Charge-Take purchase at the store, was required to show elaborate identification. "You hate to have to say, 'Look, my father owns this place,'" she says. "But in the old days that simply would not have happened."

There are also those who insist that the Bergdorf woman shopper has changed in recent years, now that the spending likes of Mrs. Foy are no more than a memory. Not only are younger women coming into the store who are looking for less expensive clothes, with the two-thousand-dollar dresses having a much harder time finding a market, but the rich women customers seem to be spending less money, or at least spending money in different ways. Two very profitable recent items, for example, had nothing to do with high fashion. They were a transparent plastic "dome" umbrella that goes over the wearer's entire head and shoulders, and something called an Isotoner — a leotard of a special fabric which, when worn, is said to firm and tone the wearer's body. Almost novelty-store items, you might say. And there is a new kind of customer, meanwhile, for the expensive items, and she might be called the non-customer. She is a great source of annoyance to Messrs. Goodman and Hankin because, after lunch and a few cocktails, she sweeps with a friend into Bergdorf's, buys like a mad thing for an hour or so, and then the next day — her friend having been suitably impressed — she returns everything for credit. There are also those who say that the store has let down its side badly, and there were startled looks on the street floor the other day when a modishly dressed young girl, all beads, chains, hair, and fringe, emerged from an elevator with her male escort who, above the belt of his tie-dyed jeans, wore nothing at all besides a headband. "In the old days, he would not have been permitted inside the store," a salesgirl whispered.

"We used to run a store for the rich woman and the kept woman," Leonard Hankin said recently. "We can't any more." Still, there are enough of the old breed around to allow the store to retain some of its air of gentility and comfort, including one longtime customer who wrote to Andrew Goodman to suggest that her name be taken off the store's mailing list. She was in her eighties now, and infirm, she explained, and hardly ever went out any more, "and it makes me feel a little guilty knowing you are spending that postage on me."

"Oh, I so hope the FTC approves!" Minky Taylor said, when the decision was still pending, as though she longed to have the great weight of the famous store thrown forever from her slender Goodman shoulders; as though she yearned for one of the last "family" stores for the super-rich to pass out of the family and into the hands of a super-super-rich conglomerate; as though she knew that the idea of such former "right" places as Bergdorf's was dying, and that it must be allowed to die as gracefully as possible. Within weeks, her prayers were answered. The FTC approved, and the conglomeration was complete.

What changes will take place when Bergdorf's — so small and special and private — becomes a part of Broadway-Hale? Well, certainly there will be branches of Bergdorf Goodman opening across the landscape, from Scarsdale to Atlanta. Branchification was something the Goodmans always scorned (though, as an inducement to Eddie, a branch store — to give him his head, and his own place — was for a while considered in Chicago). But the greatest loss, most people feel, will be the personal touch of the Goodman family. Not long ago a candy manufacturer approached Andrew Goodman with the idea of setting up a street-floor chocolate boutique at Bergdorf's. Andrew took a box of chocolates home, tried a few pieces, and didn't like it. So there was no boutique. In the Broadway-Hale conglomerate, who will taste the candy? Who will ever care?

Photo by Marc Riboud, Magnum

$5,000 a lecture — Yevtushenko

13

The Circuit:
Tell Us All

IN a recent burst of enthusiasm for his profession — lecture management — Dan Tyler Moore, director general of the International Platform Association, announced that on a certain evening in the spring of 1968 no fewer than forty thousand speakers were holding forth in as many auditoriums *in the city of New York alone.* If true, and figuring that lecture audiences generally consist of anywhere from two hundred and fifty to fifteen hundred people, this would have meant that every resident of the five boroughs, man, woman and child, had simultaneously sat down to be talked at, along with several million other people who could only have come from out of town.

Mr. Moore's claim is all the more astonishing measured against the fact that, in the lecture business, New York is not considered to be a "good talk town." Sophisticated New Yorkers, it seems, tend to prefer less cerebral pastimes — such as cocktail parties, lovemaking and theater-in-the-nude — to going to lectures. It is in the allegedly culturally barren hinterlands, smaller cities such as Buffalo, Grand Rapids, Kansas City, Fort Wayne, Dallas, Shreveport, Spokane, Iowa City and Bakersfield, that lecture audiences are trotting out in the hundreds of thousands to be edified, or just to listen to the sound of another human voice. But the Moore statement does draw attention to something undeniable: the lecture business is big business and getting bigger. This year more than a hundred million dollars will be spent on what might be called just a lot of hot air. In other words, when the new American moneyed middle class is not traveling, skiing, shopping, or dining out, it is avidly pursuing self-improvement. Sitting in front of a speaker's lectern is clearly one of the new places to be when you've nowhere else to go.

Furthermore, the 1940's image of the lady lecturer created by the late Helen Hokinson — corsaged speaker addressing a sea of flowered hats (following a chicken-in-timbales luncheon), on the subject of Flower Arranging or Secrets of Slipcovering — is now hopelessly out of date. So is the picture of the effete critic who has come to the woman's club to talk on the Joys of Poetry. Today congressmen, senators, Joint Chiefs of Staff and Supreme Court justices have taken to the lecture platform, along with ballplayers, sopranos, columnists, doctors, lawyers, composers, gurus, women's liberationists and ballet dancers. Lecturing has become an important second source of income for actors between plays, authors between books, singers between concerts, even photographers between assignments. Bosley Crowther, former film critic for the New York *Times,* claims he put his children through college by lecturing. Senator Barry Goldwater in 1968 made sixty thousand dollars in lecture fees alone and is the envy of all his Senate colleagues. Everyone whose name shines with the slightest glint of fame scrambles to climb aboard the gold lecture wagon to join those who are currently making money at it — such diverse figures as Harry Golden, Risë Stevens, Art Buchwald, Dick Gregory, Bob Feller, Kitty Carlisle, George Plimpton, Philippe Halsman and Madame Claire Chennault.

Matching — indeed outweighing — the eagerness of those willing to lecture and be paid for it are the organizations with budgets they are eager to spend on lectures. These, too, are a far cry from the club luncheons Miss Hokinson sketched. Women's groups no longer have a corner on lecturers' services. It is as though in the last decade, in a spirit of uplift, men's organizations all over the country decided to put aside their traditional evening of drinking and card-playing in favor of listening to the reminiscences of Baroness Maria von Trapp, whose life story was turned into *The Sound of Music.* Or to hear the powdered accents of the Duke and Duchess of Bedford, whose joint lecture, titled "An Evening of Elegance," is, according to Their Graces' agent, "really just a plug to get tourists to come and visit their castle."

The greatest demand for lecturers comes from colleges. "They're the bread and butter of our business," says Alan S. Walker, president of the Program Corporation of America. "Look at it this way: every single college and university in the country books between ten and fifteen speakers every year. That adds up to a tremendous market." Whatever the reason for this activity, one lecture bureau, the American Program Bureau of Boston, takes in about three million dollars every year from college campuses, three-quarters of the agency's revenue. With more than four thousand colleges and universities, there is an audience of over seven million people — and they have money to pay.

There is another reason why the college audience is particularly enticing to lecturers and the agencies. This big, rich audience turns over every four years. This means that a lecturer can be booked again — and again — at any given college. This is not the case in, say, the annual Republican Club Fund Dinner in Tulsa. After one engagement a speaker becomes "dead" for that organization for as long as a dozen years, and he may even be dead for all of Tulsa. This is because this year's program chairman has got to come up with something better than last year's speaker; if not, it would be like arriving in last year's hat. "With colleges," says one lecture agent taking a hardboiled view, "you can send them a speaker and maybe he's lousy. So what? Two, three years later nobody will remember whether he was or wasn't."

Which brings up the inevitable question: How valuable, or how entertaining, are the lectures being peddled — and delivered — to this seemingly insatiably lecture-hungry public? The answer, needless to say, is that it depends. There are, to begin with, two basic kinds of lecturers. There is the person who, having achieved a certain amount of fame or recognition in his field, decides, as it were, to cash in on it with "a little lecturing on the side." These are people who regard lecturing as something else to do, an added source of income, an excuse to get away from their wives (or husbands) for a few weeks each year. These might be called the casual lecturers who are really only as good as their names happen to be. At the moment, for example, Arthur Ashe is considered one of the "hot" lecture properties and his signature is being sought by a number of agencies, though of course no one knows — or cares — whether Mr. Ashe is as skillful on the platform as he is at the net.

Lecturers of this type, however, tend to have relatively short careers. According to an agent, "The first year we have them we can book them anywhere — they can be just as busy as they want. The second year there's a slip. By the third year, unless they're awfully good, they're dead." And yet it is this group that composes the majority of the lecturers in the business. According to W. Colston Leigh, who runs a New York agency often called "the Tiffany's of the lecture bureaus," "Ninety per cent of the people in this business are no damned good. It's like any other profession. Only the dedicated and talented minority really succeed."

The dedicated and talented minority are, of course, the second group. These are men and women who take their lecturing seriously, who work at it with full strength, who believe in what they're doing — and saying — and work on their platform performances with as much intensity as a painter works on a canvas. They learn how to establish rapport with an audience, how to build a mood and control it, how to get a laugh or a tear. They learn how to judge an audience's reaction and how to attune themselves to the subtleties of the composition of a group, and to tell instinctively when an anecdote that might be appreciated by one kind of audience will not by another. These lecturers leave their audiences enriched or entertained or both, and needless to say, these lecturers are the more durable sort, in demand year after year.

Into this category fall such people as Louis Untermeyer, who, in his mid-eighties, recently retired from a long career of lecturing, and Emily Kimbrough, who loves lecturing so much that she lectures, then writes a book about lecturing, then lectures about writing a book about lecturing. Edward Weeks, editor emeritus of the *Atlantic,* is another of this long-lasting breed, as was the late critic John Mason Brown. Eleanor Roosevelt, for years a Colston Leigh client, was still another who — though never really a very good speaker — managed, by some magic of her personality or spirit, to hold audiences enthralled with her fluty voice.

Since the lecture industry has, for the last decade, been enjoying a seller's market, with more organizations clamoring for speakers than there are speakers to speak — and since the speakers themselves are subject to such a high turnover rate — the lecture-bureau business has become highly competitive. Everybody, as Jimmy Durante used to say, wants to get into the act and is furiously beating his own drum. In the scramble to out-celebrity each other, lecture bureaus have been known to adopt practices which, while not actually illegal, might be considered a bit unsporting, and in their efforts to lure Famous Names to their lists their most important tool has been the greatness of the size of the human ego. For example, a familiar tactic has been for a lecture agent to call up a Supreme Court justice or similar luminary and say, "If I can get you a lecture engagement paying a top figure of five thousand dollars, may I represent you?" In most cases the celebrity, flattered at the thought that such a high price is placed on his words, says yes right away, and then, in a few days, forgets all about it. No five-thousand-dollar engagement may ever come, but in the meantime the celebrity's name has been printed on hundreds of thousands of brochures scattered to organizations across the country, lending prestige to the lecture bureau — and to the other speakers, less well known, whom the bureau represents.

The new student power on college campuses has also been shrewdly put to use by certain less-than-scrupulous lecture bureaus. Today undergraduate managers and student committee members have complete and final control of "special events" at the great majority of colleges and universities. Only on a few campuses must students refer their choice of speakers to officials for approval, and though the students do their best, they are often unprepared for some of the more "sophisticated" selling methods of the lecture agencies. For example, a familiar way to offer lecturers to colleges is in a series, and nearly every lecture series has at least one star. Let us say, then, that college X has decided to buy a ten-lecture series, the capstone of which will be an address — to take a ridiculous example — by Queen Elizabeth II. We assume that the Queen does not know that she has been offered. The other nine lecturers are a prize-winning electroplater from Detroit, a world's-record-breaking speed typist, and so on, but it was the Queen, really, who sold the series, for it is *her* opinions on pot and black militancy that everybody at college X wants to hear.

The lecture bureau has told the students that the cost of the ten lectures will be five thousand dollars — five hundred dollars apiece, which is modest enough — and has piously added that, in the event that any of the speakers fails to make his engagement, the five hundred dollars for that speaker's date will be cheerfully refunded. It is all put in writing and a contract is signed — all legally holeproof. Alas; on the day the Queen is expected she is stricken with laryngitis and has taken to her bed. For her nonappearance, five hundred dollars is promptly sent back to the college. The lecture bureau has made forty-five hundred dollars for nine mediocre speakers, and a campusful of unwitting students has been gulled. Unfortunately, practices like this are too common to be funny and are extremely difficult to detect.

But lecture agents have headaches to put up with, the commonest of which are the clients who — in order to avoid paying the commission, which can run anywhere from twenty to thirty-five per cent of the fee — accept speaking engagements on their own without telling the bureau. When he finds out about it all the lecture agent can do is scold. If he fires his client the client will simply trot off to another agent who will be glad to have him — such is the demand today for anyone with the slightest gift of gab. And clients have peculiar quirks that must be catered to. The popular Emily Kimbrough, for instance, dislikes flying, and her tours must be slowly and tortuously routed over railroad tracks.

Beginning lecturers, initially entranced at the heady thought of money to be made, occasionally have agonized second thoughts. This happened in the case of Andy Warhol, who agreed to a schedule of fifty college bookings for the American Program Bureau — or as it later turned out, the APB agreed to deliver Andy Warhol to fifty colleges before actually asking Andy Warhol how he felt about it, just assuming that, like most people, he would be delighted. He wasn't. Well, the APB argued, why couldn't he go along and show the colleges some footage from his underground films? Warhol agreed to this, but at the last minute, overwhelmed by stage fright, he sent a "double" with hair dyed silver (like Warhol's) and some of Warhol's clothes. The double toured in Missouri, Montana and Oregon and was quite a success. "That boy was more what the kids really wanted,"

Warhol says. "They liked him better. He smiled prettier. He was friendlier. He was a flower child." Nonetheless, when the deception was discovered, a red-faced APB was forced to return many fat fees. Since then Warhol has kept his in-person dates, but he goes accompanied not only by film footage but also by two cohorts, Viva Superstar and Paul Morissey. They answer questions for him. He merely stands there, rigid and mute, thus becoming the gab circuit's first non-speaking speaker.

And even the old pros have lapses now and then. Vincent Sheean, normally a popular and reliable platform performer, once spent a few bibulous hours with friends before a California lecture date. At some point during the cocktails Sheean apparently forgot whether he was supposed to deliver a lecture or attend one. When he got to the auditorium he paid a dollar for his ticket and took a seat in the audience. When he looked at the program and saw that he was the speaker he took his ticket back, collected his dollar, and took his place at the podium. Those who heard him testify that he was never in better form.

This was not the case with another speaker who had undergone a somewhat more alcoholic encounter prior to his lecture. After being introduced he rose, a bit unsteadily, to the lectern, gazed for a long moment at his notes, then said, "Thank you very much," and sat down.

The pitfalls of lecturers abound. When a certain novelist, who must be nameless, heard that a critic whom he particularly hated had taken to the lecture circuit, the novelist chose a brilliantly cruel, if expensive, mode of revenge. Using a false name, he engaged the critic as a lecturer, hired a hall, and appeared as an audience of one. When the critic stepped onto the bare stage to face an empty house, the novelist sat back comfortably in his seat, smiled, and said, "Okay, let's hear you do your stuff."

There is also a danger which I, in my own somewhat limited experience as a lecturer, have named the Mrs. Oppenheim Syndrome. The Mrs. Oppenheim Syndrome is most likely to be experienced in smaller cities, where warring social factions may exist within the community or within the sponsoring organization itself. I first met up with it in Scranton or Wilkes-Barre. It doesn't matter which; the two

Pennsylvania cities, near each other and sharing an airport, hate each other. Each thinks the other is its social and physical inferior and rarely do the two see eye to eye on anything. Following my talk at the "after-party" — a formidable part of the engagement in itself — I was cornered by a Mrs. Oppenheim of Scranton (or Wilkes-Barre) and a female ally presumably from the same place, was pressed between them into the corner of a triangular banquette table, and then engaged in heavy conversation. After half an hour or so, unable to move, I became aware of a heightening mood of tension in the room. The opposing Wilkes-Barre (or Scranton) part of the gathering was beginning to feel that I was dividing my time unfairly, possibly committing the unpardonable sin of snubbing the Sponsoring Organization. But, trapped as I was by Mrs. Oppenheim and her friend, I felt there was nothing I could do short of crawling across one of the ladies' laps. Twenty minutes later it was too late. From the corner of my eye I watched as the offended Wilkes-Barre (?) group stood up as if by a signal and, with marvelous precision, marched to the door, faces frozen and noses in the air, and left the party.

I have also been the victim of the overindulgent, or backhanded, compliment — another commonplace lecturing hazard. It goes like this: You are approached by an effusive woman who says, "You know, you have *me* to thank that you're our lecturer tonight. That's right. Nobody else in the whole organization wanted you. But I went to bat and I fought and fought and *fought* for you, and I finally won!"

A lecturer friend tops this by reporting that when she was thanked following her lecture she was told: "That was simply a wonderful talk. We loved it. Of course we also have really important lecturers come to us to talk about really important things — but you were simply swell." Compared with these, the tight plane schedules, the airless hotel rooms with clanking radiator pipes and all the other familiar details of a lecturer's life seem as nothing at all.

In the industry itself, the harshest critics of the lecture business complain of "high-pressure, strongarm selling techniques" used to sell lecturers of inferior quality with little of value to say. Most heavily under attack for investing the business with Hollywood show-biz flackery have been such relative newcomers as Richard Fulton and Robert Walker of the APB. Walker, who likens his clients to an "intellectual smorgasbord," and has offered in the past, in addition to Andy Warhol and Dr. Timothy Leary — who opened his lectures by crying into a microphone, "Am I turned on?" — such colorful figures as "our ghost-catcher, Hans Holzer; Sybil Leek, our séance lady and witch; our word man, James McConnell, our yoga woman, Marcia Moore; and our tremendous fish person, Roger Conklin."

The more staid, respectable, old-guard bureaus are more selective. They regard theirs as a high calling, and they conscientiously avoid anything that might be interpreted as pressure selling or sharp practices. They plan their clients' schedules to their clients' preferences. Some lecturers prefer to go out on grueling six- or eight-week tours once a year and have it over with. Others, like Art Buchwald, prefer to go out for no more than a day or two at a time, yet don't mind making one of these short trips every week. Good lecture agents warn their clients of the hazards of lecturing. Author-explorer Peter Freuchen, for example, on a lecture tour, ran up a flight of stairs with his suitcase and died on the landing of heart failure. Other hazards are social, for local hostesses in small cities will stop at nothing to get visiting celebrities to their dinner tables. Art Buchwald was once met at an airport and whisked off to what he was assured was "the official pre-lecture party." When he got to the lecture he was greeted by a roomful of icy faces. The *real* official party, where he had been expected, had been held elsewhere. He had been the victim of a simple kidnapping.

The more staid and conservative bureaus will not sell a lecture series at a blanket price but will instead price each lecturer in the series at his established worth. Colston Leigh, furthermore, insists on the signature of at least one college official on every college lecture contract. The student organizers grumble about this but, if they wish to engage a Colston Leigh client, they comply.

W. Colston Leigh, an easygoing crew-cropped man in his sixties, who has been in the lecture-bureau business for over forty years, says: "I'm extremely good, but I'm not a genius. There's a lot of room for exploitation in this business, but I don't believe in exploitation. I think of this business as a service. People want to be informed and they want to be entertained. We serve this need with our speakers. We establish a market price for a speaker and we stick to it, and we keep track of how much money various organizations have to spend. We wouldn't try to sell a thousand-dollar speaker to an organization with a two-hundred-and-fifty-dollar budget. We also keep track of what our audiences think of our speakers. We ask for comments. If the comments are bad we pass them right along to the speaker with a suggestion that he shape up. Yes, the answer to this business is *service* — service to the public — and we won't send out speakers who won't deliver this kind of service." With a twinkle in his eye Mr. Leigh adds, "Oh, there's a lot to this business, believe me. If you've got time, I'll deliver a whole lecture on it."

Part Four

HOW NOT TO DO IT

Photo by Elliott Erwitt © *1968 Magnum Photos*

Truman Capote greets some of his guests
at his celebrated New York party

14

U.S.A.:
The Dwindling Pleasures of the Rich

THOSE not blessed with wealth or lofty social position often presume that when the rich and well-placed entertain they do so both effortlessly and faultlessly, with perfect ease and taste, unhampered by the work and cares that beset the ordinary host and hostess when they undertake a party. Alas, like so many illusions about the other half and how they live, this one turns out to be no more than that — nowadays, at least. In fact, as the new moneyed American middle class has been turning its attention to culture, travel, education, and other accoutrements of gracious living, they have also discovered the joys — and the importance — of entertaining well, of serving good food and wine in attractive surroundings. The social rich, in the meantime, have been letting down the side badly. In other words, while the new rich have been learning how to do it, the old rich have been forgetting.

In Philadelphia, for example, when the John Ingersolls have friends in for cocktails (it is said in Philadelphia that when a Biddle is drunk he *thinks* he's an Ingersoll), it works this way: Mr. Ingersoll takes a bottle of inexpensive domestic gin, empties a little into a cup, and then pours a corresponding amount of inexpensive domestic vermouth into the gin bottle. He then shakes the resulting mixture vigorously, and splashes his concoction — at room temperature — into his guests' glasses. This procedure, which would horrify not only connoisseurs of the martini but most ordinary mortals as well, is standard procedure here where, after all, Ingersolls are Ingersolls and always have been, and there is little more that need be said.

In New York, meanwhile, Mr. and Mrs. Wyatt Cooper — she is the former Gloria Vanderbilt — are among the town's most elegant couples. Mrs. Cooper is not only rich and beautiful, with a model's figure and a collection of antique dresses and costumes to go with it, along with drawerfuls of jewelry, much of which she has designed herself, but she is also a celebrated painter in her own right. Mrs. Cooper has decorated her East Side town house in a fantasy style so that when guests step inside the door they will have, as she puts it, "a feeling of entering a total collage." (One bedroom is completely upholstered — walls, floor, ceiling — with a collection of old patchwork quilts.) Gloria Cooper also cares about the way her house smells, and when she has a party, she lights dozens of scented candles (imported from France at twenty-five dollars apiece) and places them in nooks and crannies throughout the house. They are intended to suffuse the air with sweetness and give the place a fairyland glow.

Now all these exotic and costly touches might be delightful to behold — if they always worked. But they don't. At a recent Cooper party, a seated dinner for twenty-six — with five courses from poached trout to *mousse au chocolat,* and three wines — all would have been well if it had not been, of all things, for the weather. New York had been having, for early spring, an unseasonably hot night — with the kind of heavy, sticky heat for which New York is infamous. The Cooper house is not air-conditioned, and cannot be: tall French windows throughout prevent the installation of individual units. Though windows were thrown open, not a trace of a breeze stirred in the city, and all the lighted candles seemed merely to add to the heat's sullen oppressiveness. "I really thought I was going to have to call the party off, it was so uncomfortable," Mrs. Cooper said. But then she had an idea. She sent out for a number of large industrial-type electric fans, and had these placed as unobtrusively as possible in the corners of the various rooms.

As the Coopers' guests crowded in, their bodily presences added to the evening's heat even more and, when it was time for her perspiring friends to be seated at the table, Gloria Cooper whispered to a servant to turn on the fans. The fans came on, with a noise approximating that of a jet takeoff and with a wind that immediately blew out all the candles, plunging the evening's proceedings into semidarkness and, at the same time, dislodging wigs, hairpieces, and even one pair of false eyelashes. It became a question of breathless heat or windy, noisy darkness. The guests, with wind-tossed hair but cooling brows, reluctantly voted for the latter.

Back in Philadelphia, guests have not forgotten the debutante party of not too many years ago when, as part of the decor, thousands of exotic white butterflies — flown in live from Hawaii — were to be prettily released from a huge satin balloon suspended from the ballroom ceiling. At the scheduled moment, the balloon was opened, and the butterflies came cascading down — all dead, killed by the fire-preventive spray with which the room had been treated.

In Washington, party-giving capital of the country, Mrs. George Bunker, wife of the president of the giant Martin Marietta Company, recently gave a large seated dinner that included, as a first course, Strasbourg pâté. In the kitchen, Mrs. Bunker's Portuguese-speaking cook apparently confused the tins of costly pâté with some cans containing food for the Bunker cats. By the time the hostess noticed what had happened, her guests were already delightedly exclaiming over the cat food — which had arrived in iced bowls, decorated with watercress and truffles — and so she decided, probably wisely, to let the incident pass without comment. In Westchester County, New York, a hostess in a similar plight was required to use considerably more ingenuity when she saw, to her horror, that her guests, instead of the macédoine of brandied fruits she had ordered, had been served as dessert the combination macaroni-tuna-cheese casserole, left over from a supper that had been fixed for the children several nights before. The guests politely did their best to deal with the chilly and gluey substance, and finally someone asked, "My dear, what is this *extraordinary* dessert?" The hostess, taking a deep breath, replied, "It's a *niçoise* country pudding I discovered in the South of France."

Obviously, when one entertains on a large scale, things can go wrong in a big way. The Edgar Bronfmans — he is the liquor tycoon — can seat fifty comfortably for dinner in the dining room of their country place, but when Mr. Bronfman wants to attract his wife's attention on the other side of the room, he must resort to lobbing peanuts at her. On the other hand, not all the rich entertain elaborately or at great expense, and a number of them regularly cut corners in ways that verge on the miserly.

In Washington it has long been the rule in the household of Wiley T. Buchanan, former U.S. Chief of Protocol under President Eisenhower, that only guests who are of national prominence may be served their drinks in the Buchanans' expensive Steuben crystal. Less important guests drink their cocktails in less costly glassware. The practice seems to have something to do with the fact that many of the Buchanan parties are semiofficial entertainments, with press photographers present. The sort of people who get their pictures in the paper, therefore, are photographed at the Buchanans' sipping from Steuben. The Anchor-Hocking group consists of those about whom the press could not care less.

Washington is a city where entertaining is done for show as well as for business — the business, usually, being politics. Mrs. Perle Mesta, the city's famous hostess and the inspiration for the musical comedy *Call Me Madam,* keeps an apartment these days at the Sheraton-Park Hotel — where, according to a persistent rumor in this persistently rumor-ridden city, she is given a nominal rate in return for the phenomenal publicity her parties bring to the place. The Sheraton-Park is certainly very nice to Mrs. Mesta. It performs such extra services, for instance, as opening up any vacant rooms and suites surrounding the Mesta suite when Mrs. Mesta entertains, so that her apartment, actually not all that large, will look larger.

Now, when they *are* entertained, are the rich dispensers of elaborate hostess presents, or even thank-you notes? It is not so much that they are rude, but, after all, when one goes out so much — there just isn't enough time in the day to write bread-and-butter letters. At best, a quick telephone call will have to suffice. The same reluctance to spend much time, or money, or even very much thought can be noticed when it comes to such things as wedding presents. At the wedding of Joan Pillsbury, a flour and baking-products heiress, to Jeffery Dupree, it was therefore no surprise to see that one of her mother's friends had sent her a set of a dozen plastic glasses "for the pool." An observer also noticed that the wedding gifts included no fewer than eight copies of Webster's Collegiate Dictionary.

In "dining-out" cities, such as New York, Chicago, and San Francisco (as opposed to eating-at-home cities, such as Boston, Philadelphia, and Detroit), it is possible for the rich to entertain very cheaply simply by going to the most fashionable restaurants. Odd though this sounds, it is much easier to sign an imposing dinner check at a restaurant such as New York's elegant Le Pavillon than it is to pay cash. The ensuing bill can then be ignored for months — sometimes for years. The richer one is, the longer one can put off paying bills like these. The fancy restaurant (unlike the plumber or even the dentist) would not dream of suing to collect a bill from a rich or famous customer. If it did, it would mean losing that customer's prestigious, decorative, and publicity-valuable trade. Stuart Levin, the usually unflappable owner of Le Pavillon, merely rolls his eyes and groans when asked about the frequency with which his wealthiest — and most regular — customers pay for their meals and parties.

It is also possible for the rich to entertain in certain restaurants, and never get any sort of bill at all. This is particularly true in New York, a city which has become restaurant-poor, with more expensive dining-out places than it really seems to need. All one needs to give a lavish party for nothing is determination, a certain amount of *chutzpah* — and an ability to sniff out the right restaurant. Ideally, it should either be a new and therefore struggling place, or one that is older and having trouble clinging to the prestige it enjoyed in an earlier day. Truman Capote's celebrated party at the Plaza Hotel is an example of the latter sort and, though those who were not on Mr. Capote's guest list were offering bribes for invitations, the great bash itself cost the author rather little. The publicity the affair engendered helped reestablish the old ballroom as New York's best address for public functions, and the hotel, in gratitude, picked up most of the tab.

Truman Capote, you say — of course, a famous author; *he* could get away with it, but what about an ordinary person? Well, what about Mrs. Edwin I. Hilson? Hers was not exactly a name to conjure with, but she did get the late Duke of Windsor and his Duchess to agree to come to a party and, led by the Duke and Duchess, all sorts of other famous and social people fell into line. The Four Seasons restaurant was happy to provide the place and the party — no charge.

If, in other words, you are not a famous person yourself, all you need is a famous friend to use for social leverage.

If you happen to be the least bit shy, in New York, about operating this way (it requires, after all, telephoning restaurants and laying your cards on the table, and restaurant owners are generally a hardboiled lot), you can always hire a publicist to do the below-stairs work for you. Your friendly publicist, who will work for a mere five hundred dollars a month, will not only help you put together free and near-free parties, but will also see to it that you get "on the list" for all the other free and near-free parties. Considered the *grande dame* of *haute publicité* in Manhattan is a pretty, vivacious blonde named Marianne Strong. No one knows quite how "Mimi" Strong does it, but when she issues a casting call, out from the woodwork come the old guard, the new guard, and "hot" new actors and actresses, best-selling authors, rich people, beautiful people, right people, and just enough of the wrong people to reassure all the others of their vast superiority. Mrs. Strong's specialty is finding new, offbeat — and therefore fun — places to have parties. She was the first, for example, to toss a party at the Seventy-ninth Street Boat Basin, a public marina operated by New York's Recreation Department — which charges only a trifling sum to people who want to have parties there.

New Yorkers have become so blasé about the dozens of free parties that are available on any given evening that they hardly give the matter any thought. One night at the Grenadier Restaurant — a slightly newer and more hungry one — one could have spotted Patricia Kennedy Lawford, Keir Dullea, Tammy Grimes, Maureen Stapleton, Joan Bennett, Patricia Neal, and some twenty-five other people, all sitting down to a dinner that had started with unlimited cocktails, and that had a menu headed by filet de boeuf Wellington and two wines. No one was under any illusions that this was anything but a party that no one was giving — except the promoters of the restaurant — nor did anyone care. Next day, a paragraph in *Women's Wear Daily* made it a success.

In Philadelphia, meanwhile, which is not at all a dining-out sort of town, things are somewhat different and, at the same time, somewhat the same in that they prove that the rich, when they entertain, operate under different rules and get away with more — up to, if not including, murder. In the bosky exurbs around Unionville, an area heavily favored by members of the du Pont family, a du Pont hostess announced to recent house guests that she thought it would be fun to cook dinner herself, since her cook had taken to her bed with a cold. "I can do either spaghetti or chop suey," the hostess announced. The vote, after some discussion, was for chop suey.

The hostess departed for her kitchen and emerged, several hours later, looking weary but happy, and bearing a large serving dish which contained a very strange-looking, dry, and lumpy concoction. Eagerly — since they were by now quite hungry — the guests dove in. But soon there were expressions of concern. "This doesn't taste like *most* chop suey," someone said. "Well," the hostess explained cheerfully, "I telephoned the grocer and asked him to send over everything that goes into chop suey. He did, and I put it all in a frying pan and heated it through." After several throat-clearings, another guest said, "It seems to need — more moisture." "Oh," the hostess exclaimed, "that must be what this is for —" and she hurried to her kitchen and returned with a bottle of soy sauce.

In glamorous Hollywood, meanwhile, entertaining is done with perhaps even less glamour and more dispatch. Several years ago, Elizabeth Taylor discovered the chili served at Chasen's restaurant in Beverly Hills. She became addicted to Chasen's chili, and even had it flown to her, frozen, while she worked on *Cleopatra* in Rome. Eventually she wangled the recipe out of Chasen's chef. Today, it is the dish the Richard Burtons serve most often when entertaining. Here is the recipe for Elizabeth Taylor Burton's chili, as passed along to the author:

½ pound pinto beans	2½ pounds chili grind beef
5 cups canned tomatoes	¼ cup chili powder
1 pound chopped sweet peppers	½ cup chopped parsley
1½ tablespoons salad oil	2 tablespoons salt
1½ pounds chopped onions	1½ teaspoons black pepper
2 cloves garlic chopped fine	1½ teaspoons cumin
1 pound ground lean pork	1½ tablespoons monosodium glutamate

Wash beans. Soak overnight. Simmer until tender in soaking water. Add tomatoes and simmer for 5 minutes. Sauté peppers in salad oil. Add onions

and cook until tender. Add garlic and parsley. Sauté meat 5 minutes. Add
to pepper mixture. Add chili powder and cook for 10 minutes. Add beans
and spices. Simmer covered for 1 hour. Uncover and simmer 30 minutes.
Skim off fat.

The above recipe, Mrs. Burton says, will serve eight handily, and
can be put together for under ten dollars at most supermarket prices.

And so it would seem that the rich do have it better than the rest
of us when they entertain. Not that they give better parties, but they're
privileged with more freedom from troubles. They are either, like the
du Ponts and the Ingersolls, too confident and secure in their positions
to worry about how to do it, or even to take the time considering which
fork to use. Or else they are like jet-setty New Yorkers, too cynical and
aware of what's in their publicity-oriented world to mind that much of
the entertaining that goes on is commercial, or ego-centered, or mere-
tricious. It's all a part of the scene. Pauline Trigère, the enormously
successful designer of expensive dresses, was being picked up by her
escort at her Park Avenue apartment the other day. After a drink at
the apartment, Miss Trigère and escort headed for a taxi; and, in the
taxi, Miss Trigère stifled a yawn and asked, "By the way, who's giving
this party, anyway?" Her escort, stifling another yawn, replied, "I
really don't know. It's probably just another freebie. If you like, when
we get there, I can ask."

The Annenbergs at peace with the Embassy eagle. (Mrs. Annenberg's daughter, Mrs. Wallis Weingarten, at left)

15

London:

His Excellency, the Ambassador

EERO Saarinen, in an institutional mood, designed the United States Embassy which occupies the entire western flank of London's Grosvenor Square. "Occupies" is the right word. The huge structure, of glittery Portland stone and glass, is certainly out of harmony with its neighbors, all stately Georgian mansions of mellowed brick, and the British, who relish nothing more than criticizing American taste, have made the building the subject of attack ever since its completion in 1960. Vulgar Americans have been taken to task for "spoiling" London's loveliest square, and the Embassy façade has been likened to everything from a recumbent air conditioner to the grille of a giant Edsel.

A feature of the design is an enormous eagle, as big as a World War I biplane, which perches on the roof and which seems about to sweep down on all the pigeons in the park (who, with pigeon-like perversity, ignore the threat and line up along the eagle's broad wingspan). And, to the British critics, this monster bird represents American aggression from 1776 to our present involvement in Vietnam. Thus it was when Walter H. Annenberg, the Philadelphia communications tycoon newly appointed United States ambassador to Great Britain by President Nixon, announced, in all innocence, that one of the first things he intended to do in office was take the eagle down.

His gesture, obviously, was meant as one of goodwill to the British critics. What ensued, however, was the first of a series of tempests in

English teapots, large and small, that have made Ambassador Annenberg the most controversial and most criticized ambassador to Britain since Joseph P. Kennedy. Once more a rich man seemed not to know how to do it.

Immediately, art and architectural groups flew to the defense of the building, the eagle, and the ghost of the late Mr. Saarinen. The eagle, they pointed out, was an integral part of the building's total concept, had been commissioned and approved by Saarinen himself, and could be stripped off the top of the building only at great aesthetic peril. The eagle's sculptor, Theodore Roszak of New York, cried out that any attempt to tamper with his eagle would be a violation of the First Amendment by denying an artist his freedom of expression. Various congressmen, meanwhile, pointed out that Mr. Annenberg had grossly overstepped his authority. It is not up to an ambassador to make architectural decisions about public buildings, including embassies, which are the property of American taxpayers. Senators who had been opposed to the Annenberg appointment to begin with muttered darkly that he would be lucky if he got to choose the color of the carpet in his office, much less tear down eagles. Senator Karl Mundt, in an attempt to make light of the matter, announced that he would agree to the removal of the eagle if, in return, the Queen would take down the pair of lions that guard the entrance to the British Embassy in Washington. Finally, admitting that he had spoken unwisely, or at least naïvely, Mr. Annenberg announced that he and the eagle had arrived at "a firm and friendly understanding," and that "the eagle speaks no ill of the Ambassador, and the Ambassador speaks no ill of the eagle."

For years, it has been standard American political practice to appoint wealthy men to prestigious diplomatic posts in glamorous European capitals. These appointments are given out, as everybody in the world realizes, as rewards for generous political contributions. London's American Embassy is one of the right places where a rich contributor to a winning presidential candidate can expect to find himself. It has been a long time since such men as Benjamin Franklin, the first Minister Plenipotentiary from the American States to France, have been expected to have real diplomatic training and the power to negotiate important treaties, sign world-shaping documents, or even

remove mighty eagles from their perches. Today, with such men as
Mr. Henry Kissinger roaming the world on vital and secret missions,
the role of American ambassador has shrunk to that of a social func-
tionary with little more to do than make friends and shake hands and
smile for photographers. Clearly, to President Nixon, Walter Annenberg was one of the right men for one of these socially and politically
right posts. Then why did he seem, all at once, so inexcusably wrong?

It was probably Ambassador Annenberg's naïveté and newness at
his job that caused his subsequent embarrassments and predicaments,
and that were responsible for the fact that during the first six months
of his tenure he was the unhappy recipient of a perfectly terrible
press, particularly in Britain. He had never claimed to have any great
diplomatic experience and, for a while, to newspaper readers and
television viewers, this seemed almost painfully apparent. As he was
getting his feet wet as our ambassador to the Court of St. James's, he
kept putting his foot in it, again and again.

To begin with, there was the episode of his presenting his credentials to the Queen, an event which was immortalized on television
film. What happened was that the Queen asked him, "Are you living
in the Embassy?" The Ambassador's longwinded reply was, "We are
in the Embassy residence, subject of course to some of the discom-
fiture as a result of the need for elements of refurbishing and rehabilitation." Ambassador Annenberg had no sooner uttered these
words than the British press leapt upon them with wild little squeals
of joy, sticking little pins into the ambassadorial syntax. The British,
who have always felt that no one speaks the English language properly
but a Briton, and certainly not an American, went to great lengths to
point out that the noun form of *refurbish* is *refurbishment,* not *refurbishing,* and that *rehabilitate* means to restore to health. Had the
Embassy residence been ailing? If not, Mr. Annenberg's answer contained a pathetic fallacy. Did it all matter? To the British, apparently,
it did, and for a while it seemed as though these would become the
twenty-six most quoted — and misquoted — words in London.

No one, meanwhile, troubled to point out that the Queen had asked
a particularly vacuous question, and might herself have been called
guilty at least of having her facts wrong. "Are you living in the
Embassy?" The Embassy in London is an office building and closes at

SIX P.M. It contains no living facilities. The Embassy *residence,* a huge
mansion originally built by Barbara Hutton for the second of her many
husbands, is miles away in Regent's Park, and was being refurbished
— as Ambassador Annenberg was attempting to explain to Her Majesty.

Then there was the weighty matter of whether or not Mr. Annenberg's daughter, Wallis (Mrs. Seth Weingarten of California), accompanied her father to the presentation ceremony. A reporter from the
mass-circulation *Sunday Express* wrote that she did go along, and
treated it as a *gaffe* of the first water, since for members of an ambassador's family to accompany him on this mission is something
"never done" in Britain. Immediately, everybody denied that Mrs.
Weingarten had done more than wave goodbye to her father from the
Embassy steps when he went to see the Queen. Ambassador Annenberg denied it ("Ridiculous!" he said), Mrs. Weingarten denied it,
and Buckingham Palace denied it. Whether the *Sunday Express* made
an honest error or maliciously made up the story, no one knows.

Ambassador Annenberg seems to share the Nixonian habit of overexplaining ("Let me make this absolutely clear"), a habit which can
make each clarification of the issue at hand seem even cloudier. Thus,
each time the story of Mrs. Weingarten tagging along to meet the
Queen was denied, and the more her actual whereabouts during the
ceremony were explained, the more the story spread and the more
people began thinking that she did, even though she most emphatically did not.

Instead of letting his remarks to the Queen die a natural death in
the press, Ambassador Annenberg has kept on issuing new explana-
tions of why he made them, thus keeping the long sentence alive —
to the delectation of reporters. "You must remember I had never met
Her Majesty before," he said. "I had never been inside the environ-
ment of Buckingham, and you must realize the impact of a thousand
years of history. You must remember along with that I'm an inex-
perienced diplomat. I'm basically a businessman. So if you add all that
together, all together in white tie and tails with your letters of cre-
dence, and the letters of recall of your predecessor, what could have
had a greater impact on somebody, a neophyte in the arena. I'd never

in my life experienced anything like it. I responded in formal terms to a formal occasion. Was I so wrong? I don't reckon so."

And Leonore Annenberg, his pretty blonde wife, added, "I think, and most of the people who remember it think, my husband carried off a difficult situation extremely well. And yet this remark keeps haunting us. It's so unfair."

What Ambassador Annenberg did not explain is that as a youth he suffered from a crippling stammer. It is only as a result of years of work, determination, and professional help that he is able to speak at all. He taught himself to speak by the arduous method used by, among other stammerers, the late W. Somerset Maugham. He composes his sentences — literally "writes" them — in his head before putting them into words. This is why his utterances so often have a stilted ring. The stammer still catches up with him at times, and his lips work to form words. The letter *w* is particularly difficult for him, and it is part of his training, not pomposity, that causes him to refer to himself using his full name — as he does when he asks, "Why do they write such things about Walter H. Annenberg?" Television cameras, as they do many people, cause him to freeze. Because of the stammer he will not conduct press conferences. Also, he has suffered all his life from partial hearing. Conversation — particularly the banal sort of social chitchat which is practically the only sort one hears in British Court circles ("Are you living in the Embassy?") is an ordeal for him — and so meeting the Queen in front of a battery of cameras was, as no one knows better than his wife knows, a difficult situation carried off well.

But it was overexplaining again that got both Ambassador and Mrs. Annenberg involved in still another brouhaha with the press about, of all things, finger bowls. Someone quoted Ambassador Annenberg as saying that the former occupants of the residence, the David K. E. Bruces, "didn't even" have finger bowls. The comment would hardly have created more than a bitchy column's morning giggle if the Annenbergs hadn't risen to the bait with another explanation. "My husband," Mrs. Annenberg announced, "was merely observing to a few friends that certain dishes were used on certain occasions and casually observed that Mr. and Mrs. Bruce did not appear to have the proper finger bowls when we took up residence. Really! Does it matter?"

Well, now. The answer to her question might have been "No, it doesn't," if Ambassador Annenberg had not come forward with this explanation of his wife's explanation. "We were merely intrigued," he said, "at the British custom of serving finger bowls only after artichokes, asparagus, or fruit — rather than the American custom of serving them after every meal, which makes less sense." "Those wretched finger bowls!" his wife cries. Quite clearly Mrs. Annenberg has been even more disturbed and dismayed by the hostile British press than her husband — and he has been disturbed and dismayed considerably.

What, then, is "wrong" with the Annenbergs as far as the British are concerned? Why have they seemed such a bitter pill for the British — particularly the perfumed circles of British upper-crust and diplomatic society — to swallow?

Walter H. Annenberg, at sixty-four, is stockily built with ruddy good looks, silvering hair, a hearty, meaty manner and a big handshake. Outwardly, he is an eager, friendly Saint Bernard of a man, but there is a steely glint in his eye that promises he would be a tough person to cross. His wife, by contrast, is coolly poised and looks very much like the actress Joan Fontaine. "When we heard Walter had been named ambassador, we all thought that it should have been Lee," one of Annenberg's sisters says. Leonore Annenberg's diplomatic skills have been tested by the fact that when she married her husband — the only son out of a family of eight children — she acquired seven sisters-in-law. All the Annenbergs are extremely rich, and the family fortune is one of the largest in the world. The Annenbergs are so rich that none of them can say with any accuracy just how much they are worth, since the size of the fortune, depending on fluctuations in the stock market, the art market, real estate, and so on, rises and falls by tens of millions of dollars from day to day. "Let me just say that it is vast," says Mrs. Leo Simon, one of Ambassador Annenberg's sisters.

All the Annenbergs enjoy living on a grand scale, and a passion for building and decorating huge houses and apartments amounts to a family obsession. One sister, Mrs. Joseph Hazen, recently bought the twenty-seventh floor of New York's Hotel Pierre — over the telephone.

Someone told her she would like it, and so she bought it. Another, Mrs. Simon, has redecorated the large Fifth Avenue duplex that formerly belonged to Joan Crawford. All the Annenbergs have multiple addresses, with houses in New York, Westchester, Palm Beach, and Beverly Hills. Walter Annenberg has an estate on the Philadelphia Main Line and another, much larger, called Sunnylands, in the desert near Palm Springs, California. Sunnylands has, among other things, its own golf course with, according to the owner, "only nine holes, but the course is laid out in such a way that a total of twenty-seven holes can be played." There are eight golf carts with blue and white hoods, thirteen man-made lakes and a swimming pool that cascades down on various levels, like a natural stream, and a giant beaucarnia tree — the largest tropical tree that grows — imported from Mexico via Los Angeles. Sunnylands requires a staff of forty-five to run it, and to make sure that his golf course would always have water, Walter Annenberg bought the local water company. The place has guesthouses, equipment houses, and a main house with a fountain copied from the fountain at the Museum of Natural History in Mexico City. The entrance to the house is a room with a high vaulted ceiling through which sunlight pours down into a reflecting pool. Beside the pool, Rodin's *Eve* is placed. All the rooms of the house are placed so they view the beaucarnia tree. There is a sculpture garden, a cactus garden, two hothouses — one just for orchids — and Lee Annenberg's private garden, just off her bedroom suite, is a simple affair: a circle of white chrysanthemums enclosed in a square of Japanese pebbles set in grout, the whole enclosed in a holly hedge. Gardeners make sure that Mrs. Annenberg's chrysanthemums are always fresh. Visitors to Sunnylands go on picnics with insulated hot and cold picnic baskets, and are driven about in a Mini-Mok, a housewarming present from Frank Sinatra. The list of pleasures available at Sunnylands goes on and on.

The source of all this was a Prussian immigrant named Moses L. Annenberg who came to Chicago at the age of seven, and whose first paying job was as a messenger for Western Union. Moe Annenberg also sold newspapers on the street, swept out livery stables and, before he was eighteen, worked as a bartender in a saloon on Chicago's tough South Side. In 1900, a brash, rich young man named William Randolph Hearst came to Chicago. Moe Annenberg's older brother, Max, went to work for Hearst and his new paper, the *American,* and Max hired Moe. These were the days of the great Midwest newspaper circulation wars, and presently Moe Annenberg was proving himself to be a genius at promoting circulation. Mr. Hearst, seeing this, put Moe Annenberg in charge of his operations in Milwaukee.

Though Moe Annenberg certainly possessed a flair for selling newspaper subscriptions, Walter Annenberg likes to recall that his father's "first important money" was made as a result of an idea suggested by Walter's mother. Looking around for a new circulation gimmick, Moe Annenberg asked his wife, "What is the one thing you're always running out of?" Oddly enough, her answer was teaspoons. Thus the "State Teaspoon" promotion was launched whereby a housewife, for coupons clipped from six daily papers and one Sunday — plus twenty-five cents — received a sterling silver teaspoon embossed with the seal of one of the forty-eight states. Naturally, every woman wanted a full set. Under an arrangement with the International Silver Company, Annenberg sold millions of spoons, and millions of copies of the Milwaukee *News.* Walter Annenberg remembers sitting with his seven sisters on weekends, wrapping spoons. It is curious that a fortune begun in teaspoons should wind up in a flurry over finger bowls. From then on, Moe Annenberg was into taxicab companies, electric automobiles, restaurants, bowling alleys, grocery stores — into the *Racing Form,* which he bought for four hundred thousand dollars cash wrapped in old newspaper, into the Philadelphia *Inquirer,* then the *Morning Telegraph,* and on into the foundation of what today is the massive Triangle Publications, Inc., which owns radio and television stations and publishes, among other things, *Seventeen* magazine and the fantastically successful *TV Guide* — all still completely family-owned.

By the 1920's it was time for the Annenbergs to buy the George M. Cohan estate on Long Island for a million dollars, a place in the Poconos, a villa in Miami next door to the Firestones, and a ranch in Wyoming that covered eighteen miles, with a fabulous trout stream and a house that had curtains made of yellow calfskin embroidered with turquoise beadwork, handmade by the Indians. Two Annenberg

family sales made news within weeks of each other — Walter's sale
of his Philadelphia *Inquirer* and *Daily News* for $55,000,000, and his
sister Harriet Ames's sale of one of her big diamonds that she had
grown tired of, for an undisclosed price. The gem, which weighs
69.42 carats, went on display at Cartier's, where it drew record crowds
and was sold to Richard Burton for his wife for $1,050,000. At the
time, it was rumored that "the Annenbergs must be going broke."
Nothing could be further from the fact.

At the same time, the cost of all this wealth has been great in terms
of human suffering. As occasionally happens in great dynastic families
— one thinks of the Kennedys, or the Greek House of Atreus — it is
as though the Fates demanded that great men be somehow punished
for their greatness. The most shattering blow of all, of course, was
Moe Annenberg's indictment, in 1939, for income tax evasion, and his
subsequent prison sentence. When released, in June 1942, he was a
broken man and died a few months later. Few children loved their
father more than Annenberg's son and seven daughters. "We worshipped him," Aye Annenberg Simon says. (She was her father's "A
Number One Girl," he used to say, which earned her her nickname.)
"We thought him all-powerful. During electric storms, when there'd
be a flash of lightning, he'd say, 'Now I'll push the thunder button,'
and of course the thunder would come. We thought he was God."
The Annenbergs continue to insist that their father's tragedy was the
result of no wrongdoing. There may have been discrepancies in his
accounts, they say, but after all he was by then the head of over
ninety corporations; for tax advice, he relied on a battery of lawyers
and accountants, some of whom may have been unreliable. Certainly,
his children say, he did not prepare his own income tax returns, nor
did he set about deliberately to cheat the government. Moe Annenberg
had entered the New Deal era as a Roosevelt supporter, but when
Roosevelt attempted his Supreme Court–packing plan, Annenberg
withdrew his support and attacked Roosevelt in a series of editorials.
Roosevelt accused Annenberg of being a "traitor," but Annenberg
persisted with the editorials. The word went out from Washington to
"get Annenberg"; then came the tax indictment. Their father, his
children believe, was simply the victim of a particular political era,

just as Eugene Debs, the Rosenbergs, Alger Hiss, and Dr. Spock have been the scapegoats of theirs. What happened to their father in 1939, their lawyers have told them, could not happen in 1972.

The pattern of tragedy has continued. Walter Annenberg's only son, considered brilliant, was a suicide, and Annenberg was so staggered by this blow that news of it was withheld for a week, as though he could not bring himself to believe that it had happened. One of his nieces was also a suicide, and another died tragically of cancer. A nephew, Robert Friede, was involved in a drug-manslaughter scandal several years ago for which he served a prison sentence. All Walter Annenberg's sisters except one — a widow — have had divorces, and Walter's own first marriage was a particularly unhappy one. The Fates at times must have seemed relentless.

And yet it is absolutely certain that His Excellency Walter H. Annenberg, United States Ambassador to the Court of St. James's, would not be the man he is or where he is if it had not been for the grim day in 1939 when he heard the verdict passed down against his father. Walter was thirty-one at the time. Up to then, he had been a shy, withdrawn young man living in his father's shadow. Suddenly he was head of the house, responsible for his mother and the seven sisters, older and younger. Ever since, he has worked diligently to enrich his family — as he certainly has done, to the point where, barring the most unusual circumstances, Annenberg heirs will be wealthy for many generations to come — and has worked even more doggedly to vindicate his father, to clear and elevate his father's name. Engraved in gold on a wooden plaque, prominently displayed in all his offices wherever he goes, are the words:

CAUSE MY WORKS ON EARTH TO REFLECT
HONOR ON MY FATHER'S MEMORY

This has been the single most important, most consuming, mission in Walter Annenberg's life. He may not always have succeeded, but he cannot be faulted for not trying. Sitting behind his big desk at the Embassy in London, he said, "Tragedy will either destroy you or inspire you, and I continue to have many inspirations to reflect credit on my father. In fact, I feel sorry for people who do not have great incentives in their lives. Great incentives can be sobering and inspiring." Walter Annenberg is a man who lives by mottoes; in fact, he has his favorite quotations typed up and printed on mimeographed sheets so he can carry them with him and refer to them for inspiration. Some of the ones he finds most comforting and reassuring are: "Today, well lived, makes every yesterday a dream of happiness and every tomorrow a vision of hope" — William Osler; "Our main business is not to do what lies dimly at a distance, but to do what lies clearly at hand" — Thomas Carlyle; "The high places occupied by those who are genuinely repentant cannot be reached even by the righteous" — the Talmud. His favorite is this, from an unknown source: "There is no misfortune but to bear it nobly is good fortune."

Annenberg says, "For every advantage a citizen has, he has a corresponding responsibility. Having had more than my share of personal success, I have felt my obligation particularly strongly. All my life I have endeavored to be a constructive citizen." He has endeavored to be constructive through philanthropy, and heads three charitable foundations, one named in his father's memory. He has given the Annenberg School of Communications to the University of Pennsylvania, and the Annenberg Library and Masters' House to the Peddie School, the latter given in honor of the masters who taught him as a student there. He has also toiled for the Philadelphia Art Museum and, in the process, has assembled an imposing collection of nineteenth- and twentieth-century paintings which he has been generous in lending to galleries and museums. He has striven to have the Annenberg name linked with philanthropy and public service, and clearly he feels that his ambassadorial post is just another way he can "reflect honor" on his father's memory.

But is he the right man for the job? Or is he, as his harshest critics say, actually hurting U.S.-British relations with his ineptitude and lack of experience? Of course, much of the criticism of the Annenberg appointment started in America and preceded his arrival in London. It was pointed out that he knew little of Britain, except as an occasional tourist, and that his biggest newspaper, the *Inquirer* — since sold — didn't even employ a foreign correspondent. Much was made of the fact that two Annenberg publications were racing papers, "a service that supplied bookies with racing results." This, of course, is rather

like calling the *Wall Street Journal* "a service for illegal manipulators
and shady speculators," because Annenberg's *Morning Telegraph*,
after all, is the official newspaper of the Thoroughbred Racing Association and of the National Association of State Racing Commission-
ers. It lists among its subscribers none other than Queen Elizabeth II,
who knows more about horses than about ambassadors' addresses.
Needless to say, at the time of the appointment, Moe Annenberg's tax
troubles were taken out and dusted off.

Leading the criticism in America was the New York *Times* — now
known in the Annenberg family as "The goddamned New York
Times." In a sharply worded editorial, the *Times* took President Nixon
to task for "returning now to the unhappy practice of parcelling out
key embassies to major campaign contributors" and said that Kennedy
and Johnson had "scrapped" this tradition. Today, Walter Annenberg
carries the *Times* editorial, slightly dogeared, in his date-book, and
appears to have it committed to memory — the way actresses sometimes memorize bad notices. He takes it out, brandishes it, pounds the
desk as his gorge — and voice — rises. "I made no political contributions!" he cries. "I have not one nickel. This is an editorial based on
falsity. This is a textbook example of yellow journalism!" He also
claims that at least two ambassadorial appointments of which he has
personal knowledge — Matt McCloskey as envoy to Ireland, under
Kennedy, and Frederick Mann, to Barbados, under Johnson — were
both the result of money contributions. He knows this, Ambassador
Annenberg says, because both President Kennedy and President Johnson telephoned him and told him so at the time.

On this rather important point — whether or not Walter Annenberg
gave money to the Nixon campaign — it is hard to get a definite
answer. Back in New York, John B. Oakes, the *Times*'s editorial director, expressed astonishment that Annenberg had accused the *Times*
of lying, and said, "Why, it's been part of my general knowledge that
Annenberg has been a big contributor," which seems a somewhat
flimsy basis for an editorial claiming this to be a fact. Since the
appointment, the *Times* has continued to needle Annenberg, once
commenting that a room in the Embassy where a reception was being
held "looked like a place where people gulp down a quick, cheap
lunch." With the British press continuing to be hostile or mocking or

both, there were signs, by the fall of 1969, that the Annenbergs were visibly wearying of the attack and that Annenberg might indeed offer his resignation by mid-1970. Later, though, the British press became kinder, led by the *Evening Standard,* which commented that "Mr. Annenberg has impressed independent observers by his sincerity and determination. Perhaps the critics will relent a little when they get to know him better." Even the New York *Times* has adopted a gentler tone.

Socially, the Annenbergs still have problems. In this, it is a question of the Annenberg style. No two men could be more unlike than Walter Annenberg and his predecessor, David Bruce. Bruce was elegant, urbane, soft-spoken, polished — a trained diplomat of many years' experience. Annenberg is bluff, tough, forthright and — in some of his overexplanations — incautious. To the mannered world of social London he seems — well, coarse. The Annenbergs have never been exactly shy about admitting how rich they are and, to social London, talking about one's money is something "not done." When asked how much the Annenberg collection of paintings was worth, the Ambassador replied, "Priceless." When asked if it was true that he was personally spending over four hundred thousand pounds of his own money on "refurbishing and rehabilitation" of the residence in Regent's Park, he exclaimed, "It'll be closer to five hundred thousand pounds!" Social London tittered, and *Queen* magazine noted that the Annenbergs' decorator was William Haines, "a former star of silent screen, who appeared in 'The Fast Life,' 'Tell It to the Marines,' and 'Get-Rich-Quick Wallingford,'" adding that the new ambassador possessed an honorary doctorate of laws degree from Dropsie College. In yet another interview, the Ambassador was asked whether he could be photographed on an exercise slab where he works out for ten minutes each morning. "I do that without any clothes on!" he roared. "May I tell you that as a representative of the President, I've got to consider the dignity of my office." Tee-hee, went smart London.

The ambassadorship to the Court of St. James's has become a social post, and was certainly used that way by the very social David Bruces. The job is not one that is considered "politically sensitive." Though it is the most prestigious post an American can occupy, it is also — from the standpoint of politics and American diplomatic goals — one of the least important. What does the American ambassador in London need to do besides go to parties? There are signs, however, that Walter Annenberg may see his role as a somewhat broader one than the purely social one it can easily be. "Our overriding goal," he said, "should be to contribute to the Anglo-American relationship and to show in tangible and visible ways to the British people the depth of our common interest." He intends, he claims, to extend himself deeper into British life than that part of it populated by dukes and duchesses. He has instituted a series of lunches with both business and labor leaders, and recently enjoyed a miners' gala in Durham. He is also eager to prove himself a *working* ambassador. In a recent 77-day work period, he made 45 official calls, received 189 callers, went to 35 lunches, 24 receptions, 53 dinners and 16 excursions, including the miners' gala.

David Bruce is a very *English* American, and Walter Annenberg is a very *American* American. He champions traditional American values — motherhood, virtue, President Eisenhower. His house in California has an "Eisenhower room," with nothing in it but photos and mementoes of his late friend and golfing companion. He also has a "Mother's room," in memory of his mother, with a pale pink carpet — his mother's favorite color. Her portrait, in soft pastels, dominates his private study now in the house in Regent's Park. He calls Mrs. Annenberg "Mother." He dislikes swearing, hippies, student activists, Democrats, and he and his wife take turns at writing a long and chatty weekly newsletter, headed "Dear Family," that goes out to all his sisters and other relatives.

Jocelyn Stevens, publisher of the *Evening Standard,* is not only an influential Briton, but also a very dashing young man about London, with all proper social credentials. "It's really gotten to be very bad," he says. "You're invited to a party, and your hostess will say, 'I'm afraid we're having the Annenbergs.' On the other hand, do the bitches matter? Do they count, in the long run? I tend to suppose that, once their house is finished and they throw a few good parties, people will come around."

It's true. All the costly refurbishing had held the Annenbergs back, because they had been unable to entertain. Now that William Haines's ministrations are complete and the great paintings are hung on the walls, the doors at Regent's Park are open, music is playing and wine is flowing. Certainly in Philadelphia no one ever complained about an Annenberg party, where, needless to say, few expenses were ever spared.

And Walter Annenberg is a tough, determined man, and one gets the impression that he will not let social London get him down. Still, at times, he displays a certain nervousness, small signs that he is under a strain. Not long ago, speeding across London in his long limousine, on his way to pay an official call upon the Rumanian ambassador, his car drew up to the curb. The chauffeur hopped out and opened the door for Ambassador Annenberg. Suddenly, in an anxious voice, he asked, "Are you sure this is the place?"

"Yes, sir, this is it. Number one Belgrave Square."

The Ambassador seemed unconvinced. "Are you positive?" he asked, touching his chauffeur's sleeve. "Are you sure I'm where I'm supposed to be?"

Part Five

SO THE RICH ARE
LIKE YOU AND ME

Emil "Bus" Mosbacher at the helm

16

Yachting:
Everybody's Doing It

"THEY have all been individualists, and they have generally all been gentlemen," said Mr. Cornelius Shields of Larchmont, New York, several years ago. "This has helped the sport of sailing have the feeling of a knit thing." Mr. Shields, grand panjandrum among international yachting figures, was commenting on yachtsmen in general, but specifically on the men who, over the past hundred and twenty years, have competed in what is easily the world's most portentous yachting match, the America's Cup Race.

With all due respect to Mr. Shields, who was born in 1895, he may have been being just a bit nostalgic. And he does, after all, qualify his comment by saying that America's Cup yachtsmen have "generally" been gentlemen. But there are other observers of today's yachting scene who feel that being a great yachtsman takes just about what it take to be a great ambassador — lots and lots of money. As one Old Guard sailor puts it, "The America's Cup used to be a clubby thing, but look at it now. Everybody's into it — even Jews." In other words, a bit of the flashy glitter of Fort Lauderdale has come to the stately shores of old Newport.

Individualists, meanwhile, have certainly not been in short supply. In Florida, after mouthwash heir Gerald B. Lambert had joined the list of unsuccessful aspirants for the honor of defending the Cup, he announced in a sour-grapes way that his new Palm Beach house would not face out to sea but would instead, face inland across Lake Worth.

His wife, on the other hand, was of the exactly opposite frame of mind. As those familiar with the area know, the sandbar which composes Palm Beach is divided by U.S. Highway A-1A, and it is technically not possible for a house to overlook both the ocean and the lake. The architect's solution was to build the house underground, under the highway, and today Mrs. Lambert never, never ventures from her side to look at the lake, and Mr. Lambert will not cross over to view the Atlantic. The room in the center of the house, over which the roadbed passes, is known as the music room.

Mad Captain Ahab would have understood the nuances of the America's Cup at a glance, and probably would have pursued the Cup with as much zeal as he pursued the whale. From the beginning, the America's Cup competition has been fraught with not only intrigue and derring-do but with non-sequiturs, inconsistencies, illogic, and sheer expensive — *very* expensive — zaniness. As one yachtsman puts it, "The thrill of the America's Cup competition is exactly like standing for hours in an icy shower, tearing up thousand-dollar bills, and watching them wash down the drain." Though considered the ultimate "gentleman's sport," the Cup race over its history has taken place in the atmosphere of a frontier free-for-all — a very well-dressed frontier free-for-all, to be sure.

"If the America's Cup is so famous," as the late Gracie Allen might have asked, "how come no one's ever heard of it?" She would have had a point. The America's Cup was in the beginning a kind of club, a clique, an "in" thing to which both money and connections were required to gain entrée. It all began in 1851 when Queen Victoria, casting about for something for her young husband, Prince Albert, to do, suggested that Britain organize the first World's Fair. A yachting race was proposed as part of the fair, and it was suggested to Albert that an American yacht be invited to England to take part in the competition. There is every indication that the smug British assumed without hesitation that any American boat entered in such a race would have to lose. After all, the American boat would have to sail across the Atlantic Ocean — a debilitating trip in those days — just to enter the competition. But the invitation caught the fancy of John Cox Stevens of New York, founder and commodore of the then fledgling New York Yacht Club, and he accepted the British challenge. Stevens quickly put together a syndicate and set about to build "a schooner yacht that would be the fastest afloat." George Steers, a leading marine architect, was commissioned to design the boat, and on May 3, 1851, the vessel was christened *America,* and set sail for England from New York's East River.

By July, the schooner had made it to within sight of England, and she was met by the British cutter *Laverock,* which immediately tried to lure *America* into a test of speed. The skipper and crew of the U.S. yacht were reluctant, but game — and won this initial race hands down. After this somewhat humiliating experience, the British committee withdrew to its drafting rooms to consider its strategy; there was even some rather unsporting talk of calling off the match altogether. But at last, on August 22, an open regatta was scheduled around the Isle of Wight, with a trophy valued at one hundred guineas as the prize.

From the beginning, it had been clear to Skipper Browne of *America* that, because of her considerable weight, her best speeds could only be attained in heavy winds. Alas, on the morning of the twenty-second the winds were discouragingly light and, sailing against fourteen of England's finest yachts, *America* was the last to cross the starting line. Throughout the early part of the course, *America* lagged behind. An experimental "flying jib" was tried, but without success. Finally, Skipper Browne decided on a desperate course. As sailors know, often when there are no winds one or two miles out to sea, there will be brisk ones farther in, close to land. Browne decided to take *America* in, along the island coastline, into uncharted waters full of dangerous rocks and shoals. When the British yachts saw what *America* was up to, "they wondered that the Americans had lost their minds." But Browne — his crew making desperate soundings as they went — found the winds he wanted, and *America* took the race, finishing a full eight minutes ahead of her nearest competitor. This has been called the most glorious moment in the history of yachting.

The United States crew sailed homeward with its hundred-guinea trophy — an odd-shaped, goosenecked ewer of silver with an improbable handle — which became, then, literally the *America's* Cup, since *America* had won it. Someone pointed out that the cup-pitcher was somewhat useless, since it contained no bottom, but the absence of a

proper bottom was put to good use when the cup was securely bolted
into its display case at the New York Yacht Club on West Forty-fourth
Street, where it stands to this day. In the years between, neither Britain
nor any other nation has been able to wrest the Cup from its American defenders. The English, Scots, Canadians, Irish and Australians
have all tried in vain to win it. In 1970, there was a French challenger.

To be sure, in the early years of the America's Cup race, the odds
that the United States would retain the Cup were rather heavily
weighted in our favor. Races were originally held in Lower New York
Harbor, where a general familiarity with the winds, tides, and pattern
of commercial harbor traffic were something of an asset to a skipper;
foreign yachtsmen were slower to grasp such mechanical intricacies.
Also, visiting skippers used to complain that the enthusiastic spectator
fleet that turned out to watch the challenge managed, perhaps acci-
dentally, to get in the way of the challenging craft. Hard feelings,
never far from the surface from the beginning, were expressed on all
sides. In 1870, the British schooner *Cambria,* owned by James Ashbury, whose father had invented the railway carriage, came to New
York to try to gain back the Cup and was met by no fewer than
twenty-three defending yachts. Needless to say, against this armada,
Cambria's chances were small. Ashbury returned huffily to England
and, a year later, came back with another challenger yacht, *Livonia.*
This time, there were only four American defenders to meet him, but
otherwise the race was hardly orthodox. *Livonia* lost her first two races
to the American yacht *Columbia,* but won the third. The Americans
then substituted *Sappho* for *Columbia,* and when *Sappho* won the
next two races the Americans declared the match was over — our side
having won four races out of seven. This was too much for Ashbury,
who hurled insults and threatened lawsuits and, eventually, stalked
home to England to devote himself to ground transportation. The fuss
Ashbury kicked up, though, resulted in the rule that no challenger
may be forced to race against more than one defending yacht.

In 1876, the Royal Canadian Yacht Club became the first non-
British challenger for the Cup with *Countess of Dufferin,* from the
Great Lakes. Needless to say, *Countess* was a freshwater yacht, and in
the unwritten hierarchy of yachting snobbism there has always been
the strong feeling that anyone who sails on fresh water is guilty of

doing something that is *infra dig* and is therefore probably not a gentleman. Consternation in the ranks of the New York Yacht Club! In any case, the American schooner *Madeleine* easily defeated *Countess of Dufferin*. Five years later, another freshwater boat — after an embarrassing trip down the old Erie Canal — suffered a similar defeat, and more rules were adopted. Among them was the rule that the challenging yacht must be constructed within the country it represents; a challenger, in other words, must be transported bodily from the country of challenge in order to compete, which makes it somewhat more costly to challenge than to defend the America's Cup. Also, it was ruled that any challenge, to be valid, had to come from an organized yacht club of a foreign country "having for its annual regatta an ocean water course on the sea or an arm of the sea." This handily eliminated further challenges from upstart lakes.

The low point in the history of the America's Cup matches occurred in 1895. The autocratic Earl of Dunraven brought his *Valkyrie III* to New York to challenge the American *Defender*. *Defender* won the first race; and in the second, *Valkyrie III* fouled her and was disqualified. Just before the third race was to start, *Valkyrie III* withdrew from the contest, complaining of prejudicial interference from the members of the spectator fleet. Dunraven also accused the American boat of having added illegal ballast — to give it a longer waterline, which makes a sailboat go faster. Dunraven was attacked as a quitter, a poor sport, and no gentleman, and he returned to England licking his wounds. In an investigation that followed, the American *Defender* was found guilty of no wrongdoing, and, for his insult, the Earl of Dunraven was advised that his honorary membership in the New York Yacht Club had been canceled. The race went to the Americans, but nowhere was the shine of sportsmanship of purest ray serene.

For years, contenders for the America's Cup were required to conform to no particular size or design formula, and the competing yachts varied greatly. Elaborate handicaps had to be devised in order to keep contestants on a more or less equal basis. Then, in 1920, a Universal Rating Rule was adopted in order to make America's Cup yachts uniform. It was the first real attempt to bring into some sort of order the chaotic rules and rituals of the event. Today, the America's Cup is restricted to yachts of the 12-meter class — which sounds simple enough, but actually means that the competing craft must conform to a complicated arithmetical formula. In the formula, L is the corrected length at approximately 7 inches above the waterline: D is the "girth difference," or the remainder between a "chain measurement" from deck to deck under the keel at the widest point, and a "skin measurement," which follows all the cross-sectional contours at the same point; SA stands for the mainsail plus 85 per cent of the fore triangle. Thus the emerging formula is:

$$\frac{L + 2D + SA}{2.37} = 12 \text{ meters}$$

Since the early days in Lower New York Bay, the America's Cup races have moved to Sandy Hook, to Sea Bright, New Jersey, and out to sea to the Ambrose Lightship, but in 1920 Newport, queen of the ocean resorts, was selected as the regular site of the match, and a standard course of 24.3 nautical miles was laid out.

Between 1920 and the 1970 challenge, there were only seven runnings of the America's Cup race. "After all," as one yachtsman says, "we've never wanted to turn it into an annual thing like the Kentucky Derby." True enough, and it is also important to remember that a yacht race, despite the size of the spectator fleet it attracts, is not really a spectator sport. It is not a sport designed for an audience. "Watching a yacht race is kind of like watching the grass grow," one man says. There are all those sails, almost motionless on the horizon. Even with the strongest glasses, it is hard to determine which sail belongs to whom. The sails shift backward and forward against the afternoon light, and the "spectators" spend their time waving and calling hello to their friends, catching up on a summer's worth of gossip, and making sure there is plenty of ice and vodka. With a bit of doggerel called "A Tragic Day at the Races," the Denniston L. Slaters of New York used to remind themselves of the terrible consequences during a regatta when "our trusty tub ran out of gin":

> *The spinnaker she would not spin.*
> *How could she? We were out of gin . . .*

Yacht racing has been a social sport. But it has been, most of all, an expensive one. In 1851, *America* cost around thirty-five thousand dollars to build, sail, and win her hundred-guinea cup. In those days, this was a considerable sum of money. The America's Cup — and the little club and the mystique surrounding it — remained the bailiwick of only the world's richest and most privileged men, the George Schuylers, the Sir Thomas Liptons, the Earls of Dunraven, the Oliver Iselins, the Harold S. Vanderbilts. It was a far cry from J. Pierpont Morgan's celebrated comment about the cost of yachts: "If you have to ask, you can't afford one." It was a case instead of "If you can afford one, you know who you are, along with the ten other men in the world who can afford one too." The America's Cup race tried to keep itself a relic of Victorian England, a living museum piece, a last vestige and appurtenance of what the gentlemanly sporting life was like among the nineteenth-century aristocracy. There were even those who, from that point of view alone, argued that the event should be government-subsidized. But today, syndicates the size of million-dollar corporations are required to create an America's Cup contender — and, of the huge sums of money laid out for an America's Cup yacht, none of it is legitimately tax-deductible. Nor is it really possible for a syndicate to be a gentleman.

There have been one or two beneath-the-surface and decidedly ungentlemanly ripples in the world of yachting. One of these occurred in 1962 when Mr. Emil ("Bus") Mosbacher skippered the American yacht *Weatherly* to victory (as he managed to do again with *Intrepid* in 1967). Mr. Mosbacher was, it appeared, not a member of the club. At least one of his credentials was out of order: he was Jewish. According to ancient tradition, winning America's Cup skippers have *always* been taken into membership of the New York Yacht Club. And after a certain amount of huffing and puffing, Mosbacher was taken in. But there were some tense moments and, today, as one member says, "No one talks about it."

It has also been inevitable that a certain amount of commercialization should have entered the America's Cup scene. Several years ago, Mr. Rudy Schaefer, who heads the company whose beer bears his name, and who is an ardent sportsman and yacht-fancier, hit upon the idea of having an exact replica of the original *America* made, a complete copy in every detail — the original having crumbled into decay during World War II. Researched by the Smithsonian Institution, built by the finest marine architects, engineers, and sailmakers he could find in the world, Mr. Schaefer had in mind to have his elaborate toy join the spectator fleet at the 1967 Cup races. The new *America* was launched on May 3 of that year, exactly one hundred and sixteen years after her namesake, and Schaefer — who won't tell the exact cost — says that his line-for-line copy set him back "about thirty times" the price of the original, or somewhat in excess of a million dollars. Schaefer's *America* is indeed a lovely thing and, at the moment, rides the waves in New York's City Island Harbor. Her cabin contains a large keg of you-know-what beer, and she is used for promotional tours, meetings and Schaefer executive junkets. At the moment, Schaefer is having a disagreement with the Internal Revenue Service over whether *America* is or is not a deductible business expense. The IRS seems to feel that Schaefer's *America* is not commercial *enough* to be considered part of the brewery's advertising effort. "If we painted 'Schaefer' in red all over the sails, they'd be happy," a Schaefer executive says. But that, of course, would be bad form. It has been claimed, but not proven, that if the new *America* were placed in competition today, she would do as well as her predecessor and beat all the others cold — to borrow the slogan of another beverage company.

In 1970, it all happened again. In Newport, the great old "cottages" were opened up to party after party, all leading up to the glorious event itself. An America's Cup race was all that social Newport needed to remind itself that it, too, is a living monument to upper-class values, however ephemeral they may seem. The 1970 cast of characters was a particularly colorful one. There were two challengers. There was blustery, burly, self-made Sir Frank Newson Packer, known as "Big Daddy" of a vast Australian communications chain which includes newspapers, magazines, and television stations all over the archipelago. It is estimated that Sir Frank's worth may run to over a hundred million Australian pounds. The yacht whose syndicate he headed was *Gretel II,* and she arrived in Newport from Sydney. The second challenger was a titled Frenchman, Baron Marcel Bich, the suave industrialist whose BIC pens have become household standards wherever ballpoint touches paper. Baron Bich spent, it is said, over two million dollars on the yacht *France,* in order, hopefully, to bring the bottomless cup from West Forty-fourth Street to the Champs Élysées.

Defending "our" cup were four yachts: *Intrepid,* the 1967 winner — souped up and refurbished — entered by a syndicate headed by William Strawbridge and Briggs Dalzell. Then there were *Weatherly,* the 1962 defender, and *Valiant,* designed by Olin Stephens (who also designed *Intrepid*) and owned by a syndicate headed by Robert Mc-Cullogh (oil) and George Hinman (banking); McCullogh was his own skipper. A third yacht, and something of a dark horse, was *Heritage,* which was designed and skippered by a brash newcomer named Charley Morgan, Jr., of St. Petersburg, Florida. Morgan had what amounted to a one-man syndicate, a terrific gamble. Also, *Heritage* was the first Florida-built boat in the America's Cup. Morgan and *Heritage* were the long shot.

Gentlemen all? Well, perhaps, if one does not press the point too hard. Baron Bich at least had a title, but there were a number of nit-pickers who didn't think Bich was playing quite by the rules. His challenging *France* was a glorious sight afloat — her spinnaker billowing and emblazoned with the Great Insignia of the Province of Paris. But the fussers of small points noted that while *France* seemed to comply with the rules in every way — completely built in France, that is — the man who *designed her sails* was an American. Shouldn't this disqualify *France?* they argued.

In any case, in the selection races between *Gretel II* and *France,* *Gretel II* was victorious. And in the trials for the defense, *Intrepid* won the honor against the newer boats. The contest itself was the closest in America's Cup history, even though the challenger won only a single race. The first race went to *Intrepid,* and in the second, *Gretel II* was disqualified due to a collision at the start — making it the first time in America's Cup history that a race was lost on a foul. *Intrepid* then won the third race, but *Gretel II* came back to win the fourth, lifting the hopes of the Australians and "Big Daddy" Packer, who was exceptionally bitter over the previous disqualification. But *Intrepid* then won the final race, retaining the Cup for our side, maintaining America's honor.

And so the Cup remains, slightly tarnished, in its resting place —

reminding those who bemoan the commercialization of yachting and complain that it's a sport now that anybody can play, anybody with money, and particularly — like the folks who are now giving you Bergdorf Goodman — a rich conglomerate. To some, the Cup is somewhat remindful of a funerary urn — bolted down, in its niche on West Forty-fourth Street.

Photo by S. Hedding Fotch. Courtesy of the Saint Andrew's Golf Club

The dawn of golf in America; Yonkers, N.Y., 1888

17

"Come and Join Our
Exclusive Club . . . Please?"

W HEN novelist John O'Hara was gathered to his ancestors, lit-
erary and otherwise, not long ago, it was noted in the press that
few authors have written more, or more accurately, about the intricacies and subtleties of that peculiarly American institution, the country club. Remember the country club? It was that cozy old place
where all the best people in town, along with those who wanted to
be, met for locker-room gossip before Sunday golf games, sat down
for endless creamed-chicken lunches, and showed up for boozy Saturday night dances where sweet-smelling girls in pretty dresses could
sometimes be coaxed out onto moonlit fairways and no one minded because it was all "people we know."

The critics also pointed out that O'Hara's was an oddly truncated
vision, that his focus had remained rooted on the kind of country-club
world that had existed before 1930. What seemed overlooked was the
fact that O'Hara's view was a nostalgic one of a world that ceased to
exist long ago, and that, as a result of a variety of social, economic, and
political factors, has changed utterly in the years since — and is bound
to change even more. Not even twenty years ago, for example, when
Donald Ruggoff, a film distributor who operates a chain of New York
movie houses, was about to marry his non-Jewish wife, his future
father-in-law warned the couple, "You'll never be able to join the
Worcester Country Club, you know!" In the 1950's, these were words

to be taken seriously. Today, they would be greeted with a hoot of laughter.

It is significant of the predicament in which private clubs find themselves that one of several dark little clouds which Judge G. Harrold Carswell found hanging over his nomination to the Supreme Court was his involvement with, of all things, a country club in Tallahassee, Florida. It seemed that Carswell had assisted with the club's transfer from a municipal to a private, segregated, status. Here, a matter that would have been ignored twenty years ago had become one of pressing seriousness. It helped lose Carswell his approval by the Senate.

But there is more plaguing private clubs these days than the conflict between civil rights and the social "right of private association." In Westchester County, one golf club is wondering how it is to pay for the winter potholes that have appeared along its miles of private roads, and another closed its beach facility because it had received an offer for the property that was too lucrative to resist. In Dallas, a club is worried about spiraling costs of labor, maintenance, and taxes — and about the reluctance of its wealthy membership to agree to higher dues. In San Francisco, a club in which literally "someone had to die," up until a few years ago, before a new member could be taken in, there is now an energetic drive to recruit new members to fill its sagging rosters. In the cases of "certain especially desirable new members," the once-mandatory five-thousand-dollar initiation fee is being waived. In New York, the cutoff age for junior membership was recently and discreetly raised from forty to forty-five in the hopes that an influx of the less well-heeled will fill the cavity left by the departing rich. Other clubs have taken to using such devices as offering "house memberships" which, for a reduced fee, give members only partial club privileges — everything but golf, for instance. New York's American Yacht Club used to insist on the distinction that it was a *sailing* club, and motor vessels were sneeringly referred to as "stinkpots." Today, the American seems delighted with its fairly lengthy list of stinkpot-owning members, as well as with a number of new members who have no interest in yachting — motorized or nonmotorized — whatever, and who are happy just to sit on the terraces, watch the races, and eat the meals which are being advertised as "very much improved."

The same sort of thing is happening in clubs all across the country
— at Boston's Somerset Club, Philadelphia's Racquet Club, Washington's Metropolitan, and San Francisco's Pacific Union. "We have decided for a variety of reasons," commenced a letter from one of these
august clubs to its members not long ago, "to accept a certain number
of new members in the Club. Such new members, of course, should
be of a calibre compatible to the present membership." And not long
ago, a visiting Englishman was lunching at New York's Knickerbocker
Club, and could not help but notice how many luncheon tables for
two were occupied by one elderly and pink-scalped gentleman, and
one pink-cheeked and longish-haired youth. Had upper-class Americans, he inquired, adopted the somewhat sophisticated European convention of *"le petit ami"*? Gruffly he was told that there was nothing at
all unnatural going on between these luncheon couples. It was simply
the Knickerbocker's drive to attract new members.

In other words, there is today a new and poignant meaning to
Groucho Marx's famous comment, "Any club that would take in me
as a member I wouldn't want to join." Now, any club that will take
you in as a member will also take in any number of friends you want
to bring along.

To the would-be clubman, this is very much a buyer's market, and
newcomers — particularly to the suburbs of the larger cities, where
there are many clubs to choose from — are well advised to shop
around. Not long ago, when applying to a supposedly "exclusive" club
on Boston's North Shore, a man was asked to supply his "Mother's
Maiden Name." He couldn't recall it, and left the space blank. He
got in anyway, which — as the old-timers shake their heads and say —
would never have happened in the days John O'Hara knew so well.
And faced with a sea of problems in a sea of change, the owners and
managers of American social and recreational clubs have banded together to form the National Club Association, with headquarters in
Washington, and the Association has been holding agonized meetings
about the current state of what is accurately called the "club industry"; the main question seems to be whither-are-we-drifting.

One of the problems with clubs in America may be that they are
suffering from growing pains — that they have proliferated so rapidly
that there are suddenly more clubs than we need. As an institution,

the country club is not really very old, and its growth has almost exactly paralleled the growth in popularity of golf. Golf first made its appearance in the United States as early as 1779, when an advertisement appeared in *Rivington's Royal Gazette* which read:

To the Golf Players! The season for this pleasant and healthy exercise now advancing. Gentlemen may be furnished with excellent CLUBS and the veritable Caledonian BALLS, by enquiring at the Printers.

But it was not until more than a century later that golf received any sort of national attention, and this happened in 1887 when a Yonkers man named Robert Lockhart returned from a trip to Scotland with a set of clubs and a supply of balls. Lockhart interested his friend John Reid in the game, and the two men laid out a crude course over several acres of Westchester pastureland. It was Reid's suggestion that a club be formed, and thus the St. Andrews Golf Club — the first in America — came into existence, and it continues to exist in Ardsley-on-Hudson, New York.

Up to then, all the best clubs in America had been the men's city clubs, where the men of society retreated elaborately from their wives and families. The most venerable of these include New York's Union Club and Knickerbocker Club, Philadelphia's Philadelphia Club and Fish House and Rabbit Club, and Boston's Somerset Club and Tavern Club. It was not until 1903 that New York got its all-lady Colony Club — founded by such as Mrs. John Jacob Astor III — and clubs which admitted children as well as women would have been considered downright un-American. But golf got the club idea out of the city into the countryside, and, once there, women proved a hard species to keep out. In the beginning, country clubs sprouted across the face of the land — before the sexual barriers were broken down. Next came the age barriers. Today, a few clubs have firm rules about when women and youngsters are permitted on the golf course, but these are always under attack, and in most places, the country club — with its kiddies' wading pool, its swings and teeter-totters, its hairdressing salon, baby-sitter service, snack bar, ladies' sauna and ladies' card room — is very much a family preoccupation.

Women have certainly helped diminish the importance of the once-powerful men's clubs. In the dining room of New York's Union Club not long ago, a woman glanced icily across the room and commented to the headwaiter, "I see you now also admit the mistresses, as well as the wives, of members." The headwaiter replied, "Only if they are also the wives of other members, madam." And meanwhile, the same sort of thing is going on across the street, as it were — at the once-exclusive women's clubs such as New York's Colony and Cosmopolitan, Boston's Chilton Club, Philadelphia's Acorn, and San Francisco's Franciscan Club. These clubs now admit men. They are also, in as ladylike a way as possible, going after new members. Because they also are languishing.

Part of the trouble has been the steady decline in the quality of service the social clubs have been able to offer. It is increasingly difficult to staff a club with bowing and scraping waiters and superb chefs, and to surround a member with the cozy sensation of belonging to some place decidedly privileged and special. Not long ago Colonel and Mrs. Charles A. Lindbergh arrived for dinner at the Cosmopolitan Club in New York, where Mrs. Lindbergh has maintained a membership for years. The Lindberghs of course had a reservation, but when the headwaitress approached them she inquired rather crossly, "Name, please?" "Charles Lindbergh," replied the Colonel politely; and of the man who, for a while at least, was the most famous figure in the world, the headwaitress asked, "How do you spell it?" And at New York's august Union Club a member was startled when a young waiter approached him and asked to borrow money. "Just till payday," the waiter said.

Meanwhile, back in the country, golf has achieved such an enormous popularity that what had started out as a polite sport for the propertied gentleman is now taken up not only by women but by men who actually work for a living. Today, golf is enjoyed by the milkman as well as the millionaire and has been taken over by those the sociologists group as the "upwardly mobile middle class." Today, accordingly, there are country clubs designed to suit almost every social and economic bracket. Starting times at local golf courses are announced over local radio stations. Big companies, which for a number of years have been paying the initiation fees of their executives to help them get into the best clubs in an area — on the theory that membership in the best club enhances the reputation of the company — have started building country club–like facilities for their lesser employees. So have labor unions, for their members. Then, since World War II, there has been a rash of municipal clubs, with memberships open to all residents of a certain town or city. Often these municipal clubs have come about as, for taxes, a community has bought up the languishing facilities of a private club. Then, of course, there are always the public golf courses.

All this golf-playing by the so-called silent majority has had a profound effect upon the old-line country clubs — the clubs à la John O'Hara's novels — which were built for the so-called effete snobs. Much of the effect is economic. Costs have risen, as have taxes, and members have taken to asking, "Why should I pay five hundred a year to belong to the country club when I can play golf for a pittance a week on the public course?" To make ends meet, private clubs have been forced to go into something very closely resembling the hotel business. They have taken to catering outside parties and offering to sell their facilities for weddings, debuts, and bar mitzvahs. They have even gone after convention business, offering "outings" — days when the club will be closed to regular members and turned over to a corporation for meetings, followed by golf. But at this sort of thing a club must be careful. Tax laws specify that if a club earns more than fifty per cent of its revenue from outside sources it can lose its special club status. The club industry, understandably, complains that it is being "persecuted" by the Internal Revenue Service.

It may well be that the IRS is exerting indirect pressure in hopes of breaking down the traditional social structure in the traditional club. Built into the whole club concept, right from the beginning, was the principle of "exclusivity," and there is no question that those who practice exclusivity are more concerned with keeping people out than with letting them in. Apologists for the concept argue that humans have an essential right to privacy, and to mingle and associate only with others of their own choice; that a group of friends may choose whatever criteria it wishes for admission to the group. This notion, of course, has come under attack in recent years as flying in the face of the broader, more urgent cause of civil rights, and the clubmen have had a hard time trying to defend the special tax status of clubs which are known to discriminate, as well as the fact that members of these clubs have been allowed to treat their dues as standard business income-tax deductions.

But right from the beginning in 1887, racism and anti-Semitism were part of the whole private-club idea. This, the post–Civil War era, was when racial and religious hate first became apparent as facts of life in America; they existed before, of course, but no one noticed them. The earliest country clubs were structured along racial and religious lines. To counteract anti-Semitic clubs, Jews developed clubs of their own which were intended to be equally exclusive. In Westchester County, for example, the Century Country Club was intended as the specifically Jewish "answer" to the exclusive, non-Jewish Apawamis Club. The Century, furthermore, was designed as a *German* Jewish Club and, as one member put it, "mostly Wall Street, though we have a couple of token Gimbels." Other Jews — Russians and Poles, for example — were consigned to the Old Oaks Country Club, where they were said to be "waiting to get into Century." This is less true today, as even the Century has had to look elsewhere than in the German elite for its membership.

In New York City, meanwhile, old Spanish and Portuguese Jewish families — fixtures of New York life since before the Revolution — had been taken into the city's best clubs indiscriminately for generations. These people looked askance, however, at the upstart Germans, who had then to organize a club of their own, the Harmonie.

Discrimination in clubs has been attacked for longer than most people realize. After his defeat by Franklin D. Roosevelt in 1940, the late Wendell Willkie went to Hobe Sound, Florida, for a rest, where he found that Hobe's Jupiter Island Club accepted no Jews. He immediately and vociferously objected, threatening never to come back, and the club hurriedly announced a shift in policy. More recently, Kennedy in-law Stephen Smith was criticized by New York broadcasting head R. Peter Straus for taking his family to the Lake Placid Club, a club "that is known openly to discriminate against Jews," according to Straus. Senator Robert F. Kennedy stalked out of Washington's Metropolitan Club soon after that, announcing that he had discovered the club was not taking in diplomats from the new African nations. New York's University Club — though it boasts the Yale insignia, in Hebrew, on its McKim façade — has for years been notoriously anti-Semitic and under attack from Jewish groups since in most cities the University Club is open to any college graduate. Recently, the University Club announced a softening of this hard line.

The late Ward McAllister, who invented the phrase "the Four Hundred" for Mrs. Astor's parties, once wrote: "Men whose personality is not remarkably brilliant and who, standing by themselves, would not be apt to arouse a great deal of enthusiasm among their associates on account of their intellectual capacity, very frequently counteract these drawbacks by joining a well-known club. Thus it will be seen that a club often lends a generous hand to persons who, without this assistance, might ever remain in obscurity." Today, the exact opposite seems to be the case, and it is the clubs, not their members, which are becoming obscure. Has, for example, the celebrity of David Ogilvy, the advertising man, been enhanced in any way at all by his membership in the "exclusive" Brook Club? Roy Chapin, Joseph Alsop, Gardner Cowles, David K. E. Bruce, Roger M. Blough, Winthrop Aldrich, C. Douglas Dillon, and Henry Ford are all members in good standing of the Links. And yet their famous faces are, nowadays, only rarely seen within the clubhouse. His memberships in the Knickerbocker, the Century, and the University Club did not help lift Nelson Rockefeller from obscurity, nor did the Tuxedo, the Union, and Washington's Metropolitan Club offer a "generous hand" to Averell Harriman.

The classic clubman — overstuffed, with his after-lunch cigar, dozing in his huge leather chair — is becoming a dying breed. A generation ago, nothing added more spice and relish to the dinner-table conversation than tales of this or that rich man who tried, but didn't "make" the club — how the elder J. P. Morgan, enraged that he could not get a friend of his into the Union Club, built himself a whole new club, the Metropolitan. Today, all this sort of thing has begun to seem hopelessly old-fashioned. And when, not long ago, at a membership meeting of the Knickerbocker Club, a candidate's name was proposed, someone said, a little tentatively, "Of course you know he's Jewish . . ." the immediate reaction to the speaker was: "What do you mean? Do you mean you want to keep the man *out*?"

At the same time, the traditions and the rules which the social clubs imposed upon their members have begun to seem not only antiquated but ridiculous. A sign — NO LADIES ALLOWED ON THE THIRD FLOOR FOR ANY PURPOSE WHATEVER — which for years hung in the Metropolitan Club in Washington finally became the object of so much derision that it was removed. Equally the object of fun is the notice posted on a door in Boston's Somerset Club which reads: THIS WATER CLOSET FOR EMERGENCY USE ONLY; OTHER WATER CLOSETS AVAILABLE ON THE SECOND FLOOR. At one New York club, it has long been a firm rule that no business could be discussed over the club luncheon tables; also, because everyone was supposed to know everyone else in the club, there was a rule that no introductions could be performed. In recent years, members have found these rules increasingly silly and restrictive, and several resignations from the club resulted. Today, these rules have been relaxed, and prospective new members are eagerly urged to pay the old rules no heed.

Perhaps the trend that members of the National Club Association fear the most, however, is that today's young people seem to be turning their backs on the whole idea of private social clubs. It is very like what is happening on campuses, where the young are rejecting fraternity and sorority memberships on the grounds (the phrase of the moment) that they are "not relevant," preferring instead to join activist and political groups trying to end pollution and the Vietnam War. Such staid New York organizations as the Links Club — often considered the most exclusive club in America — are worried about being rejected by youth. The Links, chartered in 1916 "to promote and conserve throughout the United States the best interest and true spirit of the game of golf in its ancient and honorable traditions," includes so many giants among its members that it has been said that "walking through the Links locker room is like walking through a nude Industrial Hall of Fame." But the sons of the giants are heading, it would seem, in another direction altogether. Who will be in the Links thirty years from now?

There is still another social fact at work here. Not only the young, but the oldest guard of society have been gradually placing less emphasis on club memberships. A random glance at a couple of issues of the New York *Social Register* tells a curious story. Take the case of Mr. and Mrs. Harvey Dow Gibson (she is the former Helen Whitney). In 1950, the Gibsons belonged to a total of fifteen clubs — the

Links, the Piping Rock, the Metropolitan, the Meadow Brook, and River, the National Golf Links, the Creek, the Union League, the University, the New York Yacht, the Turf & Field, the Westminster Kennel, the Racquet & Tennis, the Colony, and the Daughters of the American Revolution. By 1967, the Gibsons had cut their club memberships by exactly two-thirds, to a mere five — River, Creek, Piping Rock, Colony, and DAR. The same sort of thing is true of the Winthrop W. Aldriches, who, in 1950, belonged to eighteen clubs. Seventeen years later, they had trimmed their list to a mere eleven. Is it possible that as clubs have become the target and the province of the middle class, they have been falling out of favor with the upper?

Meanwhile, the National Club Association is busy. It has, after all, an industry involving hundreds of thousands of people, who do everything from manicure golf greens to manicure fingernails, to support. The NCA recently announced a new and successful club called the Mill River, in Upper Brookville, Long Island. Its charter stipulates a membership equally divided between Jews and gentiles, and is intended to reverse the trend of other Long Island clubs "to go one way or the other."

In New York City, a new men's social club has been announced, to be called the New Yorker Club. It will be "private, distinguished, but unexclusive in the usual sense. It will be devoted to interracial friendship." The New Yorker Club will restrict itself to one thousand members, the only qualification being that members either work or reside in the New York metropolitan area. Behind the club are Richard V. Clarke, a Negro who heads a minority-group consulting firm; Holmes Brown, chairman of the New York Board of Trade; Herbert J. Farber, a prominent public relations man; Senator Jacob K. Javits and Senator Charles E. Goodell; Charles Luce, chairman of Consolidated Edison; Arthur Goldberg, former delegate to the United Nations; Theodore W. Kheel, labor consultant; Orin Lehman, chairman of the New School for Social Research; and advertising man David Ogilvy. Initiation fees for corporate membership will be twenty-five hundred dollars and "must include either the chairman or president of a company."

Perhaps the New Yorker Club is the private club of the future. One can only speculate, and agree that it is a new departure. Meanwhile, for those who long for the days when the band, in raspberry tuxedos, played sweet songs on Saturday nights for sweet-smelling and compliant girls, perhaps you had better go back to Mr. O'Hara's novels.

In London, meanwhile, the great social clubs — White's, Boodle's, St. James's, the Saville — upon which American social clubs were originally modeled, are still flourishing. In fact, there are some who feel that socially it is more important today for a young London businessman to ally himself with the right club that it ever was before, that the helping hand and lift from obscurity are still provided by clubs on that side of the Atlantic. A recent item from *The Times* of London would seem to confirm this. The item reported that a certain London gentleman — not named in the story — had applied for membership in a certain club so often, and had been turned down with such gonglike regularity, that he had finally pleaded, "If you'll just let me join this club, I promise I'll never so much as set foot inside it."

There are some tales that one longs to have be true, but that one suspects cannot really be. The above story is one of these. Can this actually have happened? Or was it a slow day at *The Times* reporter's desk and, for his own amusement, did he tap out this little vignette for his newspaper — just to see if it would get past the copy editor's desk, perhaps? It seems like something very close to sacrilege to doubt the authenticity of a news item from, of all places, *The Times* of London. But do *you* really believe that story? *Do* you?

An Erno Laszlo "symposium," Dallas

18

Where to Get Young and Beautiful

THERE is hardly any point in having money — old money or new — if you can't use it to look your best, is there? While country clubs and city clubs may be languishing, health and beauty spas are flourishing all over the world, and with but one design in mind — to help the rich stay young and pretty.

Staying young, to begin with, takes time, and time, to use a more than familiar phrase, is money. If you have money, you can buy time — other people's time. A person who has servants to help around the house can find time for a little nap in the afternoon, little naps that keep you looking youthful and rested. With servants to do her household chores, a woman can spend time before her mirror with creams and masks and jellies, tweezers, brushes, teasing combs, and eyelash curlers. She can take the time to study her face, to experiment with different kinds of cosmetics, to find which shapes and shades flatter her best and make her appear younger. She has time, in other words, to *think* beautiful.

Or she can take the time to turn herself over to others — to the masseuse who, for fifteen dollars and up an hour, will tug and twist and push and pound her body into shape as many times a week as a client wishes; to an exercise instructor, like those at Kounovsky's in New York (where Mrs. Onassis goes and where Mme. Louis Arpels wears diamonds with her leotard), where the calisthenics a woman needs to keep her firm and fit are made a gay social occasion, and not the chore and bore they are when done, alone, on the bedroom floor at home; to a salon, such as Elizabeth Arden's, where a whole "Day of Beauty" (costing a hundred dollars and up, depending on how far you want the Arden people to go) will tackle the entire woman, from hairstyle to pedicure. With time, a woman (and a man, too, of course) can take up all the sporty, outdoorsy things — golf, tennis, swimming, riding — that are so good for one. With time, a woman can take a week — or two, or three — at a place like the Greenhouse in Texas, where, for about one thousand dollars a week plus tips, a woman can go through a programmed ritual of health and beauty, involving diet, exercise, massage, skin treatments, hair treatments, makeup lessons, manicures, pedicures, fashion lectures, and, for good measure, a little culture (travelogues). With time, which is money, the list of things available to help you look younger is almost endless.

"To me, it is a crime — a *crime*," cries Jolie Gabor, "for a woman not to look her most beautiful, her most glamorous for her husband or her lover. When he comes home at night, she should be freshly bathed, in her most exquisite perfume, in her most beautiful dress, her loveliest makeup, every hair in its place!" Well, yes, but the servantless woman, whose day has been spent with housework and laundry and small children, and who is exhausted by the time she has the roast in the oven, must certainly be forgiven for collapsing on the sofa in her blue jeans rather than stepping into a perfumed tub.

"Household help is absolutely the one essential thing," says a New York housewife who happens to be without it at the moment. "If you have help, *everything* about staying young and looking good becomes much, much easier. Even dieting is easier. I mean, I *know* it's easier for Jackie Onassis to keep her figure than it is for me. If she steps on the scales and sees she's gained a pound, she simply tells her cook, 'All I want for dinner tonight is a cup of yoghurt and some fresh strawberries' — and it's *done!* She doesn't have to fix the kids' dinner, so she couldn't possibly — *ever* — catch herself licking the spoon from the mashed potatoes. And if John-John brings home an uneaten half of a peanut-butter sandwich in his lunch box, it isn't *Jackie* who finds it there and eats it."

The older one gets, the more it costs — in time and money — to stay young. This is a sort of natural law — that the richest are able to stay looking youngest longest. There is, for example, the matter of cosmetic surgery, which most doctors now view more favorably (or at least with less disfavor) than they did in the past, on the basis that anything that improves a patient's appearance will improve his outlook and thus make him feel better. On the other hand, plastic surgery is costly; fifteen hundred dollars is an average cost of a face-lift, and it is not covered by Blue Cross; and since any surgery is a shock to the system, recovery takes time and involves some discomfort.

The number of cosmetic operations performed in America has escalated enormously — some say by as much as five hundred per cent in the past ten years. At the same time, surgeons who specialize in this work have become much more skillful, sophisticated, and ingenious. The face-lift is now the most commonplace of these operations, and one woman who had checked into a Connecticut hospital for the removal of some varicose veins decided to have the doctor lift her face as well, "just for the fun of it." Men, in the meantime, have also been getting facelifts in hugely increasing numbers, but not for fun at all. They have found that the lack of puffy eyes and jowly chins has become a definite business asset and — for that purpose — can become tax-deductible.

Today, there is virtually no part of the body that cannot be put into trimmer, more youthful shape by the removal or addition of snips and pieces here and there. Women who have weight problems, impatient with diets, now frequently order themselves instantly slimmed, through surgery. According to one doctor, whom his colleagues consider "particularly clever," if a woman is "too chesty, too busty, I give her my little pinch pleats."

While all this has been going on, it is inevitable that some of the business of keeping wealthy people young has slipped into the hands of those who — though not certifiable quacks — possess qualifications somewhat more tenuous. After all, the business of keeping wealthy people young has become big business, and everybody wants a bit of the action. The relatively new (in the United States, that is) technique of facial peeling is still the subject of much controversy, and a number of practitioners have found themselves in serious difficulties with the courts and have even gone to jail. The process, by which the outer layer of skin — along with the accompanying wrinkles — is peeled away through the application of chemicals, must, to be legal, be performed by a licensed M.D. It is reasonably uncomfortable, and for a time after the operation, peeled people do not look very presentable and are well advised not to appear in public. But this does not mean that peeling cannot be fun. Mrs. Marjorie Merriweather Post Close Hutton Davies May, an elderly beauty, makes a game of it. Every year or so, she invites her doctor and three close friends to her Palm Beach house and all four ladies have themselves peeled. In the sequestered days that follow, they are a congenial foursome for bridge.

In Los Angeles, the presiding lady genius of skin-peeling is Venner Kelsen, who says that she has the title of "doctor," but prefers, for reasons of her own, not to use it. Her treatment, which takes three reasonably lengthy appointments, followed by a two-week recuperative period, costs from seven hundred and fifty to fifteen hundred dollars.

Venner Kelsen can, she boasts, make a forty-five-year-old face look thirty, and most clients find that their Kelsen peelings last at least five years. At this point, according to her, nearly every major film star in Hollywood — men as well as women — past the age of forty has passed through her doors. In the cases of older clients — she has worked on women of seventy-five — Miss Kelsen works cooperatively with such celebrated California plastic surgeons as Dr. Michael Gurdin. "He handles the structural problems; then I go to work on the skin," says Miss Kelsen.

Meanwhile, a more superficial sort of peeling can be done by licensed operators in beauty salons. This process is less painful ("The face experiences only a warm glow," says one operator), can be done in a day, and the recipient is ready to be viewed and admired immediately afterward. It also costs less (a hundred and fifty dollars) and doesn't last as long — about a month. The process is also called "lysing" — lysis, according to Webster, is "a process of disintegration or dissolution (as of bacteria or blood cells)" — and the instruction booklet for one of these cell-disintegrating compounds is delightfully vague on the subject of just what the sticky — it looks like Elmer's glue — and rather unpleasant-smelling material consists of. It is, says the booklet, a "biological construction of the preparation with the characteristic combination of the various kinds of silicic acid and traces of elements, calcium and so on." The booklet was printed in Vienna, which may be why it seems so uninformative.

It also says "A lysing . . . should be made before starting a cosmetic treatment, or if the skin is plain, too oily, too dry, too smooth or too coarse. [This just about includes everybody, doesn't it?] If the skin has no more the power to eliminate the cells of the epidermis, when they are only loosened at its borders but still fasten [sic] and when looked at with a magnifying glass appear like little horn-leaves [whatever those are] covering chinks and pores, when the skin — examined through the skin microscope — looks cracked, when the pores are obstructed by dust or fat particles — then the receptibility of the skin for nutritive preparations is reduced and the best products applied on the skin remain uneffective. . . . A treatment . . . should be made either before each cosmetic skin-treatment or at least each second one. . . . [This product] is after all the best preparation to normalize the skin and blemiches [sic] will pass completely."

Well, there has always been a certain amount of fantasy and hocus-pocus surrounding every aspect of the beauty world, and anyway, women — and men, too — are coming in for lysing treatments in droves.

Peeling, or peeling done in conjunction with plastic surgery, is certainly the most fashionable way to stay young today. Silicone injections, which had the same end in mind, were very much the thing a few years back, but now they have fallen into disrepute — to the extent that they are against the law. Silicone, it seems, had one unfortunate habit. "It travels," says Venner Kelsen. A wad of silicone, in other words, which is injected in the forehead to remove worry lines, may descend, following the laws of gravity, into the eyelids. Material placed to relieve lines around the nose may sink and settle in the upper lip. "And once it's there," says Miss Kelsen sadly, "it seems that there just isn't any way to get it out." A number of people who received silicone injections in order to achieve more youthful and pretty faces have, it seems, wound up with results that were just the opposite.

At the same time, the beauty world is always spawning cults, and easily the most passionate recent cult — the fervor of the cultists approached that of a religion — was the one that had New York's Dr.

Erno Laszlo as its chief guru. Laszlo, who says, "I have degrees from all the best universities in Europe," is a black-mustached, hand-kissing Transylvanian who has labored on the skin problems of women such as Gloria Vanderbilt Cooper and the Duchess of Windsor. Laszlo's own skin — creamy, smooth and clear — is one of his best advertisements, and naturally his competition in the beauty business claims that he had had his own face lifted. "He's had it lifted to the skies!" says one woman. Laszlo denies this.

Though he no longer personally sees clients, his was quite an operation. In a semidarkened room, with his subject in a hospital gown on a hospital bed, Laszlo went to work with strange, mad-scientist-looking electrical instruments of his own design which made the face muscles jump and twitch — "vacuum the pores," was his expression — and "calm down the capillaries." He then prescribed a variety of secret (and very costly) potions and lotions and instructed each client to wash her face three times a day with his "sea-mud soap," each washing followed by thirty rinses. His sea-mud soap cost ten dollars a cake. He pooh-poohs the suggestion that all this washing and rinsing could be a chore and says that he has rinsed his face as many as ninety times a day. Laszlo is opposed to makeup, and when, not long ago, designer Bill Blass decreed that women should not wear makeup during the day, Bill Blass fans wrote to Laszlo for his ministrations.

A twenty-minute consultation with the Master, which most members of the Laszlo cult considered a continuing essential — Laszlo lectured on sex, drinking, smoking, dietary, and toilet habits, all of which, he says, directly affect the skin — costs seventy-five dollars. One did not tip a man who keeps a signed photograph of Doris Duke on his desk, but an expensive present at Christmastime was considered quite proper. Subsequent visits, with full electric treatment and therapy, also cost seventy-five dollars, and most of the cultists — a number of whom were men — felt that a Laszlo treatment must be undergone at least twice a month. Today, however, Laszlo products — though still expensive — are mass-produced and sold in stores all over the country. And Laszlo clients are cared for by a staff of specialists.

The cosmetics industry now says that for years it has known that men were using their wives' cream and emulsions, their deodorants and hairsprays, but that until quite recently no way to cash in on the male market had been found — that American men regarded male cosmetics as sissy. Meanwhile, in Europe men had been using cosmetics for years. Probably the first male cosmetic products to become popular here were hair tonics. Then came men's colognes.

Today, Revlon's Braggi line for men includes over a dozen items; among them are a Sauna Splash for body rub, an after-shower dusting powder, a bath oil, a cake-type face powder, a face-bronzer in four shades (the darkest gives a man a smashing tan, which washes off with soap and water), a number of before- and after-shave items, and a hairspray. Essentially, these products are identical to similar products for women; they have been given a more "masculine" packaging and more manly scents (pine and lemon, as opposed to the more feminine flower essences). A home hair-coloring product for men introduced a year or so ago has been an enormous success, partly the result of some clever man-to-man advertising, but mostly the result of a whole new feeling in the air: A man now wants to look just as good, in his own way, and as young as a woman.

It is women, many in the cosmetics business say, who are responsible for this new feeling. One who thought this way was the late Eddie Pulaski, proprietor of Eddie's — one of the elegant and expensive new "hairstylist to men" shops that have been springing up along upper Madison Avenue in New York. Eddie liked to cite the case of a woman, the wife of a customer (he, too, liked to refer to his customers as "clients"), who gave her husband for Christmas a gift certificate for an Eddie's hairpiece. These run from three hundred and fifty to five hundred dollars, depending on the area to be covered. Eddie also claimed that he saw more women than men in men's shops and men's department stores — that women were the ones who set men's fashions.

Eddie was the son of a small-town barber who, during World War II, was stationed in France and, on trips to Paris, was astonished to see French-style men's haircutting — it is cut wet, after shampooing, with a straight razor, then dried with a hand dryer, teased and styled with a brush and comb, then wrapped in a hairnet and sprayed. He practiced on his fellow servicemen, and he liked to say that he introduced the French style to America.

Eddie's first customers over here were, he admitted, men from the wealthy homosexual world. But before his death in 1972 he said, "Ninety per cent of my clients are ordinary businessmen — lawyers, doctors, stockbrokers." Executive-placement agencies send clients to be groomed before sending them out to be interviewed for high-paying jobs.

All this made Eddie Pulaski a wealthy man himself. He lived in a penthouse apartment in the East Seventies, an address unlikely for a barber.

This has been the pattern in men's cosmetics and fashions: Whether sponsored by women or not, ideas have started in Europe, been taken up in America at first by the homosexuals, then have moved to the general businessmen. The outfit that looks a bit outré on the young elegant will, in a few years' time, have made its way to the board meeting in Wall Street.

When Eddie first opened his shop, he was called on to do one, or perhaps two, men's hair-coloring jobs a week. By 1972 he was averaging forty a day. Does He or Doesn't He? Who can tell any more? (A number of hairstylists insist, though, that LBJ colors his hair.) Many more men, too, are having their hair straightened, and Eddie's hairpiece business is growing by leaps and bounds. Ten years ago nearly every man who came in for hair coloring insisted on having it done in a private booth. Today, the majority have it done right in the barber chair, no longer ashamed to be seen by other men having their hair dyed. Hairpiece clients do, however, still like their privacy.

The hairpiece is, of course, only a partial solution to male baldness. Even the most expensive hairpieces give themselves away in little ways, and they limit the wearer's activities. One technique that is being used to give a more natural look is weaving, where hair from the sides and back of the man's head is allowed to grow longer; these strands of real hair are then artfully upswept and woven into the hairpiece. But this means that the hairpiece must remain on the head for two weeks at a stretch if the wearer doesn't want to destroy the effect.

Another system of hair transplant plucks live hairs from the sides and back and plants them anew, one by tiny one, on the bald scalp — an enormously expensive and painful operation, which doesn't always work and can leave the victim's head so scarred that a hairpiece is required to cover the damage.

The big excitement in the men's hair world is that it does finally seem that the breakthrough is imminent — that a chemical solution will be perfected that will grow hair on bald heads. One hairstylist says, intending no pun, that he has "a few kinks to work out," but claims that his product is already working on two out of five subjects.

If you are very rich and have the time, you can pursue beauty and youth all over the world, and many men and women do. In Europe particularly, where medical and pharmaceutical laws are more lenient than they are in America, all sorts of exotic stay-young treatments and products are arrayed, and each has a band of well-heeled devotees.

Olivia de Havilland, for instance, likes to take the seaweed baths at Trouville, in France, right across the river from Deauville, which is the more fashionable place to stay. The immersions in seaweed are alternated with massage and strong hosings of seawater. Afterward, one is required to lie silently, facing the sea, in a reclining chair in a large relaxing room. Meanwhile, according to Miss de Havilland, a "really serious" seaweed bath is at Roscoff, in Brittany, with seaweed gathered fresh on the beaches there. "The cure," she says, "has medical value to people with various ailments. I am told it is not at all a gay place and is for the very earnest. I go to Montecatini, too, and take the waters and baths there, even though it is known chiefly as a liver cure."

On the Mediterranean island of Ischia, radioactive mud baths are all the rage, and a prolonged series of treatments is recommended. The full course of baths consists of twelve — one each day for three days, then a day of total rest; then three more days of baths, a day of rest, and so on until the twelve days of baths have been completed. Along with the baths are various types of massage, some done with the subject submerged in radioactive water, and each day ends with a fifteen-minute inhalation of radioactive steam.

A sixteen-to-eighteen-day treatment such as this costs around eight hundred dollars, including doctors' fees, analyses, and round-trip air fare (first class) Paris-Ischia. European health and beauty resorts and spas are still less expensive than those in America; a similar stay, with treatments, at Elizabeth Arden's Maine Chance would cost nearly three times that figure.

In Paris, everyone is going in for saunas and oxygenation. Oxygen-whiffing, inhaling the straight stuff for sessions of fifteen to thirty minutes, is, indeed, becoming popular everywhere, and in Los Angeles, a number of the better beauty salons — even a few drugstores — have installed oxygen tanks for their customers. Oxygen, it is said, is particularly good for treatment of the common hangover, a malaise that often afflicts the wealthy. "Thirty minutes of oxygen are worth three days in the mountains" is the rule, and now small oxygen tanks and masks, designed to fit into a lady's handbag or a man's briefcase, are sold in stores that specialize in expensive gimmickry.

In Paris, salons have sprung up that offer not only oxygenation but massage, physical culture, swimming, food, music, paraffin baths, Salmonoff baths, haircutting, manicure, pedicure — in short, the works. While this is going on, your clothes which you brought with you in the morning are being pressed and readied for your appearance when you emerge in the evening. Another popular treatment in Paris is called Infrason, which is described as "a method of air compressing and decompressing to attack cellulite," which is French for fat.

Recently a number of health and beauty resorts — as well as "cellular" clinics modeled on those of Paul Niehans in Vevey — have sprouted in Rumania, in towns along the Black Sea. Rumania is particularly popular with West Coast people, who can fly to Bucharest over the Pole. It is said that Rumanians are definitely out to snatch some of the health business away from Switzerland.

Obviously, most of the emporia above — plus, we must not forget, the elegant private hospitals, retreats, and sanitariums where the emotional lives of the rich can be put gently back in order — offer promises of added youthfulness only to those with unlimited time and money. But it isn't true that in order to stay young one *must* be rich, though it certainly helps. One of the less expensive developments in recent years, as far as women are concerned, has been that of the estrogens, which are said to eliminate "lady problems" in a woman's middle years and generally to help women feel better, have more energy, look younger, and enjoy happier sex lives. (And the old wives' tale that sexual intercourse is good for a woman's skin may, doctors now say, turn out to have a certain basis in fact; it is male hormones, absorbed by a woman's body, that do the trick, they claim.) So-called "hot flashes," which are related to drops in hormone levels, can be virtually eliminated by estrogen. Women who get estrogen seem to have a lower cholesterol count and, consequently, better circulation and heart action. While the medical profession is not entirely agreed about who should take this hormone, one thing is certain; the pills are so inexpensive and easy to take that any woman whose doctor thinks she should have them can afford them. An eight-to-twelve-dollar supply will last four months.

And there are even less costly ways of staying young — ways, indeed, that cost nothing at all. One is what Joan Crawford, at sixty-four, calls her "basic beauty rule." With a flash of her famous green eyes, she says that this rule is "Look to the stars!" By this she does not refer to her own celebrated ambition to be tops at whatever she does but means, quite simply, that a woman, when she reaches a certain age, should keep her chin up as much as possible, to avoid jowls or a crepe-y neck. (It is no coincidence that many actresses who are over forty are careful to be photographed only when their chins are up-tilted.) Joan Crawford also stresses the importance of a youthful walk and youthful posture.

Another inexpensive way to stay young is offered by Lyn Tornabene, a writer who at the age of thirty-three enrolled in a Midwestern high school to see whether she could "pass" as a teenager, in order to write a book about it. She passed, more or less, though she admits she got some fishy looks and funny questions asked, and that one girl commented that Mrs. Tornabene had sort of an "old face." Mrs. Tornabene is also a Fairfield County housewife who does her own cooking and housework, helped only by a part-time cleaning woman, and still looks much younger than she is.

Her solution has nothing to do with injections, or radioactive mud-baths, or saunas, or hosings with hot seawater, or oxygen-sniffing. She says, "The best way to stay looking young is to stay *up* on things. Keep up with what's happening, and, as much as possible, be *for* what's happening. Take a positive attitude toward things that are different and new — don't close yourself off from new things." In other words, don't knock pop and op art or whatever comes next, at least until you've studied it to see what you can get out of it. Don't complain about the high-school boy next door *just* because his hair is down to his shoulders. Keep up with the latest books, the latest plays, the latest music, the latest films, both underground and above.

The late Elizabeth Arden, who went to her grave in her eighties looking the way most women in their fifties wish they *still* looked, once said, "The secret of perpetual youth is perpetual motion." She had a point. Staying busy and interested in what's going on is one of the most important secrets one must learn to stay young. Lyn Torna-bene says, "At a party, or in any group of people, it's the pooh-poohers, the tongue-cluckers, the gracious-what's-the-world-coming-to types who look *old!*"

The rich have learned these secrets, too (not all the rich look young, but those who do have young interests), and, of course, with more money, the rich will always have more time to stay abreast of things. It seems unfair that the rich should have a priority on youthfulness, but they do have that important edge.

What's more, the rich today begin the job of staying younger sooner than ever. It is no longer a surprise to hear of a mother who trots her ten-year-old (or younger) daughter to Norbert's or Vidal Sassoon's for a haircut, shampoo, set, manicure, et al. Venner Kelsen in California and Erno Laszlo in New York are only two of many costly skin special-ists in the country who are now doing a big business treating adolescent skin.

Youngsters today are having their teeth not only straightened, but *capped* before they reach high-school age. Eddie's like other high-priced hairstylists, is now giving seven-dollar haircuts and twelve-dollar hair-straightening jobs to prep-school boys before they go off to Andover or Groton, and his clients for hairpieces today include several Ivy League college boys. At an early age, the children of the rich are learning the importance of staying young, healthy, and attractive.

And yet it should not be said that the rich emphasize these things only out of vanity, or because they are bored or lazy and have no in-terests other than their own beautification and adornment. There is more to it than that, and a lot of it has to do with the somewhat special attitude of the American rich where, today, the most important question is not who you are or what you do — or even what's your mother's maiden name? — but "Is he *attractive?*"

This attitude grows more pronounced, and one New York society woman states it rather well. "It's part of the different role which money plays in America today," she says. "In Grandpa's day, men made money so they could wield financial power — control a railroad or that sort of thing. Today, people who have money use it almost entirely on pleasure — travel, entertaining, going out to restaurants and parties, and that sort of thing — and on improving their surroundings and, last but not least, themselves. To do that you've *got* to feel and look your best. Do you see what I mean? I mean, if you don't look young and attractive — well, for all you're worth, you might as well be poor."

Photo by Louis Mercier

The *Social Register* — is it still the goal?

19

The Dying Art of Social Climbing

IT used to be that an upper crust could not exist in the United
States without the thousands of persons clambering to penetrate
its shell from underneath. Certainly, if this had not been the case, the
crust would not have been as cohesive and recognizable as it was and
would simply have been an amorphous collection of rich people looking worried. "Blessed be the social climbers," those who considered
themselves to have been better than others must — or should — have
murmured to themselves from time to time as they contemplated their
lot; "without them, we would be unwanted."

In Europe, it was always different. Those who were of the aristocracy knew who they were, and so did everyone else, and that was that.
You couldn't *climb* into European aristocracy, not even by marrying
into it. In the United States, something more than a title was always
required to be of the topmost social level, which was probably why
the topmost social level in America often ended up resembling very
much what a European would consider the middle class — moored
there like a kite in a tree. Old Mrs. Vanderbilt, "Queen of Newport
Society," repaired to her pantry after every dinner party and pains-
takingly counted her linens and her silver. Henriette Seligman, doy-
enne of New York's Jewish society during the early part of this century, entertained like a mad thing in her Manhattan town house —
with meals that were always catered by Schrafft's.

In the United States, the social climber's relationship to society was the opposite of the mountaineer's to Everest. The social climber didn't climb simply because society was *there*. The social climber created his own mountain, and the best social climbers met at the top, at ringside tables, with all the people they moved out of Brooklyn to avoid.

With these facts in mind, social climbing has never been a difficult art. Essentially, all the successful social climber needed — like any other aerialist — was guts, determination, skin the thickness of rhinoceros hide, and a knowledge of the ground rules. Social climbing was not for the faint of heart or the easily discouraged. Even so, there were always some who were better at it than others. It helped, for example, if the climber was reasonably good-looking. If he or she had dandruff, chronic halitosis, a wooden leg, or was hopelessly overweight, his or her rise was less swift. It was, on the other hand, always helpful to look well in clothes, to have an easy smile, to be able to dance, play tennis or at least backgammon, to be witty — but not *too* funny, which was off-putting — to enjoy gossip, to be able to drink well, not to make a big thing about a person's morals, to be able to remember names and faces quickly, and to know at any given moment just who it was whom everybody hated. It went without saying, if you were interested in social climbing, that you were rich. All this was true as recently as a decade ago. But today, social climbing is becoming a dying art, and it has become so for a simple reason: Nowadays it's so easy. One cannot consider as a true art form what has become as simple as a childish exercise in finger-painting.

For example, it used to be that the kiss of death for any social climber was to be caught at it. The social climber used to have to affect an air of indifference towards his goal, to pretend not to care whether or not he achieved it, to insinuate himself gradually and oh-so-gently into the perfumed waters of the people he wanted to get to know. The social climber used the traditional avenues — hard work (or at least the appearance of hard work) for charities, hospitals, churches, and worthy civic causes, and from there into the better clubs and dinner parties. It was a climb, in other words, within the social framework that prevailed in any given city.

Today, all that has changed. Now the social climber seldom beats around the bush. If he cares at all, he simply lays his cards on the table and says, in effect, "Look, here I am. I want to get in, and if it costs

I'm willing to pay." Needless to say, this makes for a cut-and-dried situation, but one that is not without a certain amount of excitement. It may be exciting for others to know that here, now, is a person nobody had heard of a year ago — with money, or at least some money, from God knows where — willing to put himself on the line to get to mix with whoever are supposed to be the right people in town.

Today, the main thing the climber needs is recognition. Someone should say, "Here comes So-and-So," when So-and-So enters the room or the restaurant door. Recognition means the press, the name or the photograph, or both, in the social columns. It used to be that this could best be achieved through the use of a social publicist who, for a fee ranging from five hundred to a thousand dollars a month, "placed" items in columns about his clients. The publicist could also arrange for his clients' names to appear on certain lists, on the committees for certain benefits, and for them to be invited to certain art and theater openings as well as to parties given by people the clients would like to know. The publicist is still a climbing tool of sorts. "They dress them up in a David Webb pin, put them in Sarmi pants and trot them around," says one public relations man. Marianne Strong, who has taken on socially ambitious clients in the past, now says, "All we can do is take them around to parties and introduce them to people. After that, they're on their own."

Today's climber, however — in today's less constrained, less self-conscious mood — has discovered that the social publicist may have become superfluous. If you want publicity, you can do it yourself. If you want your party written up in Leonard Lyons's column, why not just invite Leonard Lyons to your party? In a recent, and brilliant, example of the dexterity with which this can be handled, an attractive woman had a large dinner party in her New York apartment with three important columnists present — three powerful and competitive women who do not really like each other. It was all right; they stayed in different corners of the room, and the hostess was mentioned in three newspapers in the morning.

If climbers take on this task for themselves there are a few simple basics to bear in mind. Here, then, are ten easy rules for today's upstart:

    1. Find something about yourself to promote, get a label. That way,

people will say, "Oh yes, I've heard of her," even when they haven't. The label can be based on anything, no matter how tenuous. Have a gimmick, an identifying fetish. Be "Mrs. Anne Kerr Slater, whose inevitable blue-tinted glasses and huge diamond solitaire . . . etc.," or "Mrs. Reed Albee, who wears nothing but white in winter, nothing but black in summer," or anything equally silly. People, including the columnists, will learn to spot you.

2. Be generous to your friendly society columnist at Christmastime. "I used to pay a publicist once a month, now I pay just once a year," says one woman, obviously pleased with the results of her economy. Cash gifts, however, are frowned upon. A hand-me-down designer dress, on the other hand, is not.

3. Find a designer and spend a bit on his clothes. When asked, "Whose dress is that?" don't look puzzled and say, "Mine." Designers employ publicists too, and if you spend enough their publicists will publicize you — for free. They will feed your picture to *Women's Wear Daily* and make sure that it is a picture of you looking your loveliest.

4. Latch on to, by all means — up to, if not including, threat of bodily harm — someone *big*, preferably from out of town, even more preferably from out of the country, certainly from out of your league, whom everyone will flock to your house in droves to see. Mrs. Robert R. Young built a whole house just to entertain the Windsors in, and when they were in residence, her parties were the most popular in Palm Beach. Royalty still carries weight down there, at least. Once you have made your Very Important Friend, cherish and cosset her. Lavish her with gifts and flattery and she will serve you well. Don't be shy. Zero in on the top people around. Remember that quite often the top people are sitting around twiddling their thumbs on a Saturday evening. Often they are the easiest to get because everyone else is too in awe of them to ask them to dinner. Splendor can create isolation.

In Washington, once upon a time, Mrs. Gwen Cafritz discovered that Supreme Court justices and their wives were so loftily regarded that they were being socially shortchanged. She fixed all that, made them her special property, and decorated her parties with justices again and again. Mrs. Cafritz's technique lives on. There is also the old but still workable technique of calling one Important Friend to say you're having a party for another Important Friend, and then calling the second one to say you're having a party for the first one. Then you hold your breath and hope that at least one of your guests of honor shows up.

5. Be Jewish. Many of the most publicized "new" names recently have been Jewish, and this has nothing to do with anything in the so-called Jewish character. It is simply that it is better, in big-city society, to be Jewish today than it has ever been before. Never has social anti-Semitism been so unfashionable, nor have so many people been out to prove that they are liberal-liberal-liberal. If you can't be Jewish, sprinkle your guest list liberally with fashionable Jews and — even more important — with blacks. This is more than your social conscience at work if you are a climber. It is because you know that most reporters of metropolitan newspapers nowadays are liberal in their outlook. Your mixed racial and religious gathering will get more attention and more praise and sympathy than if you confine yourself to old-hat WASPs.

6. Pay for the photographs that come to you in the mail unsolicited. Increasingly, at social gatherings — openings, benefits, private parties — photographers roam about the premises, shutters clicking. The pictures, when they arrive — often handsomely displayed in leather frames — can become a costly item (the bill enclosed with the pictures always urges you to return them, and no hard feelings). But the photographers feed society columns, and if you don't buy their wares they have ways of taking their revenge. "They get very skillful at taking your picture while you're scratching yourself," one woman has said.

7. If you're a woman, lunch out selectively — both as to restaurant and as to luncheon companion. It's not a bad idea, for instance, to lunch with a man other than your husband. This helps create talk, and might even become a column item. If you go to the "in" restaurants, be sure to tip your captain, as well as your waiter, handsomely, until you have successfully worked your way up to the best tables and are greeted, when you come in, by name. Be willing to withstand the humiliation of rebuffs, blank stares, and placement in "Siberia" as you progress toward your goal. In New York, the five most "in" restaurants are La Grenouille, La Côte Basque, La Caravelle, Le Pavillon,

and Lafayette, in more or less that order. But even more "in" than lunching at one of the above, which are all French, is having a corned beef sandwich in the workroom of a pet designer, such as Halston, so there you are. Perhaps this is why several of the formerly "in" restaurants — Chauveron, the Colony — have closed, for lack of interest.

8. Knock, for all they're worth, all the old traditional society institutions — the Colony Club, Newport, coming-out parties, the Junior League, fox-hunting, Foxcroft, beagling, billiards, the *Social Register*. These institutions are hopelessly out of date, at least as topics of conversation. This does not mean that if asked to go to something involving one of them you should not treat the invitation seriously.

9. Become involved with Art. Art has become one of the most effective avenues and the most rewarding for the social climber. Also, as far as Art goes, anything goes for Art these days, which makes it all the easier. Go to gallery openings. You do not even need an invitation to most of these, where gate-crashers are expected. Sign the guest book, and the gallery concerned will promptly invite you to its next opening. An evening's roam of galleries can be, according to one art expert, "the easiest free drunk in town" — that is, if you like the least expensive brands of domestic champagne. Start a collection of art. Give your art away to museums or send it on tour. Get on the board of directors of a major art museum, and you will have arrived.

Aside from the importance of art, how you decorate your house matters less today than ever before. It is not considered smart to admit to using an interior decorator (interior decorators today try to be called "designers," but the old label sticks.) In your house, order an atmosphere of cultivated clutter and, as soon as the decorator is out of earshot, claim to have done it all yourself.

10. When you entertain, serve good food. Remember that not just women but men too have a say in which invitations are accepted and which are not. His wife may call you "that silly little climber," but if he knows that you will reward him with a spectacular meal at your table, they will more than likely both show up. (Superb food is, after all, available in only a handful of restaurants and clubs in the world.) In most cities, the most fashionable night to entertain is Monday. Next comes Thursday. No one knows why. Friday and Saturday nights are

for entertaining in the country. Sunday is for cocktail parties. Think twice before giving a cocktail party.

Go, if you must, to charity balls — but go selectively, favoring only the best ones, that is, those for the best charities. Go to these by making up a table, which, being a climber, you'll want to be ringside, up front. Go, and don't be too surprised if you spot, at the ringside table next to yours, a few of the old crowd from Brooklyn. After all, it's a fact of life that social climbers meet mostly other social climbers. You will also see, at other nearby tables, numberless nameless faces, which is because these tables have been purchased by large corporations and filled up with their employees and friends.

Where, then, are real society, the Old Guard, the founding families of our cities, the great names to conjure with? Well, some of them have moved out of town — to Arizona, to a ranch in Wyoming, or just to Manhasset. Others have simply tired of the sort of thing you're having so much fun doing, and you'd find them very boring. The rest have simply died.

But don't worry. Now that you've been climbing, and have made it up so far, you've undergone certain important changes. Social climbing is supposed to be self-improving, and the new you is much more happy than the old. And if you take another look at that old Brooklyn crowd, they're looking better too.

Not long ago, New York's famous old El Morocco — which had fallen upon sorry days under a series of different managers — was reopened as a strictly private, members-only club by that prince (real Russian title and all) of publicists, Serge Obolensky. Everyone from the Onassises on down turned out for the opening, and the club has been a huge popular success with what passes for society in New York today. Exclusivity has been the club's keynote and touted cornerstone. In addition to the ability to pay five hundred dollars a month dues, new members must be sponsored by at least two older members, plus two members of the august Board of Governors. When, the other day, a public relations man had a client who wanted to join El Morocco, he spent an hour or so on the telephone calling members and governors, asking them to sponsor his client. By the end of the afternoon, the client had all the sponsorship he needed. Not one of the sponsors knew, or had even heard of, the prospective member before that afternoon. One sponsor even let the prospective member sign the sponsor's name on the application; it seemed like too much trouble to send the application over to his office. The new member went sailing in.

And so, having mastered the simple rules of modern social climbing, you must ask yourself: Was it worth the candle? Or wasn't there some point you missed? Wasn't the point that today's society, where the right people get together in the right places, is everywhere and everyone? Perhaps, without knowing it, you are *there* already. Mr. Fitzgerald might have found the present-day situation confusing, or even disappointing. But now that the rich *are* you and me, there are really no more places that are closed to life on earth.

Index

Index